T0340359

The Political Economy of Patriarchy in the Global South

Recent decades have witnessed both a renewed energy in feminist activism and widespread attacks taking back hard-won rights. Despite powerful feminist movements, the Covid-19 pandemic has significantly undermined the progress women have struggled for decades to achieve; how can this be? What explains this paradox of a strong feminist movement coexisting with stubborn patriarchal arrangements? How can we stop the next global catastrophe initiating a similar backlash? This book suggests that the limitations of social theory prevent feminist strategies from initiating transformative changes and achieving permanent gains. It investigates the impact of theoretical shortcomings upon feminist strategies by engaging with two clusters of work: ungendered accounts of capitalist development and theories on gendered oppression and inequality. Decentring feminist theorising grounded in histories and developments of the global North, the book provides an original theory of the patriarchal system by analysing changes within its forms and degrees as well as investigating the relationship between the gender, class and race-ethnicity based inequalities. Turkey offers a case that challenges assumptions and calls for rethinking major feminist categories and theories thereby shedding light on the dynamics of social change in the global South. The timely intervention of this book is, therefore, crucial for feminist strategies going forward.

The book emerges at the intersections between Gender, International Development, Political Economy, and Sociology and its main readership will be found in, but not limited to these disciplinary fields. The material covered in this book will be of great interest to students and researchers in these areas as well as policy makers and feminist activists.

Ece Kocabıçak, Ph.D., is currently working as a lecturer in the Department of Sociology at the Open University, United Kingdom. For more than two decades, Ece has been involved in feminist politics in Turkey, Egypt, Cyprus and England. She has written for a variety of publications including academic books and journals, newspapers and magazines.

Routledge Studies in Gender and Economics

For more information about this series, please visit www.routledge.com/
Routledge-Studies-in-Gender-and-Economics/book-series/RSGENECON

The Political Economy of Patriarchy in the Global South

Ece Kocabıçak

Routledge
Taylor & Francis Group
LONDON AND NEW YORK

First published 2023
by Routledge
4 Park Square, Milton Park, Abingdon, Oxon OX14 4RN

and by Routledge
605 Third Avenue, New York, NY 10158

*Routledge is an imprint of the Taylor & Francis Group,
an informa business*

Trademark notice: Product or corporate names may be trademarks or registered trademarks, and are used only for identification and explanation without intent to infringe.

British Library Cataloguing-in-Publication Data
A catalogue record for this book is available from the British Library

Library of Congress Cataloging-in-Publication Data
A catalog record has been requested for this book

ISBN: 978-0-367-51578-2 (hbk)
ISBN: 978-0-367-51579-9 (pbk)
ISBN: 978-1-003-05451-1 (ebk)

DOI: 10.4324/9781003054511

Contents

Conclusion: Drivers & Dampeners of Social Change   182

Figures

Tables

Acknowledgements

Questions concerning the persistence of gendered oppression and inequality have had a theoretical and practical significance for the feminist politics that I have been involved with in İstanbul, İzmir, Cairo, Nicosia, London, Manchester and Lancaster. Asking big questions, in my opinion, is necessary to develop effective feminist strategies. In this respect, I am deeply grateful to Sylvia Walby for encouraging me to develop those questions and consider the complexity of social transformation. Her support, expertise and guidance made this work better. Discussion and debate with Valentine Moghadam and Gülnur Acar Savran altered my thinking on some key issues addressed in this book. Colleagues who read and commented on the manuscript also deserve special thanks. Heidi Gottfried, Valentine Moghadam, Sylvia Walby, Emel Memiş, Gamze Çavdar, Eren Düzgün, Peter Redman, Necla Açık, Sevgi Adak, Kate McNicholas Smith and Berfin K. Emre Çetin gave me patient, consistent and discerning feedback. Several others also helped me develop key ideas. Special thanks to Anouk Patel-Campillo, Diane Perrons, Cynthia Cockburn, Isabella C. Bakker, Bob Jessop, Imogen Tyler and Şebnem Oğuz.

I benefited greatly from discussions and debates in the varieties of gender regimes research network (thanks to Karen Shire), the dynamics of gender inequality in the Middle East, North Africa and South Asia research network (thanks to Massoud Karshenas), the women's access to paid work in South Asia and the Middle East and North Africa workshop (thanks to Naila Kabeer), the Open University seminar series on gender and social policy (thanks to Lorena Lombardozzi), and the gender studies department at London School of Economics and Political Science. I completed the book at the Open University. I am grateful to my colleagues at the School of Social Sciences & Global Studies for their support and the shared passion for social justice. Another set of thanks goes to my postgraduate students who participated in the Gender, Development and Globalisation module at London School of Economics and Political Science. Their questions and interpretations immensely helped me. I am particularly indebted to my editor, Kristina Abbotts, and the entire Routledge team to make this book possible. Special thanks to Jo Armstrong for her writing support. Her professionalism and suggestions were very helpful in communicating my ways of thinking in a different language.

Some personal acknowledgements are also essential because this book would not have been possible without their care and support. Special thanks to my friends Berfin K. Emre Çetin and Sevgi Adak, particularly indebted to Sevgi for her generous support during this journey of writing and publishing. I am also grateful to my mother Sevinç Kocabıçak and my sister Evren Kocabıçak for their enthusiasm about what I am doing. Thank you both for your support and motivation. The joy that a little person, River Zeliha, has brought to my life immensely supported me during this time period. And finally, I especially thank my partner, Kate McNicholas Smith from the bottom of my heart for her critique, companionship and support.

INTRODUCTION
THE CONTEMPORARY PARADOX

Today, geographies of the global North and the global South are marked by a paradox of a strong feminist resistance coupled with stubborn patriarchal injustices. Feminist movements and other forms of mobilisations have achieved numerous worldwide successes, from challenging the gender discriminatory laws, regulations and the patriarchal norms and attitudes as well as targeting gendered violence and increasing their influence over international institutions. The increased strength of the movement, particularly in the global South, has come at a cost; feminists have risked imprisonment and death penalties to further the cause (Hong Fincher 2018; Hoodfar and Sadeghi 2009; Fleischmann 2018; Lim 2018; Kışanak 2018). Such a vibrant and resilient feminist resistance, nonetheless, appears to be accompanied by regression in terms of the changing forms and degrees of patriarchal regimes (Evans 2017; Enloe 2017; Gilligan and Richards 2018; Folbre 2021; Shire and Walby 2020; Moghadam 2020).

Indeed, the Covid-19 pandemic has shown that gendered oppression and inequality not only persist, but can also increase by taking back women's hard-won rights.[1] Evidence from more than a hundred countries confirms that during Covid-19 lockdowns, gender gaps in care work and domestic work and unemployment have significantly widened (UN Women 2021, 2020). Following stay-at-home orders, women's time spent on housework and care work has increased more than that of men's and, at the same time, domestic violence has increased in every country (Kabeer, Razavi, and van der Meulen Rodgers 2021). Under lockdown measures, the market-led provisioning of care, particularly for children, has become somewhat redundant underlining the fragility of work-life reconciliation mechanisms (İlkkaracan and Memiş 2021). While women have lost their jobs to a greater extent than their male counterparts, evidence shows that the employment of Black and minority ethnic women has taken the hardest hit (Holder, Jones, and Masterson 2021; WBG 2020). As UN Women Deputy Executive Director, Anita Bhatia, concludes, everything women worked for, that has taken 25 years, has been endangered within a year during the pandemic (Lungumbu and Butterly 2020).

DOI: 10.4324/9781003054511-1

Despite powerful feminist movements at the national and global levels, the pandemic has significantly undermined the progress women have struggled for decades to achieve; How can this be? What explains this paradox of a strong feminist movement coexisting with stubborn patriarchal arrangements? How can we stop the next global catastrophe initiating a similar backlash? This book suggests that the shortcomings of social theory prevent feminist strategies from initiating transformative changes and achieving permanent gains. I use the concept of feminist strategies to refer to the gender equality policies promoted by national and global policy makers, trade unions and non-governmental organisations together with the demands and strategies of transnational feminist networks and grassroots mobilisations. In this book, I investigate the impact of theoretical shortcomings upon feminist strategies by engaging with two clusters of work: ungendered accounts of socio-economic transformation and theories on gendered oppression and inequality. While the former neglects the ways in which gender regimes diversify the trajectories of capitalist development as well as shape state formation and civil society, the latter cluster has increasingly omitted analysis of patriarchal labour exploitation from their theoretical frameworks thereby initiating a shift in attention away from the causes and towards the consequences of gendered oppression and inequality.

1   Reconsidering the determinants of socio-economic transformation

Not only the neoclassical, but also the classical and Marxist accounts of socio-economic transformation appear to assume that the dynamics of capitalist development are the only determinant of social change. Development scholarship, for instance, ignores that gendered oppression and inequality in rural areas are effective factors preventing the labour migration from agriculture to capitalist sectors, as well as constraining labour supply and putting upward pressure on urban wages (Gollin 2014; Fields 2004; Griffin, Khan, and Ickowitz 2002). While Marxist analyses of agrarian change do not consider the patriarchal path of agrarian transformation whereby male peasants uphold a strong control over landownership and women's unpaid family labour (Bernstein 2010; Byres 2009; 2003), theories on the significance of non-capitalist classes in the global South draw on an ungendered account of the peasantry as well as dismissing their influence over the state (Moore 1966; Amin 1976; Düzgün 2019; 2017). Despite their differences, theories of the state dismiss the impact of the patriarchal (or racist) characters and functions of the state upon socio-economic transformation thereby failing to provide a detailed account of state formation (Amsden 2001; Chang 2002; Wade 2003; Jessop 1990; Poulantzas 1969).

In the context of the global South, the above theoretical shortcomings tend to become even more pronounced. Considering that the global Southern contexts are marked by diverse trajectories of capitalist development, scholars are quick to claim that underdevelopment, dependent development or peripheral capitalism is the main reason for higher levels of gender inequality. This approach, however, dismisses the significance of domestic dynamics, particularly the respective roles of the patriarchal and racist political actors in diversifying trajectories of social change. Such capitalism-based reductionism also lends support to an essentialist perception of the cultural and religious conditions. When the main features of the capitalist system do not explain the extended variations of development trajectories in the global South, then the supposedly key characteristics of non-Western social formations (e.g. traditionalism, authoritarianism, conservativism) are portrayed as the main barrier to the development of modern institutions, including the democratic state. This quick slide from capitalist determinism to cultural essentialism perceives some cultural and religious settings – particularly that of Islamic culture and religion since the 9/11 attacks – as backward, authoritarian or inherently patriarchal and thereby gives rise to ahistorical and essentialist explanations.

Feminist research provides an invaluable critique of development theories and strategies; however, one particular approach adopted by their accounts tends to reduce the relationship between gender and development either to *the gendered outcomes of* or *the gendered prerequisites for* capitalist development.[2] It is certainly important to investigate the ways in which development strategies affect women differently to men and, at the same time, understand how the capitalist system can utilise women's unpaid labour as well as benefit from gender inequality in the labour market. However, the significance of uneven gender relations in shaping capitalist transformation also needs to be examined in order to avoid the negative implications that capitalist or culture and religion based reductionisms have for feminist research. Scrutinising the ungendered accounts of capitalist development, this book investigates the extent to which patriarchal labour relations effectively diversify development trajectories as well as shaping capital accumulation strategies and having an impact on state formation and civil society.

2 Bringing the causes of gender inequality into the focus of feminist analysis

Feminist research has increasingly dropped the analysis of patriarchal labour exploitation out of their theoretical framework and as such either reduces the dynamics of gendered oppression to the capitalist system or obscures the causes of gender inequality. In this book, I engage with two most influential approaches towards gendered oppression and inequality. The first one followed by social reproduction theorists subordinates women's oppression and inequality to the logic of capital accumulation and class struggle. The second perspective followed by varieties of gender regime theorists tends to lead to a shift away from the causes and towards the aspects of gendered inequality and thereby prevents a detailed analysis of the gender-based division of labour and the role played by the (cis-gender) heterosexual family.

Critically engaging with the social reproduction approach,[3] the book examines if the dynamics of gendered oppression and inequality can be subordinated to the capitalist system, or whether patriarchal property and labour relations can shape capitalist transformation. By investigating the determinants of the gender-based division of labour in agriculture, I further assess the accuracy of biologically deterministic accounts adopted by the social reproduction approach. I then explore whether household production is limited to non-market goods and services, especially care, as the social reproduction approach assumes, or whether men in their positions as household heads and small producers exchange the surplus produced by women's unpaid labour, thereby forcing women to produce for the market. In doing so, I assess how far the analytical divide between production and reproduction is useful in understanding the experiences of women in the global South.

My research contributes to varieties of gender regime scholarship[4] by theorising the uneven and combined development of gender transformation on the grounds of patriarchal labour exploitation. Consequently, I elaborate on how far the cis-gender heterosexual family *mediates* the relationship between male appropriators and female producers, and in so doing, extend the current debate on the significance of family for varieties of patriarchy (Shire and Nemoto 2020; Moghadam 2020; Walby 2020b). In this book, I further address neglected varieties which are significant in the contexts of the global South. Differentiating two major forms of patriarchal domination, gender-based exclusion and gender-based segregation and subordination, gender regime scholarship conceptualises the domestic and the neoliberal and social-democratic forms of public gender regimes. Providing a detailed account of the patriarchal property and labour relations in rural and urban households, I conceptualise *the premodern* and *the modern forms of domestic patriarchy*.[5] In my analysis of the non-linear and unidirectional trajectories of patriarchal transformation, I provide a geopolitical analysis of the shift from women's unpaid labour towards the double burden of paid and unpaid labour. The account of gender transformation provided in this book, therefore, points to patriarchal relations of labour exploitation as the key dynamic sustaining gendered oppression and inequality.

3 Advantages of historical materialism for feminism

As well as examining the implications for feminist strategies of the shortcomings of social theory, this book assesses the limitations of existing methodologies and ontologies and offers an alternative theoretical framework. Critically engaging with the feminist adaptation of complexity science as well as current interpretations of historical materialism, the book draws on French Materialist Feminism[6] and proposes that the historical materialist methodology and ontology is significant and necessary to abolish gender, class and race-ethnicity based oppressions and inequalities. Yet the influence of mechanical materialism, especially the Althusserian base/superstructure approach, needs to be eliminated from our theoretical trajectories. In order to do so, I explore the potential contribution of Hegelian Marxism to a feminist thought by developing the concepts of collective subject, self-consciousness, mediation, and totality as well as the notion of the unity of the material and the social within the context of gendered oppression and inequality.

Drawing on the Hegelian Marxist interpretation of historical materialism, I argue that cis-gender heterosexual men in their position as the dominant gender constitute a patriarchal collective subject that serves to reinforce the system of gender-based exploitation of labour, whereas the capitalist collective subject maintains the class-based system of labour exploitation. At the same time, varieties of race-ethnicity based oppressions are reproduced by the racist collective subject. Investigating the negotiations between these political collective subjects, I propose that the relationship between the patriarchal and capitalist systems and the racist regimes cannot be reduced to one of harmony or contradiction. Nor can the capitalist system be perceived as the major determinant of social change. In avoiding such determinisms, I draw on the notion of a mutual interaction amongst multiple inequality regimes (Walby 2020a, 2009; Folbre 2020, 2021) as well as an intersectionality of manifold oppressions (Hill Collins and Bilge 2020; Hill-Collins 1990; Crenshaw 1991). However, I do so critically, recognising that while these approaches are useful, the argument that everything determines everything or the emphasis on the intersecting power relations of race, gender and class can obscure the distinctive characteristics of exploitation and oppression based inequalities, and lead to a shift away from the causes and towards the aspects of patriarchy, capitalism and racism.

In order to go beyond this limitation, I differentiate the patriarchal, capitalist, and racist categories of *mediation* as well as investigating the ways in which each category of mediation maintains the gender or class based labour exploitation and race-ethnicity based oppression. According to my framework, the system or the regime having categories of mediation of the highest level of complexity is challenged to a lesser degree than others. Therefore, the more complex mediating categories are, the more influence the system or the regime in question has over others and the concrete totality. The proposed theoretical framework, therefore, does not only allow for an assessment of the ways in which the patriarchal and capitalist systems of exploitation and the racist regimes of oppression are maintained, but also sheds lights on the historically and geographically diverse relations of *over-determination*.

4   The patriarchal, capitalist and racist case of Turkey

Turkey is an upper-middle income country with significant manufacturing capacity and competitiveness in the global market yet, at the same time, patriarchal labour relations predominate. The majority of women's labour is confined to household production (including care work) meaning substantial gender gaps in paid employment. In 2021, around 31% of women of working age (15 – 64 years old) had access to paid employment in formal or informal sectors (ILOSTAT 2022). Furthermore, the capitalist and patriarchal agendas of the state have been historically intertwined with the Turkish Muslim racist agenda. In other words, the trajectory of capitalist development in Turkey is intertwined with strong patriarchal labour relations and a persistent aggression towards its non-Muslim and non-Turkish populations. The selected case study, therefore, enables a detailed assessment of the interaction between the patriarchal, capitalist and racist collective subjects, and thereby allows an assessment of the mediating categories of each and every system of exploitation and regime of oppression.

Turkey further shares a similarly gendered pattern of agriculture to countries in North Africa (such as Egypt and Morocco), and South and Southeast Asia (for example, India, Pakistan and Bangladesh); accordingly, it provides a suitable context for an in-depth analysis of the multiple dynamics of socio-economic transformation in the global South. The pattern of small landownership in the country has remained largely unchanged: since the 1950s, only 8% of agricultural holdings have comprised large-scale farms (20 hectares or larger) and 80% of agricultural holdings are smaller than 10 hectares (TURKSTAT 2016). The predominance of small landownership is also associated with a marked gender-based division of labour and gender gaps in unpaid family work: approximately 80% of women in agriculture work as unpaid family workers (2015–2019) (ILOSTAT 2022). The case of Turkey, therefore, is valuable in considering the ways in which patriarchal labour exploitation in rural and urban households (i) maintains gendered oppression and inequality by diversifying its forms and degrees, (ii) leads to the divisions amongst women on the grounds of varieties of patriarchy and (iv) impacts capital accumulation strategies, thereby diversifying development trajectories and shaping state formation and civil society.

5   The plan of the book

The book contains eight chapters grouped into three parts. PART I, comprising Chapters 1, 2 and 3, provides a detailed assessment of the shortcomings of social theory and introduces the key concepts of my theoretical framework. Critically engaging with the key arguments of development economics, the Marxist perspectives on agrarian change, theories of uneven and combined development, and the key debates on state formation, Chapter 1 examines the ways theories on socio-economic transformation neglect the significance of patriarchal labour relations, and as such, give rise to capitalism-based determinism or cultural essentialism within the global Southern context. The chapter ends with a discussion considering how feminist critiques of development scholarship can be enhanced in order to effectively challenge those ungendered accounts of capitalist development.

Chapter 2 assesses feminist theories, investigating the extent to which they have neglected analysis of patriarchal labour exploitation and discussing the implications of this conceptual shift. As well as providing a brief account of the early debate on patriarchal exploitation, the chapter addresses how interruption of this debate has given rise to various approaches, two of which are outlined: one subordinating the dynamics of gender oppression to the capitalist system, and another obscuring causality in gender inequality. While the former is associated with the social reproduction approach, theories on varieties of gender regime tend to adopt the latter.

Chapter 3 starts with discussion of the political implications of neglecting patriarchal labour exploitation. Departing from such analysis, I develop the key concepts of my theoretical framework, including the gendered patterns of labour exploitation and the political collective subject as well as differentiating changes within the patriarchal state character. I further provide a detailed assessment of existing theories on rural forms of patriarchy in the global South and conceptualise the premodern and modern forms of domestic patriarchy.

PART II of the book includes four chapters containing my data analysis. Using an historical sociology-based case study method, Chapter 4 differentiates the causes and the consequences of the premodern form of domestic patriarchy from those of the modern form. The time period considered is from the nineteenth century Ottoman Empire until the early Republican period (1923- 1940s). The chapter further elaborates on the ways in which the interplay between the capitalist and the racist agendas of the Republican state provided a suitable context for men in their position as rural and urban small producers to exert a stronger patriarchal influence over state formation. I also investigate the dynamics preventing the first wave feminist movement from sustaining control over the state.

Chapter 5 examines how far the emergence of neoliberal public patriarchy has challenged the hegemony of the premodern and modern forms of domestic patriarchy in the country. The neoliberal policies in the global North date from the 1980s, but the strength of working-class movement has delayed those policies in Turkey. Therefore, I consider the time period from the 2000s onwards to assess the shift away from the domestic forms towards the neoliberal public form of patriarchy. Using the mixed methods of qualitative and quantitative analysis, the chapter investigates (i) whether the majority of women experience the conditions of the double burden of paid and unpaid labour, (ii) how far changes within the patriarchal character of the Turkish state, and (iii) the civil society domain, point to a transition away from gender-based exclusion, and at the same time (iv) analyse the extent to which state interventions in the domain of gendered violence point to a shift away from the hegemony of premodern and modern domestic patriarchies.

In Chapter 6, I provide a detailed analysis of the uneven and combined development of premodern and modern domestic and neoliberal public patriarchies in contemporary Turkey (2000s- current). Rejecting the predominant method of differentiating rural from urban areas, I conceptualise agrarian, semi-agrarian and non-agrarian cities. I further investigate the way in which women in agrarian and semi-agrarian cities largely experience premodern and modern domestic patriarchies whereas neoliberal public patriarchy occurs alongside modern domestic patriarchy in non-agrarian cities. Drawing on my geopolitical analysis of patriarchal transformation, I consider the divisions amongst women on the grounds of varieties of patriarchy. Considering varieties of racist regimes in the country, I look at how far the experiences of Alevi and Kurdish women can be distinguished from those of women with the dominant ethnicity and religious backgrounds.

My final data analysis chapter, Chapter 7, investigates the extent to which varieties of patriarchy shape socio-economic transformation. Using comparative analysis, I demonstrate the important role played by premodern domestic patriarchy in shaping the proletarianization process, subsistence earnings and urban wage levels, labour supply, and capital accumulation strategies. I further elaborate on the strategies developed by the Turkish bourgeoisie in response to the conditions imposed by varieties of patriarchy, as well as considering the implications for state formation. Counter to the essentialist accounts of culture and religion, the chapter further points to the significance of varieties of patriarchy in upholding the gender-based exclusionary characteristics of the cultural and religious settings irrespective of the dominant religion.

In light of my assessment, PART III proposes a new theoretical framework and reflects on effective feminist strategies. By comparing and contrasting the key findings of my data analysis, Chapter 8 provides a detailed assessment of theories on socio-economic transformation and gendered oppression. Critically engaging with their theoretical trajectories, it also identifies the limitations of feminist adaptations of complexity theory as well as scrutinising the Althusserian base/superstructure approach. Drawing on the Hegelian Marxist accounts of the historical materialist methodology and ontology, the chapter develops an alternative theoretical framework which can go beyond the existing theoretical shortcomings. By focusing on the drivers and dampeners of the transition away from premodern and modern domestic patriarchies, the conclusion provides a detailed discussion on the key strategies that the feminist movement needs to consider in order to bring change.

Notes

1 The COVID-19 is the name of an infectious diseases caused by a newly discovered virus. People across countries are infected by this virus between 2020 and 2022. In order to prevent and slow down transmission, every country has announced lockdown measures by encompassing stay-at-home orders, curfews, quarantines, cordons sanitaires and similar societal restrictions.

2 E.g. (Razavi 2009; Razavi, Pearson, and Danloy 2004; Kabeer 2001, 2003; Molyneux and Thomson 2011; Dunaway 2014), for details see Chapter 1.

3 E.g. (Federici 2014; Vogel 2014; Giménez 2018; Ferguson and McNally 2014; Ferguson 2008; Arruzza 2016; Bhattacharya 2017), for details see Chapter 2.
4 E.g. (Walby 2020a, 2009, 2020b, 2011b; Moghadam 2020; Shire and Nemoto 2020; Lombardo and Alonso 2020), for details see Chapter 2.
5 Walby (2011a, 1997) stresses that in her analysis the terms patriarchy and gender regime mean exactly the same thing. Therefore, in this book, I often replace her terminology of gender regime with the term of patriarchy.
6 E.g. (Delphy 1984; Delphy and Leonard 1992; Guillaumin 1995; Wittig 1992; Mathieu 1996), for details see Chapter 2 and Chapter 8.

References

Amin, Samir. 1976. *Unequal Development: an Essay on the Social Formation of Peripheral Capitalism*. New York: Monthly Review Press.

Amsden, Alice. 2001. *The Rise of "The Rest": Challenges to the West From Late-Industrializing Economies*. Oxford: Oxford University Press.

Arruzza, Cinzia. 2016. "Functionalist, Determinist, Reductionist: Social Reproduction Feminism and its Critics." *Science and Society* 80 (1):9–30. doi: 10.1521/siso.2016.80.1.9.

Bernstein, Henry. 2010. *Capitalism and Development*. Halifax: Fernwood Books.

Bhattacharya, Tithi. 2017. *Social Reproduction Theory: Remapping Class, Recentering Oppression, Mapping Social Reproduction Theory*. London, New York: Pluto Press.

Byres, Terence J. 2003. "Paths of capitalist agrarian transition in the past and in the contemporary world." In *Agrarian Studies: Essays on Agrarian Relations in Less-developed Countries*, edited by V.K. Ramachandran and M. Swaminathan. London: Zed Books.

Byres, Terence J. 2009. "The Landlord Class, Peasant Differentiation, Class Struggle and the Transition to Capitalism: England, France and Prussia Compared." *The Journal of Peasant Studies* 36 (1):33–54. doi: 10.1080/03066150902820453.

Chang, Ha-Joon. 2002. *Kicking Away the Ladder: Development Strategy in Historical Perspective*. London: Anthem Press.

Crenshaw, Kimberle Williams. 1991. "Mapping the Margins: Intersectionality, Identity Politics, and Violence Against Women of Colour." *Stanford Law Review* 43 (6):1241–1299.

Delphy, Christine. 1984. *Close to Home: a Materialist Analysis of Women's Oppression*. London, New York: The University of Massachusetts Press.

Delphy, Christine. 1992. *Familiar Exploitation: a New Analysis of Marriage in Contemporary Western Societies*. Cambridge, Massachusetts: Polity Press.

Dunaway, Wilma. 2014. "Bringing Commodity Chain Analysis Back to its World-Systems Roots: Rediscovering Women's Work and Households." *Journal of World - Systems Research* 20 (1):64–81. doi: 10.5195/jwsr.2014.576.

Düzgün, Eren. 2017. "Agrarian Change, Industrialization and Geopolitics: Beyond the Turkish Sonderweg." *Archives Europeennes de Sociologie* 58 (3):405–439. doi: 10.1017/S0003975617000194.

Düzgün, Eren. 2019. "The political economy of the transition to capitalism in the Ottoman Empire and Turkey: Towards a new interpretation." In *Case studies in the origins of capitalism*, edited by X. Lafrance and C. Post. London, New York: Palgrave Macmillan.

Enloe, Cynthia. 2017. *The Big Push: Exposing and Challenging the Persistence of Patriarchy*. California: University of California Press.

Evans, Mary. 2017. *The Persistence of Gender Inequality*. Cambridge, Malden: Polity Press.

Federici, Silvia. 2014. *Caliban and the Witch: Women, the Body and Primitive Accumulation*. Brooklyn: Autonomedia.

Ferguson, Susan. 2008. "Canadian Contributions to Social Reproduction Feminism, Race and Embodied Labor." *Race, Gender & Class* 15 (1–2):42–57.

Ferguson, Susan, and David McNally. 2014. "Capital, labour-power, and gender-relations: introduction to the historical materialism edition of marxism and the oppression of women." In *Marxism and the Oppression of Women: Toward a Unitary Theory*, edited by L. Vogel. London: Haymarket Books.

Fields, Gary S. 2004. "Dualism in the Labour Market: A Perspective on the Lewis Model After Half A Century." *Manchester School* 72 (6):724–735. doi: 10.1111/j.1467-9957.2004.00432.x.

Fleischmann, Ellen. L. 2018. "The Other "Awakening": The Emergence of Women's Movements in the Modern Middle East, 1900–1940." In *A Social History of Women and Gender in the Modern Middle East*, 89–139.

Folbre, Nancy. 2020. "Manifold Exploitations: Toward an Intersectional Political Economy." *Review of Social Economy* 78 (4):451–472. doi: 10.1080/00346764.2020.1798493.

Folbre, Nancy. 2021. *The Rise and Decline of Patriarchal Systems: An Intersectional Political Economy*. London, New York: Verso.

Gilligan, Carol, and David A. J. Richards. 2018. *Darkness Now Visible: Patriarchy's Resurgence and Feminist Resistance*. Cambridge, New York: Cambridge University Press.

Giménez, Martha E. 2018. *Marx, Women, and Capitalist Social Reproduction: Marxist-Feminist Essays, Historical Materialism Book Series* London, New York: Brill.

Gollin, Douglas. 2014. "The Lewis Model: A 60-Year Retrospective." *Journal of Economic Perspectives* 28 (3):71–88. doi: 10.1257/jep.28.3.71.

Griffin, Keith, Azizur Rahman Khan, and Amy Ickowitz. 2002. "Poverty and the Distribution of Land." *Journal of Agrarian Change* 2 (3):279–330. doi: 10.1111/1471-0366.00036.

Guillaumin, Colette. 1995. *Racism, Sexism, Power and Ideology*. London, New York: Routledge.

Hill Collins, Patricia, and Bilge Sırma. 2020. *Intersectionality (Key Concepts)*. Cambridge, Medford: Polity.

Hill-Collins, Patricia. 1990. *Black Feminist Thought: Knowledge, Consciousness, and the Politics of Empowerment*. London, New York: Hyman.

Holder, Michelle, Janelle Jones, and Thomas Masterson. 2021. "The Early Impact of COVID-19 on Job Losses Among Black Women in the United States." *Feminist Economics* 27 (1–2):103–116. doi: 10.1080/13545701.2020.1849766.

Hong Fincher, Leta. 2018. *Betraying Big Brother: The Feminist Awakening in China*. London, New York: Verso.

Hoodfar, Homa, and Fatimah Sadeghi. 2009. "Against All Odds: The Women's Movement in the Islamic Republic of Iran." *Development* 52 (2):215–223. doi: 10.1057/dev.2009.19.

ILOSTAT. 2022. Statistics on the Working-age Population and Labour Force—ILO modelled Estimates. In *The ILOSTAT database*, Geneva: The International Labour Organisation.

İlkkaracan, İpek, and Emel Memiş. 2021. "Transformations in the Gender Gaps in Paid and Unpaid Work During the COVID-19 Pandemic: Findings from Turkey." *Feminist Economics* 27 (1–2):288–309. doi: 10.1080/13545701.2020.1849764.

Jessop, Bob. 1990. *State Theory: Putting the Capitalist State in its Place*. Cambridge: Polity Press.

Kabeer, Naila. 2001. *The Power to Choose. Bangladeshi Women and Labour Market Decisions in London and Dhaka*. London: Verso.

Kabeer, Naila. 2003. *Gender Mainstreaming in Poverty Eradication and the Millennium Development Goals: A Handbook for Policy-Makers and Other Stakeholders*. Ottawa, CA: IDRC Books/Les Éditions du CRDI.

Kabeer, Naila, Shahra Razavi, and Yana van der Meulen Rodgers. 2021. "Feminist Economic Perspectives on the COVID-19 Pandemic." *Feminist Economics* 27 (1–2):1–29. doi: 10.1080/13545701.2021.1876906.

Kışanak, Gültan. 2018. *Kürt Siyasetinin Mor Rengi*. Ankara: Dipnot Yayınları.

Lim, Merlyna. 2018. "Unveiling Saudi Feminism(s): Historicization, Heterogeneity, and Corporeality in Women's Movements." *Canadian Journal of Communication* 43 (3):461–479. doi: 10.22230/CJC.2019V44N3A3379.

Lombardo, Emanuela, and Alba Alonso. 2020. "Gender Regime Change in Decentralized States: The Case of Spain." *Social Politics* 27 (3):449–466. doi: 10.1093/sp/jxaa016.

Lungumbu, Sandrine, and Amelia Butterly. 2020. "Coronavirus and Gender: More Chores for Women Set Back Gains in Equality." *BBC*. Accessed 26.03.2021. https://www.bbc.co.uk/news/world-55016842.

Mathieu, Nicole Claude. 1996. "Sexual, sexed and sex-class identities: Three ways of conceptualising the relationship between sex and gender." In *Sex In Question: French Materialist Feminism*, edited by L. Adkins and D. Leonard. London, New York: Taylor& Francis.

Moghadam, Valentine M. 2020. "Gender Regimes in the Middle East and North Africa: The Power of Feminist Movements." *Social Politics* 27 (3):467–485. doi: 10.1093/sp/jxaa019.

Molyneux, Maxine, and Marilyn Thomson. 2011. "Cash Transfers, Gender Equity and Women's Empowerment in Peru, Ecuador and Bolivia." *Gender and Development* 19 (2):195–212. doi: 10.1080/13552074.2011.592631.

Moore, Barrington. 1966. *Social Origins of Dictatorship and Democracy: Lord and Peasant in the Making of the Modern World*. Boston: Beacon Press.

Poulantzas, Nicos. 1969. "The Problem of the Capitalist State." *New Left Review* 1/58, 67–78.

Razavi, Shahra, Ruth Pearson, and Caroline Danloy. 2004. *Globalization, Export-Oriented Employment and Social Policy: Gendered Connections*. New York, London: Palgrave Macmillan.

Razavi, Shahra. 2009. *The Gendered Impacts of Liberalization: Towards 'Embedded Liberalism'?* edited by S. Razavi. New York, London, Abingdon: Routledge.

Shire, Karen, and Kumiko Nemoto. 2020. "The Origins and Transformations of Conservative Gender Regimes in Germany and Japan." *Social Politics* 27 (3): 432–448. doi: 10.1093/sp/jxaa017.

Shire, Karen, and Sylvia Walby. 2020. "Varieties of Gender Regimes." *Social Politics: Special issue* 27 (3 and 4).

TURKSTAT. 2016. Agricultural Farm Structure Survey.

UN Women. 2020. Whose Time to Care? Unpaid Care and Domestic Work During COVID-19. The United Nations.

UN Women. 2021. COVID-19 and Violence Against Women: The Evidence Behind the Talk. The United Nations.

Vogel, Lise. 2014. *Marxism and the Oppression of Women: Toward a Unitary Theory.* London: Haymarket Books.

Wade, Robert. 2003. *Governing the Market: Economic Theory and the Role of Government in East Asian Industrialization.* Princeton: Princeton University Press.

Walby, Sylvia. 1997. *Gender Transformations.* London, New York: Routledge.

Walby, Sylvia. 2009. *Globalisation and Inequalities: Complexity and Contested Modernities.* London: Sage Publications Ltd.

Walby, Sylvia. 2011a. Interview with sylvia walby. In *Feminist and Women's Studies Association (UK and Ireland) Newsletter*, edited by M. Perrier. UK: Feminist and Women's Studies Association (UK and Ireland).

Walby, Sylvia. 2011b. *The Future of Feminism.* Cambridge: Polity Press.

Walby, Sylvia. 2020a. "Developing the Concept of Society: Institutional Domains, Regimes of Inequalities and Complex Systems in a Global Era." *Current Sociology.* doi: 10.1177/0011392120932940.

Walby, Sylvia. 2020b. "Varieties of Gender Regimes." *Social politics* 27 (3):414–431. doi: 10.1093/sp/jxaa018.

WBG. 2020. BAME women and COVID-19 – Research evidence. Women's Budget Group.

Wittig, Monique. 1992. *The Straight Mind, and Other Essays.* London, New York: Harvester.

PART I
THEORETICAL SHORTCOMINGS AND POLITICAL IMPLICATIONS

1 THE UNGENDERED ACCOUNTS OF CAPITALIST DEVELOPMENT

While the predominant theories of neoclassical economics promote the idea of *laissez-faire*, the classical and Marxist political economists consider the role of unequal power relations. According to Joan Robinson, the neoclassical account represents an uncritical defence of capitalism by stressing that capitalism is a system which promotes the good of all, whereas the Marxist political economists argue capitalism is inherently problematic and that the system needs to be overthrown before it brings about its own destruction. The classical economists, she suggests, remain more optimistic and investigate the ways in which problems of the capitalist system can be resolved (Robinson 2017 [1937]). Despite their differences, the neoclassical and the classical and Marxist accounts of capitalist development all neglect the significance of gendered property and labour relations in diversifying development trajectories. In this chapter, I discuss how the failure to consider patriarchal relations of labour impedes a detailed account of socio-economic transformation and reduces the dynamics of social change to the capitalist system or the cultural and religious settings, thereby preventing effective feminist strategies.

The chapter starts with a critical discussion of development economics' dual sector analysis and continues with the Marxist perspectives on agrarian transformation (Sections 1.1 and 1.2). Later, I assess arguments regarding the significance of the non-capitalist classes for social change, as well as exploring theories on state formation (Sections 1.3 and 1.4). I then provide a critical assessment of the culture and religion based essentialist arguments (Section 1.5). The chapter ends by engaging with the feminist critique of development scholarship, exploring the relationship between gender and development (Section 1.6).

1.1 The gendered patterns of labour movement

Development economists who employ the Lewisian dual sector analysis argue that the one-sector neoclassical growth model – originally developed by Robert Solow (1956) and Trevor Swan (1956) – fails to understand the development process in the global South (Gollin 2014; Wang and Piesse 2013;

DOI: 10.4324/9781003054511-3

Temple 2005; Kirkpatrick and Barrientos 2004; Fields 2004). According to those scholars, Arthur Lewis (1954) made fundamental contributions to the field by (i) presenting development economics as a policy science, (ii) conceptualising development as a multidimensional process of economic, political, social and institutional change, (iii) examining the co-existence of modern (capitalist) and traditional (non-capitalist) sectors in developing countries and (iv) investigating the intersecting links between capitalist and traditional sectors as well as analysing the movement of labour across those sectors (Gollin 2014; Temple 2005; Fields 2004; Kirkpatrick and Barrientos 2004). Drawing on this approach, Douglas Gollin (2014) argues that for developing countries today it is important to identify the factors preventing the movement of labour from agriculture to non-agricultural sectors.

Rather than assuming countries with a relatively high rural population have an unlimited labour supply, these scholars also highlight that labour is actually *scarce* and *has to be bid away* from other uses (Fields 2004). Building on his analysis of elasticity in labour supply, Lewis argues that depending on the gap between capitalist wages and subsistence earnings in agriculture, there is a possibility that landowning male peasants may stay on their farm:

> in economies where the majority of people are peasant farmers, working on their own land... *men will not leave the family farm to seek employment if the wage is worth less than they would be able to consume if they remained at home*
>
> (Lewis 1954: 148–149, my emphasis)

As the gap between capitalist wages and subsistence earnings in agriculture influences the decision to migrate, the income of the peasantry "sets a floor for urban wages" in the non-agricultural sectors (Griffin, Khan, and Ickowitz 2002: 292).

While providing a valuable approach to think about the development process in the global South, this scholarship tends to dismiss the gendered patterns of property and labour relations in agriculture. In doing so, they fail to acknowledge that women's unpaid family labour in agriculture enabled high levels of agrarian surplus necessary for initial accumulation. Overlooking gendered patterns also prevents an analysis of the ways in which the patriarchal property and labour relations in agriculture constitute a barrier to the movement of labour from agriculture to capitalist sectors leading to constraints in labour supply as well as being significant for the gap between subsistence earnings and capitalist wages. In other words, these scholars disregard the role of gender in setting a floor for urban wages.

Drawing upon such ungendered accounts, research on Turkey disregards the association between patriarchal labour relations in agriculture and the movement of labour from agriculture to non-agricultural sectors. Alternatively, it assumes that the mechanisation of agriculture eliminated low-productivity small family farming and made peasants redundant (Kazgan 2013; İlkkaracan and Tunali 2011), yet the capacity of non-agricultural sectors is not sufficient to absorb the surplus labour (Toksöz 2012, 2011; Özar 1994). In investigating the relationship between the dominance of small landownership and urban wage levels, there is also a tendency to neglect the role of women's unpaid family labour in terms of putting upward pressure on capitalist wages (Oyvat 2016; Keyder 1987) or subsidising the low level of urban wages (Gürel 2011; Köymen 2008).

In this book, I provide a detailed account of a particular case in which the patriarchal agrarian sector exists alongside the capitalist sectors. Drawing on the case of Turkey, I investigate the role played by the patriarchal labour relations in agriculture, looking at how land-owning male peasants escape proletarianisation and examining the significant gender gaps emerging with the shift from agricultural to non-agricultural employment. In doing so, I assess the extent to which gendered property and labour relations prevent the movement of female labour from agriculture to non-agricultural sectors thereby constraining labour supply. I also explore the way women's unpaid family labour puts upward pressure on capitalist wages by increasing earnings in agriculture.

1.2 The patriarchal path of agrarian transformation

Marxist political economists provide a detailed account of the role of social property relations in diversifying paths of agrarian transformation. In their investigation of different mechanisms, forms and degrees of dispossession, these scholars highlight the importance of market-mediated forces of dispossession (Wood 2002, 1998; Brenner 2001), the necessity of coercion arising from both the state and market (Qi and Li 2019) and the importance of rural class struggle (Byres 2009; Gürel 2019; Hairong and Yiyuan 2015; Bernstein 2010b). Drawing on a rich account of the social property relations in agriculture, these scholars also identify various paths of agrarian transformation, including: (i) landlord-mediated capitalism, i.e. the English path, (ii) capitalism from above, i.e. the Russian path, (iii) capitalism from below, i.e. the American path and (iv) delayed capitalism, i.e. the French path (Bernstein 2010a; Byres 2009; 2003; 1986). The French path, for example, represents the absence of a clear movement towards capitalism. Agriculture in France, these scholars argue, remained non-capitalist until the end of the nineteenth century due to the political power of rich peasants. According to Terence Byres (2009), a rich peasant is a labourer who owns land and a plough with a pair of animals. The American path, on the other hand, refers to a landowning peasant-led transition to capitalist agriculture. The transition to capitalist agriculture occurs when landowning peasants are transformed into bourgeois farmers (Byres 1986).

Engaging with these accounts of agrarian change, the scholarship on Turkey investigates the extent to which the reproduction of the agricultural sector depends on the market. It variously suggests that there was no transition to capitalism until the 1950s (Düzgün 2019), that market dependency initiated a rapid de-ruralisation (Keyder and Yenal 2011) or that de-agrarianisation – led by the Turkish state and the transnational agribusiness companies – impoverished the rural masses (Aydın 2010). Focusing on the dynamics of proletarianisation, others have emphasised the role of capitalist transformation in establishing semi-proletarianisation in rural areas (Öztürk et al. 2017; Kentel, Emre-Öğün, and Öztürk 2017) or the increased prevalence of wage labour through contract farming (Gürel, Küçük, and Taş 2019).

While providing a useful approach to considering trajectories of agrarian transformation, Marxist analyses ignore the significance of patriarchal forces of dispossession by assuming that agrarian social property relations are solely determined by the dynamics of capitalism. Their disregard for the patriarchal property and labour relations, in turn, prevents a detailed account of an alternative path that I call *the patriarchal path of agrarian transformation* (Kocabıçak 2021). All paths of agrarian transformation are gendered, but in different ways. The dominance of small landownership in conjunction with women's exclusion from landownership results in differently gendered outcomes to those associated with large-scale capitalist farms hiring wage labour. In the following chapters, I address the gendered patterns of agriculture which are pivotal in accounting for the dynamics of agrarian change in Turkey and which have hitherto been neglected. As others have argued, the "failure to address the gender dimensions of production, accumulation and politics renders any understanding of the agrarian question, at best, as highly partial and, at worst, as wrong" (Akram-Lodhi and Kay 2010: 268).

In order to provide a detailed account of the patriarchal path of agrarian transformation, the ungendered concepts developed by Marxist political economists need to be revisited. According to my conceptual framework, self-exploitation of the peasantry occurs only when a land-owning male peasant, in his position as household head and small producer, lacks the necessary means (including gendered violence) to sustain the gender-based division of labour. Therefore, all family members work equally on the land *and* have equal access to the products of their labour. However, as Karl Marx proposed in the third volume of *Capital* (1976), small producers may exploit the labour of others:

> In this form, too, greater differences arise in the economic condition of individual immediate producers. There is at least the possibility of this, and the possibility for *the immediate producer to obtain the means whereby he may exploit the labour of others*
>
> (Marx 1976: 931, my emphasis)

Drawing on his analysis, I argue that exploitation of women's unpaid family labour in agriculture gives rise to *a patriarchal farmer*. Building on the original concept developed by Vladimir I. Lenin (1977), I argue that the patriarchal peasant is a land-owning male peasant who can sustain a strong gender-based division of labour and appropriate the surplus produced by women's unpaid family labour. Patriarchal relations of labour, in turn, allow for a certain level of accumulation. With this accumulation, the patriarchal peasantry might increase their capacity of sharecropping or contractual farming by investing in labour saving technologies, e.g. tractors. Considering that a farmer is a bourgeois farmer only if he hires the labour of others (full time or seasonal), I argue that as long as a farmer exploits women's unpaid labour (on his own land or on the land of others) his status remains patriarchal rather than bourgeois.

In a context, where agriculture in Turkey is highly commercialised and integrated into the local and global food chains, I argue that the Turkish trajectory does not represent a delay in capitalist transition (i.e. the French path), nor does it comprise a bourgeois peasant-led transition (i.e. the American path). Instead, the key features of a patriarchal path of agrarian transition point to an integration of patriarchal relations of production in agriculture and capitalist relations of exchange in the market. This integration cannot be reduced to the question of market dependency. It is preserved by the political power of a patriarchal peasantry but, at the same time, challenged by women's struggle. Next, I elaborate on the significance of land-owning male peasantry for socio-economic transformation.

1.3 Landowning male peasants as an influential political actor

The relationship between the capitalist and non-capitalist (or pre-capitalist) classes is discussed within the context of transition to capitalism. Drawing on the Marxist understanding of uneven development, Leon Trotsky (1980) argues that imperialism prevents organic growth, therefore less-developed countries experience a combined "development of development" and "development of underdevelopment". Under the conditions of such uneven and combined development, he argues, not only the capitalist classes (the national and international bourgeoisie), but also the non-capitalist classes (e.g. primitive classes in agriculture, merchants, church, tribes, sheikdoms) determine socio-economic transformation (Trotsky 1980; Novack 1957).

In contrast, the Weberian interpretation of socio-economic transformation emphasises the role of the patrimonial or rentier characteristics of the state in weakening the bourgeois classes in the global South. Such forms of illiberal states, these scholars argue, prevent the bourgeoisie from challenging the pre-capitalist classes, e.g. the aristocracy, the bureaucracy or the peasantry (Moore 1966; Tilly 1990; Heper 1985; Mardin 2006 [1967]). Critically engaging with the Weberian account, World System and Dependency scholars suggest that the capitalist world economy and the peripheralisation process prevent the creation of a powerful domestic bourgeoisie, and as such, reinforce an alliance between the bourgeois class and the pre-capitalist classes in the global South (Wallerstein 2004, 1974; Amin 1976; Alavi 1972; Keyder 1987; Boratav 2011).

The political Marxist approach makes an important contribution to the transition to capitalism debate by emphasising the significance of politics and historicism, and in so doing, initiates a shift away from the Althusserian structuralism towards social and historical specificity.[1] Building on the political Marxist account of capitalist transformation Eren Düzgün (2012a, b) suggests that the Weberian, World System and Dependency scholars assume that the bourgeoisie constitutes an inherently progressive force shifting society to liberal democracy. Instead, he argues, depending on its relation to other classes in historically specific contexts, the bourgeoisie can also play a regressive role. Drawing on the case of the Ottoman Empire, Düzgün (2018) further elaborates on the significance of a particular non-capitalist actor, *the peasant citizen-soldiers*, whose social reproduction depended on their participation in a mass army rather than the market-mediated forces of dispossession.

Theories on the significance of non-capitalist classes provide a helpful analysis of the development process in the global South. While the concept of uneven and combined development enables an assessment of the co-existence and articulation of the capitalist and the non-capitalist systems, the political Marxist accounts of transition to capitalism put a special emphasis on the political power of direct producers in retaining non-market access to their own means of subsistence. In this respect, Düzgün's analyses of the landowning citizen-soldiers and the regressive role of the bourgeois class shed light on the diverse trajectories of capitalist development. Nevertheless, those theories neglect the significance of the patriarchal property and labour relations thereby grouping all forms of political collective subjects different to the capitalist classes under the category of the non-capitalist or the pre-capitalist classes. In fact, their dismissal of the gendered patterns of property and labour relations weakens those scholars' capacity to assess the significance of the patriarchal peasantry for state formation and capital accumulation.

Subsequently, the Weberian analysis fails to identify the determinants of illiberal states which leads to an essentialist account of the patrimonial states in the global South, whereas the World System and Dependency theories (i.e. the neo-Smithian approach) reduce the dynamics of social change solely to external factors. The dismissal of the patriarchal peasantry also weakens the political Marxist scholars' capacity to investigate the gendered regimes of property. Although Düzgün (2019; 2017) is right to highlight the non-capitalist character of agriculture in Turkey, his disregard for the patriarchal labour relations prevents a detailed assessment of the qualitative features of the peasants' labour process. Moreover, a comprehensive account of the bourgeoise's motives in adopting a regressive approach requires a detailed assessment of the outcomes arising from the patriarchal path of agrarian transformation; something which the political Marxist approaches neglect.

This book starts to detail the ways in which the patriarchal peasantry constitutes an important political actor, having an impact on state formation as well as diversifying the trajectories of capitalist development. Counter to the Weberian and neo-Smithian emphasis on the weakness of the domestic bourgeoise, my investigation provides support to the political Marxist accounts by demonstrating the regressive role played by the Turkish bourgeoisie, but, at the same time, I depart from those scholars in insisting on the significance of the gendered patterns of property and labour relations. Considering the implications of the patriarchal path of agrarian transformation, I elaborate on the Turkish manufacturers' strategies of capital accumulation. In turn, this focus allows identification of the determinants of an enduring bond between the bourgeoisie and the authoritarian state regimes. Furthermore, under the patriarchal property regime, the integration with the market remains strong at the same time as the labour processes draw on the gender-based division of labour. This, in turn, leads to a particular trajectory whereby the capitalist relations of exchange in the market are integrated with the patriarchal relations of production in agriculture.

1.4 The ungendered perceptions of the state

Engaging with the Keynesian principles of political economy, development economists initially highlighted the significant role of the state in appropriating the agrarian surplus and arranging the initial accumulation necessary for early industrialisation in the global South (Lewis 1954; Rosenstein-Rodan 1961, 1943). However, since the 1980s, state formation in the global South has been dominated by the neoliberal doctrine. This doctrine has shaped the policy frameworks in ways which minimised the state's role and government's control over the economy. Rejecting such neoliberal doctrine, development economists stress that the global South should do the opposite (Amsden 2001; Chang 2002; Wade 2003); by providing a detailed account of the economic histories of the United States, Great Britain and several other countries in the global North, those scholars argue that successful development in the North was possible because of state interventions in markets (e.g. protectionism). Therefore, protectionism and active state support for new industries have a crucial role in development (Chang 2008, 2002). Engaging with the debates on the developmental state, Ziya Öniş and Fikret Şenses (2009) further suggest that the proactive state (e.g. in South Korea) utilises the policy framework to regulate the economy, whereas the reactive state (e.g. in Turkey and Latin America) does not intervene in the market except in periods of economic crisis. In light of the 2007/2008 economic crisis, others have also questioned the mainstream neoliberal policies by highlighting the significance of the state and other institutions (Serra and Stiglitz 2008; Rodrik 2007; Krugman and Obstfeld 2006; Krueger 2000).

While the above accounts focus on the respective roles of the state in regulating capitalist development, Marxist scholars address the forms and functions of the capitalist state. Analysing the transition from feudalism to capitalism, these scholars argue that the feudal appropriators needed to hold the extra-economic powers of direct coercion, but their private control over the production process was necessary for the reproduction of the capitalist appropriators (Poulantzas 1969; Wood 1981; Offe and Keane 1984). Therefore, in the capitalist system, the public character of the state mediates the private character of labour exploitation:

> The direct political power which capitalist proprietors have lost to the state, they have gained in the direct control of production. While economic power of appropriation possessed by the capitalist is separated from the coercive political instruments that ultimately enforce it, that appropriating power is integrated *more closely and directly than ever before with the authority to organise production*
>
> (Wood 1981: 82, my emphasis)

Nicos Poulantzas is one of the most important contributors to Marxist theories of the state. Drawing on the Gramscian account of hegemony, he argues that the separation of extra-economic coercion from the relations of production enables the capitalist state to promote the interests of the dominant class through the exercise of hegemony. In his analysis, hegemony does not only operate to secure the active consent of the subordinated classes, but also imposes short-term sacrifices on the dominant classes to secure long-term political goals thereby unifying dominant class fractions into a coherent power bloc (Poulantzas 1980, 1969).

As well as the multiple functions of the state, these scholars investigate varieties of the capitalist state. For example, Bob Jessop (2002) argues that the Keynesian welfare states in the global North originally managed the conflict between capital and labour through welfare policies and by following economic policies of full employment, demand management, infrastructure provision and consideration of the national scale. Accordingly, Fordist growth based on mass production and consumption was guaranteed. However, during the post-Fordist era (since the mid-1970s), there has been a shift from the Keynesian welfare state towards the Schumpeterian competitive state. This particular form of state focuses on innovation and competitiveness in the global market, attacks welfare rights, places downward pressure on national wages, plays a greater role regarding local and international governance, as well as upholding a post-national character.

It is beyond the scope of this section to provide a comprehensive assessment of state theories, but it is suffice to point out that feminist strategies must challenge the way these influential scholars overlook the patriarchal character of the state. The classical and Marxist political economists' accounts of the state dismiss the impact of the patriarchal or racist characters and functions of the state upon socio-economic transformation. Early development economists neglect that the state benefited from women's unpaid family labour in agriculture with respect to increasing the agrarian surplus and initial accumulation; whereas the contemporary development economists do not differentiate changes within the forms of patriarchal developmental state which, in turn, weaken those scholars' capacity to differentiate trajectories of development. For example, the trajectory where the state confines women's labour to rural and urban household-production needs to be distinguished from the trajectory in which women's double burden of paid and unpaid labour is regulated by the state. Disregarding the patriarchal character of the developmental state further obscures changes within the gendered social policies taking place during the shift from the Keynesian welfare state towards the Schumpeterian competitive state. While invaluable in providing a detailed analysis of the capitalist character of the state, Marxist theories do not pay enough attention to determinants of state formation other than the dynamics of capitalism. These theories thereby reduce those determinants to the logic of capital accumulation and class struggle. Subsequently, those scholars neglect the enduring bond between the state and the patriarchal or racist political actors within society. This omission leads them to overlook the ways in which, depending on the collective acting capacity of men, the state regulates the patriarchal property and labour relations.

Critically engaging with the ungendered accounts of the state, feminist research focuses on the ways in which the state shapes and is also shaped by gendered oppression and inequality. Those studies investigate a wide range of topics, from welfare provisions and policy formation (Orloff 1996; Skocpol 1985; Orloff 2017), legal codes and penal polities (Haney 1996; Crenshaw 1991; MacKinnon 1983, 1991), political citizenship and rights as well as addressing militarism, security and moral regulation (Rai and Waylen 2008; Erel and Açık 2020; Pateman 1988). Going beyond the dichotomy of whether the state is a liberating force or inherently coercive, co-opted by social inequality regimes, feminist state theory conceptualises the state as a fragmented institution working on multiple levels (Walby 2009; Haney 2000; Connell 1990). Nonetheless, I argue that these scholars do not pay enough attention to the collective agency of men in shaping the patriarchal character of the state. This oversight gives support to the ungendered perceptions of the state by pointing to the cultural and religious settings (especially Islam) or varieties of modernism or the capitalist world system as the main determinants of state formation.[2] An example of such an approach can be found within research on the Turkish welfare regime. Such studies tend to reduce the patriarchal character of the state either to the Islamic conservatism of the ruling Justice and Development Party (since 2002), neoliberalism or to the combination of both (Buğra 2020; 2014; Çavdar and Yaşar 2019; Dedeoğlu and Elveren 2012; Acar and Altunok 2012).

Drawing on the case of Turkey, this book begins to detail the determinants of state formation by investigating how far men in their position as household heads and small producers utilise their collective bargaining capacity to shape the patriarchal character of the state. It also considers the extent to which the interplay between the racist and capitalist agendas of the Turkish state has impacted on the bargaining capacity of men. I further build on varieties of gender regime theories and differentiate two major forms of patriarchal state: the domestic and the public forms of patriarchal state. While the former sustains gender-based exclusionary strategies, the latter regulates gender-based segregation and subordination. Consequently, the analysis illuminates the role of the Turkish state in sustaining the gendered patterns of property and labour relations, confining women's labour to rural and urban household production, and maintaining the gender gaps in proletarianisation.

1.5 Essentialist interpretations of culture and religion

I have thus far argued that classical and Marxist political economists tend to reduce the dynamics of social change solely to the mechanisms of the capitalist system. Their capitalism-based reductionism leads to the dismissal of the patriarchal property and labour relations as well as the collective acting capacity of men and the patriarchal character of the state and, at the same time, appears to support an essentialist perception of the cultural and religious conditions. When the key features of capitalism (e.g. dependency, neoliberalism or class struggle) do not explain the extended variations of development trajectories in the global South, the authoritarian, anti-democratic or conservative characteristics of certain cultural and religious conditions are portrayed as the main barrier to the development of modern institutions, including the democratic state. This quick slide from capitalism-based determinism towards cultural essentialism seems to be rooted in the Weberian account of the non-Western societies.

The Weberian account of modernity emphasises that the irrational characteristics of the traditional culture, religion and politics in the non-Western societies prevent the development of modern institutions (Weber 1976, 1947, 1930; Löwith 2002). Drawing on this account of non-Western societies, the pioneers of modernisation theory attempted to explain the failure of development strategies in the global South by pinning responsibility on those societies' cultural and religious settings (Rostow 1960, 1956; Huntington 1998). In their investigation of the success of the Western trajectory of development, these scholars posited an opposition between modern and traditional societies and argued that the characteristics of traditional societies prevent capitalist development. Accordingly, the local and irrational obstacles to modernisation need to be removed by diffusing modern values and institutions to those societies.

Initial accounts of the "irrationality" and "backwardness" of the non-Western social formations, therefore, portrayed certain cultural and religious conditions as incompatible with modernity and led to the assumption that a lack of capitalist modernity strongly correlates with greater gender inequality and women's oppression. By perceiving the patriarchal norms and attitudes as "traditional", rooted in the pre-capitalist social formations, those scholars understood modernity to be a prerequisite for gender equality in the global South. Drawing on this perception, Catholicism, Islam and Hinduism (Clark, Ramsbey, and Adler 1991; Psacharopoulos and Tzannatos 1989), and Islamic culture and religion in particular following 9/11, are portrayed as barriers to achieving greater gender equality and women's access to public space (Inglehart and Norris 2003b, a; Korotayev, Issaev, and Shishkina 2015).

This assumption that Islamic cultural and religious settings are inherently hostile to gender equality is problematic in many ways. First, these studies "consider the Islamic and Western civilizations as more or less homogeneous blocks" (Spierings, Smits, and Verloo 2009: 504) and thereby ignore the diverse character of patriarchal culture and religion. In addition, their account is ahistorical and thus neglects the dynamics which strengthen or challenge the patriarchal character of Islamic cultural and religious settings. Disregarding these dynamics, furthermore, serves to invalidate Muslim women's struggle and at the same time obscures the connections between culture and religion and men's control over women's labour in household production.

Rejecting these essentialist accounts, I provide a detailed account of changes within the cultural and religious settings in Turkey from the 1990s onwards. In conceptualising variations, I differentiate the gender-based exclusionary characteristics from the gender-based segregationist characteristics. Furthermore, I demonstrate the ways in which the modern civil code (1926–2002) discriminated against women in land inheritance to a greater extent than the premodern Islamic legal framework meaning that rural women sought Islamic cultural and legal settings in order to defend their access to property, including agricultural land.

1.6 Rethinking the problem

In contrast to the ungendered accounts of socio-economic transformation developed by the classical and Marxist political economists, feminist research provides a detailed analysis of the connections between gender and development. The areas addressed by this body of research include: the debates on global value chains (Yeates 2004; Dunaway 2014a; Barrientos 2019; Collins 2014), World Systems theories (Dunaway 2014b; 2001; Moghadam 2017), agrarian change (Agarwal 2016; Deere and León 2001; O'Laughlin 2012), urbanisation and the global cities (Chant 2013; Chant and McIlvaine 2016), conditional cash transfers (Molyneux 2006; Molyneux and Thomson 2011), microcredits and microfinance (Johnson 2005; Kabeer 2005) as well as the consequences of neoliberal regulations and policies for women in the global South (Razavi 2009; Razavi, Pearson, and Danloy 2004; Kabeer 2001, 2003).

These feminist scholars have provided an invaluable critical assessment of development theories and strategies; however, their accounts tend to reduce the relationship between gender and development either to the gendered *outcomes* of, or the gendered *prerequisites* for, capitalist development. So, while they provide detailed investigation of the gendered aspects of development and demonstrate that gendered hierarchy and women's unpaid/ domestic labour are preconditions for capitalist development, their lack of attention to patriarchal labour relations prevents a detailed account of the ways in which gendered property and labour relations shape trajectories of capitalist development. This limitation appears to weaken the capacity of the feminist critique to challenge the ungendered conceptions of the classical and Marxist political economists.

Nevertheless, there are exceptions. An alternative approach which focuses on the role of gender inequality in bringing about diverse trajectories of capitalist development can be found in some of the studies of feminist economists. For example, Diane Elson, Caren Grown and Nilüfer Çağatay (2000) consider the implications of gender for economic growth and identify four scenarios: (i) A win-win scenario (high growth and low gender inequality), (ii) A lose-lose scenario (low growth and high gender inequality), (iii) A lose-win scenario (low growth and low gender inequality) and (iv). A win-lose scenario (high growth and high gender inequality). According to those scholars, higher levels of gender inequality in the labour market harm competitiveness, thereby bringing short-term economic growth (Elson, Grown, and Çağatay 2007; Elson 1995). Drawing on a neo-Keynesian perspective, Stephanie Seguino (2011; Seguino and Grown 2007) also explains that gender equality would bring long-term sustainable growth by increasing productivity through skilled labour and capital-intensive goods, promoting the strategic industries that can afford to pay high wages, and targeting full employment through demand-side management. In her recent work, Seguino (2020) shows that the gender-based division of labour in paid and unpaid work effectively shape macroeconomics, including fiscal, monetary, and trade. These scholars therefore point to the ways different forms or degrees of gender inequality shape development trajectories.

I argue that the relationship between gender inequality and capitalist transformation cannot be reduced to the gendered outcomes of, or the gendered prerequisites for, capitalist development. It is certainly important to investigate the ways in which development strategies affect women differently to men and, at the same time, understand how the capitalist system utilises women's unpaid labour as well as benefits from gender inequality in the labour market. However, the significance of patriarchal labour relations in diversifying trajectories of capitalist transformation also needs to be examined in order to avoid the negative implications that capitalist or culture and religion based reductionisms have for feminist strategies.

1.7 Conclusion

The underlying assumption of the classical and Marxist political economists that the dynamics of capitalism are the only determinant of social change leads them to disregard the respective roles of patriarchal property and labour relations in shaping proletarianisation, urban wages, capital accumulation strategies and state formation. This capitalism-based reductionism further lends support to an essentialist perception of the cultural and religious conditions. When the key features of capitalism fail to explain the extended variations of development trajectories in the global South, then attention is directed to the characteristics of certain cultural and religious conditions which are then portrayed as the main barrier to gender equality. While the critical interventions of feminist research are influential in revealing the gendered aspects or prerequisites of capitalist development, it is necessary to consider the ways in which gendered oppression and inequality diversify development trajectories as well as shape capital accumulation strategies and state formation.

Rejecting both the capitalism and the culture and religion based reductionist approaches, I propose a mutually shaping relationship between the patriarchal and capitalist systems and racist regimes, and investigate the respective roles of the patriarchal property and labour relations in (i) increasing initial accumulation necessary for early industrialisation, (ii) restricting the movement of labour from agriculture to non-agricultural sectors thereby constraining labour supply, (iii) increasing earnings in agriculture and putting upward pressure on capitalist wages, (iv) affecting capital accumulation strategies, and in so doing, (v) sustaining the enduring bond between the anti-democratic state regimes and the bourgeoise thereby shaping state formation. (vi) I further analyse the connections between the patriarchal path of agrarian transformation and the gendered cultural and religious conditions.

Notes

1 Robert Brenner, Ellen Meiksins Wood, George Comninel, Frederick Guillaume Dufour, Xavier Lafrance, Charles Post, Benno Teschke, and Eren Düzgün are some of the key thinkers of this approach.
2 The exception is an early study of Jean L. Pyle (1990) in which she investigates that state personnel aim to maximise the level of support from the electorate which tends to sustain the state's patriarchal character through the demands of male voters in Ireland. The Irish state has therefore supported men in controlling women's labour within the home by protecting the traditional family form (1930s–1960s).

Reference

Acar, Feride, and Gülbanu Altunok. 2012. "The 'Politics of Intimate' at the Intersection of Neo-Liberalism and Neo-Conservatism in Contemporary Turkey." *Women's Studies International Forum* 41 (P1). doi: 10.1016/j.wsif.2012.10.001.

Agarwal, Bina. 2016. *Gender Challenges (Vol 1, 2 and 3)*. India: Oxford University Press.

Akram-Lodhi, A. Haroon, and Cristóbal Kay. 2010. "Surveying the Agrarian Question (Part 2): Current Debates and Beyond." *The Journal of Peasant Studies* 37 (2):255–284. doi: 10.1080/03066151003594906.

Alavi, Hamza. 1972. "The State in Post-Colonial Societies: Pakistan and Bangladesh." *New Left Review* 74(I):59–81.

Amin, Samir. 1976. *Unequal Development: an Essay on the Social Formation of Peripheral Capitalism*. New York: Monthly Review Press.

Amsden, Alice. 2001. *The Rise of "The Rest": Challenges to the West from Late-Industrializing Economies*. Oxford: Oxford University Press.

Aydın, Zafer. 2010. "Neo-Liberal Transformation of Turkish Agriculture." *Journal of Agrarian Change* 10 (2):149–187. doi: 10.1111/j.1471-0366.2009.00241.x.

Barrientos, Stephanie. 2019. *Gender and Work in Global Value Chains: Capturing the Gains?* London, New York: Cambridge University Press.

Berik, Günseli, Yana van der Meulen Rodgers, and Stephanie Seguino. 2009. "Feminist Economics of Inequality, Development, and Growth." *Feminist Economics* 15 (3):1–33.

Bernstein, Henry. 2010a. *Capitalism and Development*. Halifax: Fernwood Books.

Bernstein, Henry. 2010b. *Class Dynamics of Agrarian change*. Halifax, Nova Scotia: Fernwood Pub.; Sterling, VA: Kumarian Press.

Boratav, Korkut. 2011. *Türkiye İktisat Tarihi (1908–2009)*. Ankara: İmge Kitabevi.

Brenner, Robert P. 2001. "The Low Countries in the Transition to Capitalism." *Journal of Agrarian Change* 1 (2):169–241. doi: 10.1111/1471-0366.00007.

Buğra, Ayşe. 2014. "Revisiting the Wollstonecraft Dilemma in the Context of Conservative Liberalism: The Case of Female Employment in Turkey." *Social Politics* 21 (1):148–166. doi: 10.1093/sp/jxt001.

Buğra, Ayşe. 2020. "Politics of Social Policy in a Late Industrializing Country: The Case of Turkey." *Development and Change* 51 (2):442–462. doi: 10.1111/dech.12566.

Byres, Terence J. 2003. "Paths of capitalist agrarian transition in the past and in the contemporary world." In *Agrarian Studies: Essays on Agrarian Relations in Less-Developed Countries*, edited by V.K. Ramachandran and M. Swaminathan. London: Zed Books.

Byres, Terence J. 1986. "The Agrarian Question, Forms of Capitalist Agrarian Transition and the State: An Essay with Reference to Asia." *Social Scientist* 14 (11/12):3–67. doi: 10.2307/3517162.

Byres, Terence J. 2009. "The Landlord Class, Peasant Differentiation, Class Struggle and the Transition to Capitalism: England, France and Prussia compared." *The Journal of Peasant Studies* 36 (1):33–54. doi: 10.1080/03066150902820453.

Chang, Ha-Joon. 2002. *Kicking Away the Ladder: Development Strategy in Historical Perspective*. London: Anthem Press.

Chang, Ha-Joon. 2008. *Bad Samaritans: The Guilty Secrets of Rich Nations and the Threat to Global Prosperity. London*: Random House Business.

Chant, Sylvia. 2013. "Cities Through A "Gender Lens": A Golden "Urban Age" for Women in the Global South?" *Environment and Urbanization* 25 (1):9–29. doi: 10.1177/0956247813477809.

Chant, Sylvia, and Cathy McIlvaine. 2016. *Cities, Slums, and Gender in the Global South: Toward a Feminized Urban Future*. New York: Routledge.

Clark, Roger D., Thomas W. Ramsbey, and Emily S. Adler. 1991. "Culture, Gender and Labour Force Participation." *Gender and Society* 5 (1):47–66.

Collins, Jane. 2014. "A feminist approach to overcoming the closed boxes of the commodity chain." In *Gendered Commodity Chains: Seeing Women's Work and Households in Global Production*, edited by W. Dunaway. California, Stanford: Stanford University Press.

Connell, Raewyn. 1990. "The State, Gender, and Sexual Politics." *Theory and Society* 19 (5):507–544. doi: 10.1007/BF00147025.

Crenshaw, Kimberle Williams. 1991. "Mapping the Margins: Intersectionality, Identity Politics, and Violence against Women of Colour." *Stanford Law Review* 43 (6):1241–1299.

Çavdar, Gamze, and Yavuz Yaşar. 2019. *Women in Turkey: Silent Consensus in the Age of Neoliberalism and Islamic Conservatism, Routledge Studies in Middle Eastern Politics*, London, New York: Routledge.

Dedeoğlu, Saniye, and Adem Y. Elveren. 2012. *Gender and Society in Turkey: The Impact of Neoliberal Policies, Political Islam and EU Accession.* London, New York: I.B. Tauris.

Deere, Carmen Diana, and Magdalena León. 2001. "Who Owns the Land? Gender and Land-Titling Programmes in Latin America." *Journal of Agrarian Change* 1 (3):440–467. doi: 10.1111/1471-0366.00013.

Dunaway, Wilma. 2014a. "Through the portal of the household: Conceptualising women's subsidies to commodity chains." In *Gendered Commodity Chains: Seeing Women's Work and Households in Global Production*, edited by W. Dunaway. Stanford, California: Stanford University Press.

Dunaway, Wilma. 2014b. "Bringing Commodity Chain Analysis Back to its World-Systems Roots: Rediscovering Women's Work and Households." *Journal of World – Systems Research* 20 (1):64–81. doi: 10.5195/jwsr.2014.576.

Dunaway, Wilma. 2001. "The Double Register of History: Situating the Forgotten Woman and Her Household In Capitalist Commodity Chains." *Journal of World-Systems Research* 7 (1):2–29.

Düzgün, Eren. 2018. "Capitalism, Jacobinism and International Relations: Re-interpreting the Ottoman Path to Modernity." *Review of International Studies* 44 (2):252–278. doi: 10.1017/S0260210517000468.

Düzgün, Eren. 2017. "Agrarian Change, Industrialization and Geopolitics: Beyond the Turkish Sonderweg." *Archives Europeennes de Sociologie* 58 (3):405–439. doi: 10.1017/S0003975617000194.

Düzgün, Eren. 2012a. "Capitalist Modernity A la Turca: Turkey's 'Great Transformation' Reconsidered." *Critical Sociology* 39 (6):889–909. doi: 10.1177/0896920512451605

Düzgün, Eren. 2012b. "Class, State and Property: Modernity and Capitalism in Turkey." *European Journal of Sociology* 53 (2):119–148. doi:10.1017/S0003975612000070

Düzgün, Eren. 2019. "The political economy of the transition to capitalism in the ottoman empire and turkey: Towards a new interpretation." In *Case Studies in the Origins of Capitalism*, edited by X. Lafrance and C. Post. London, New York: Palgrave Macmillan.

Elson, Diana, Caren Grown, and Nilüfer Çağatay. 2007. "Mainstream, heterodox and feminist trade theory." In *The Feminist Economics of Trade*, edited by D. Elson, I. Van Staveren, C. Grown and N. Çağatay. London, New York: Routledge.

Elson, Diane. 1995. "Gender Awareness in Modeling Structural Adjustment." *World Development* 23 (11):1851–1868. doi: 10.1016/0305-750X(95)00087-S.

Elson, Diane, Caren Grown, and Nilüfer Çağatay. 2000. "Introduction." *World Development* 28 (7):1145–1156. doi: 10.1016/s0305-750x(00)00032-2.

Erel, Umut, and Necla Açık. 2020. "Enacting Intersectional Multilayered Citizenship: Kurdish Women's Politics." *Gender, Place and Culture* 27 (4):479–501. doi: 10.1080/0966369X.2019.1596883.

Fields, Gary S. 2004. "Dualism in the Labour Market: A Perspective on The Lewis Model After Half A Century." *Manchester School* 72 (6):724–735. doi: 10.1111/j.1467-9957.2004.00432.x.

Gollin, Douglas. 2014. "The Lewis Model: A 60-year Retrospective." *Journal of Economic Perspectives* 28 (3):71–88. doi: 10.1257/jep.28.3.71.

Griffin, Keith, Azizur Rahman Khan, and Amy Ickowitz. 2002. "Poverty and the Distribution of Land." *Journal of Agrarian Change* 2 (3):279–330. doi: 10.1111/1471-0366.00036.

Gürel, Burak. 2019. "Semi-private Landownership and Capitalist Agriculture in Contemporary China." *Review of Radical Political Economics* 51 (4):650–669. doi: 10.1177/0486613419849683.

Gürel, Burak. 2011. "Agrarian Change and Labour Supply in Turkey, 1950-1980." *Journal of Agrarian Change* 11 (2):195–219.

Gürel, Burak, Bermal Küçük, and Sercan Taş. 2019. "The Rural Roots of the Rise of the Justice and Development Party in Turkey." *The Journal of Peasant Studies* 1–23. doi: 10.1080/03066150.2018.1552264.

Hairong, Yan, and Chen Yiyuan. 2015. "Agrarian Capitalization without Capitalism? Capitalist Dynamics from above and below in China." *Journal of Agrarian Change* 15 (3):366–391. doi: 10.1111/joac.12121.

Haney, Lynne. 1996. "Homeboys, Babies, Men in Suits: The State and the Reproduction of Male Dominance." *American Sociological Review* 61 (5):759–778. doi: 10.2307/2096452.

Haney, Lynne. 2000. "Feminist State Theory: Applications to Jurisprudence, Criminology, and the Welfare State." *Annual Review of Sociology* 26 (1):641–666. doi: 10.1146/annurev.soc.26.1.641.

Heper, Metin. 1985. *The State Tradition in Turkey*. Walkington: Eothen Press.

Huntington, Samuel P. 1998. *The Clash of Civilizations and the Remaking of World Order*. London: Touchstone.

Inglehart, Ronald F., and Pippa Norris. 2003a. *Rising Tide: Gender Equality and Cultural Change Around the World*. London, New York: Cambridge University Press. doi: 10.1017/CBO9780511550362

Inglehart, Ronald F., and Pippa Norris. 2003b. "The True Clash of Civilizations." *Foreign Policy* (135):62–70. doi: 10.2307/3183594.

İlkkaracan, İpek, and İnsan Tunali. 2011. "Agricultural transformation and the rural labor market in Turkey." In *Rethinking Structural Reform in Turkish Agriculture: Beyond the World Bank's Strategy*, edited by B. Karapınar, F. Adaman and G. Özartaş. New York: Nova Science Publishers Inc.

Jessop, Bob. 2002. *The Future of the Capitalist State*. Oxford: Polity.

Johnson, Susan. 2005. "Gender Relations, Empowerment and Microcredit: Moving on From a Lost Decade." *European Journal of Development Research* 17 (2):224–248. doi: 10.1080/09578810500130831.

Kabeer, Naila. 2001. *The Power to Choose. Bangladeshi Women and Labour Market Decisions in London and Dhaka*. London: Verso.

Kabeer, Naila. 2003. *Gender Mainstreaming in Poverty Eradication and the Millennium Development Goals: A Handbook for Policy-Makers and Other Stakeholders.* Ottawa, CA: IDRC Books/Les Éditions du CRDI.

Kabeer, Naila. 2005. "Is Microfinance a 'Magic Bullet' for Women's Empowerment? Analysis of Findings from South Asia." *Economic and Political Weekly* 40 (44/45):4709–4718.

Kazgan, Gülten. 2013. *Tarım ve Gelişme.* İstanbul: İstanbul Bilgi Üniversitesi Yayınları.

Kentel, Ferhat, Perrin Emre-Öğün, and Murat Öztürk. 2017. *Kır Mekânının Sosyo-Ekonomik ve Kültürel Dönüşümü: Modernleşen ve Kaybolan Geleneksel Mekânlar ve Anlamlar.* Ankara: TUBITAK.

Keyder, Çağlar. 1987. *State and Class in Turkey: A Study in Capitalist development.* London: Verso.

Keyder, Çağlar, and Zafer Yenal. 2011. "Agrarian Change Under Globalisation: Markets and Insecurity in Turkish Agriculture." *Journal of Agrarian Change* 11 (1):60–86.

Kirkpatrick, Colin, and Armando Barrientos. 2004. "The Lewis Model After 50 years." *Manchester School* 72 (6):679–690. doi: 10.1111/j.1467-9957.2004.00429.x.

Korotayev, Andrey V., Leonid M. Issaev, and Alisa R. Shishkina. 2015. "Female Labor Force Participation Rate, Islam, and Arab Culture in Cross-Cultural Perspective." *Cross-Cultural Research* 49 (1):3–19. doi: 10.1177/1069397114536126.

Krueger, Anne O. 2000. "NAFTA's Effects: A Preliminary Assessment." *World Economy* 23 (6):761–775. doi: 10.1111/1467-9701.00302.

Krugman, Paul R., and Maurice Obstfeld. 2006. *International Economics: Theory and Policy. The Addison-Wesley Series in Economics.* Boston, Mass.: Addison-Wesley.

Kocabıçak, Ece. 2021. "Gendered Property and Labour Relations in Agriculture: Implications for Social Change in Turkey." Oxford Development Studies forthcoming. doi: 10.1080/13600818.2021.1929914.

Köymen, Oya. 2008. *Kapitalizm ve Köylülük: Ağalar, Üretenler, Patronlar.* İstanbul: Yordam kitap.

Lenin, Vladimir Il'ich. 1977. *The Development of Capitalism in Russia.* Progress Publishers.

Lewis, Arthur W. 1954. "Economic Development with Unlimited Supplies of Labour." *The Manchester School* 22 (2):139–191.

Löwith, Karl. 2002. *Max Weber and Karl Marx*: Taylor and Francis.

MacKinnon, Catharine A. 1983. "Feminism, Marxism, Method, and the State: Toward Feminist Jurisprudence." *Signs: Journal of Women in Culture and Society* 8 (4):635–658. doi: 10.1086/494000.

MacKinnon, Catharine A. 1991. *Toward a Feminist Theory of the State*: Harvard University Press.

Mardin, Şerif. 2006 [1967]. "Historical thresholds and stratification: Social class and class consciousness." In *Religion, Society and Modernity in Turkey,* edited by S. Mardin. New York: Syracuse University Press.

Marx, Karl. 1976. *Capital: A Critique of Political Economy (vol 3).* England: Penguin Books.

Moghadam, Valentine. 2017. "The Semi-Periphery, World Revolution, and the Arab Spring: Reflections on Tunisia." *Journal of World - Systems Research* 23 (2): 620–636. doi: 10.5195/JWSR.2017.724.

Molyneux, Maxine. 2006. "Mothers at the Service of the New Poverty Agenda: Progresa/Oportunidades, Mexico's Conditional Transfer Programme." *Social Policy & Administration* 40 (4):425–449. doi: 10.1111/j.1467-9515.2006.00497.x.

Molyneux, Maxine, and Marilyn Thomson. 2011. "Cash Transfers, Gender Equity and Women's Empowerment in Peru, Ecuador and Bolivia." *Gender and Development* 19 (2):195–212. doi: 10.1080/13552074.2011.592631.

Moore, Barrington. 1966. *Social Origins of Dictatorship and Democracy: Lord and Peasant in the Making of the Modern World.* Boston: Beacon Press.

Novack, George. 1957. *The Irregular Movement of History the Marxist Law of the Combined and Uneven Development of Society.* New York: Spark Publishers.

Offe, Claus, and John Keane. 1984. *Contradictions of the Welfare State, Contemporary Politics.* London: Hutchinson.

Orloff, Ann. 1996. "Gender in the Welfare State." *Annual Review of Sociology* 22 (1):51–78. doi: 10.1146/annurev.soc.22.1.51.

Orloff, Ann. 2017. "Gendered states made and remade: Gendered labor policies in the united states and Sweden, 1960–2010". In *The Many Hands of the State: Theorizing Political Authority and Social Control,* edited by K. Morgan & A. Orloff. Cambridge: Cambridge University Press. doi:10.1017/9781316471586.006

Oyvat, Cem. 2016. "Agrarian Structures, Urbanization, and Inequality." *World Development* 83 (C):207–230. doi: 10.1016/j.worlddev.2016.01.019.

Öniş, Ziya, and Fikret Şenses. 2009. "Küresel dinamikler, Ülkeiçi koalisyonlar ve reaktif devlet: Türkiye'nin savaş sonrasi kalkinmasinda Önemli politika dönüşümleri." In *Neoliberal Küreselleşme ve Kalkınma, Seçme Yazılar,* edited by F. Şenses. İstanbul: İletişim Yayınevi.

Özar, Şemsa. 1994. "Some Observations on the Position of Women in the Labour Market in the Development Process of Turkey." *Boğaziçi Journal: Review of Social, Economic and Administrative Studies* 8 (1):21–43.

Öztürk, Murat, Beşir Topaloğlu, Andy Hilton, and Joost Jongerden. 2017. "Rural–Urban Mobilities in Turkey: Socio-spatial Perspectives on Migration and Return Movements." *Journal of Balkan and Near Eastern Studies* 20 (5):513–530. doi: 10.1080/19448953.2018.1406696.

O'Laughlin, Bridget. 2012. "Gender justice, land and the agrarian question in Southern Africa." In *Peasants and Globalization: Political Economy, Rural Transformation and the Agrarian Question,* edited by A. H. Akram-Lodhi and C. Kay. London, New York: Taylor and Francis.

Pateman, Carole. 1988. *The Sexual Contract.* Cambridge: Polity Press.

Poulantzas, Nicos. 1969. "The Problem of the Capitalist State." *New Left Review* 1/58, 67–78.

Poulantzas, Nicos. 1980. *State, Power, Socialism.* London: Verso.

Psacharopoulos, George, and Zafiris Tzannatos. 1989. "Female Labour Force Participation: An International Perspective." *Research Observer* 4 (2):187–201.

Pyle, Jean L. 1990. *The State and Women in the Economy: Lessons from Sex Discrimination in the Republic of Ireland.* New York: State University of New York Press.

Qi, Hao, and Zhongjin Li. 2019. "Giovanni Arrighi in Beijing: Rethinking the Transformation of the Labor Supply in Rural China during the Reform Era." *Science & Society* 83 (3):327–355. doi: 10.1521/siso.2019.83.3.327.

Rai, Shirin M., and Georgina Waylen. 2008. *Global Governance: Feminist Perspectives.* London, New York: Palgrave Macmillan.

Razavi, Shahra, Ruth Pearson, and Caroline Danloy. 2004. *Globalization, Export-Oriented Employment and Social Policy: Gendered Connections.* Palgrave Macmillan.

Razavi, Shahra. 2009. *The Gendered Impacts of Liberalization: Towards 'Embedded Liberalism'?* edited by Development United Nations Research Institute for Social and Shahra Razavi. New York, London, Abingdon: Routledge.

Robinson, Joan. 2017 [1937]. *Essays in the Theory of Employment.* London: Andesite Press.

Rodrik, Dani. 2007. "How to Save Globalization from Its Cheerleaders." *The Journal of International Trade and Diplomacy* (1): 1–33.

Rosenstein-Rodan, Paul N. 1943. "Problems of Industrialisation of Eastern and South-Eastern Europe." *The Economic Journal* 53 (210/211):202–211. doi: 10.2307/2226317.

Rosenstein-Rodan, Paul N. 1961. *International Aid for Underdeveloped Countries.* edited by Centre for International Studies. Cambridge, Massachusetts: Massachusetts Institute of Technology.

Rostow, Walt. W. 1956. "The Take-off into Self-Sustained Growth." *The Economic Journal* 66 (261): 25–48. doi: 10.2307/2227401.

Rostow, Walt. W. 1960. *The Stages of Economic Growth: A Non-Communist Manifesto.* Cambridge, New York, Melbourne: Cambridge University Press.

Seguino, Stephanie. 2011. "The global economic crisis, its gender and ethnic implications and policy responses." In *Gender and the Economic Crisis*, edited by R. Pearson and C. Sweetman. London, New York: Practical Action.

Seguino, Stephanie, and Caren Grown. 2007. "Gender equity and globalisation: Macroeconomic policy for developing countries." In *The Feminist Economics of Trade*, edited by D. Elson, I. Van Staveren, C. Grown and N. Cagatay. London New York: Routledge.

Seguino, Stephanie. 2020. "Engendering Macroeconomic Theory and Policy." *Feminist Economics* 26 (2):27–61. doi: 10.1080/13545701.2019.1609691.

Serra, Narcís, and Joseph E. Stiglitz. 2008. *The Washington Consensus Reconsidered: Towards a New Global Governance.* Oxford: Oxford University Press.

Skocpol, Theda. 1985. "Bringing the state back in: Strategies of analysis in current research." In *Bringing the State Back In*, edited by P. Evans, D. Rueschemeyer and T. Skocpol. Cambridge University Press.

Solow, Robert M. 1956. "A Contribution to The Theory of Economic Growth." *Quarterly Journal of Economics* 70 (1):65–95.

Spierings, Niels, Jeroen Smits, and Mieke Verloo. 2009. "On the Compatibility of Islam and Gender Equality." *Social Indicators Research* 90 (3):503–522. doi: 10.1007/s11205-008-9274-z.

Swan, Trevor W. 1956. "Economic Grwoth and Capital Accumulation." *Economic Record* 32 (2):334–361. doi: 10.1111/j.1475-4932.1956.tb00434.x.

Temple, Jonathan. 2005. "Dual Economy Models: A Primer for Growth Economists." *Manchester School* 73 (4):435–478. doi: 10.1111/j.1467-9957.2005.00454.x.

Tilly, Charles. 1990. *Coercion, Capital, and European States, AD 990–1990.* Cambridge, Oxford: Basil Blackwell Ltd.

Toksöz, Gülay. 2011. *Kalkınmada Kadın Emeği.* İstanbul: Varlık yayınları.

Toksöz, Gülay. 2012. "Kalkınmada farkli yörüngeler: Kadın İstihdamında farkli Örüntüler ışığında türkiye'de kadin İstihdamı." In *Geçmişten Günümüze Türkiye'de Kadın Emeği*, edited by A. Makal and G. Toksöz. Ankara: University of Ankara.

Trotsky, Leon. 1980. *The History of the Russian Revolution.* Vol. 1. New York: Monad Press.

Wade, Robert. 2003. *Governing the Market: Economic Theory and the Role of Government in East Asian Industrialization.* Princeton: Princeton University Press.

Walby, Sylvia. 2009. *Globalisation and Inequalities: Complexity and Contested Modernities.* London: Sage Publications Ltd.

Wallerstein, Immanuel Maurice. 1974. *The Modern World-System: Capitalist Agriculture and the Origins of the European World-Economy in the Sixteenth Century.* New York: Academic Press.

Wallerstein, Immanuel Maurice. 2004. *World-systems Analysis: An Introduction.* Durham: Duke University Press.

Wang, Xiaobing, and Jenifer Piesse. 2013. "The Micro-Foundations of Dual Economy Models." *Manchester School* 81 (1):80–101. doi: 10.1111/j.1467-9957.2011.02263.x.

Weber, Max. 1930. *The Protestant Ethic and the Spirit of Capitalism.* London, New York: Routledge.

Weber, Max. 1947. *The Theory of Social and Economic Organisation.* New York: Free press.

Weber, Max. 1976. *The Agrarian Sociology of Ancient Civilizations.* London: Humanities Press.

Wood, Ellen M. 1981. "The Separation of the Economic and the Political In Capitalism." *New Left Review I,* 127: 66–93.

Wood, Ellen M. 1998. "The Agrarian Origins of Capitalism." *Monthly Review* 50 (3): 14–31.

Wood, Ellen M. 2002. "The Question of Market Dependence." *Journal of Agrarian Change* 2 (1): 50–87.

Yeates, Nicola. 2004. "Global Care Chains: Critical Reflections and Lines of Enquiry." *International Feminist Journal of Politics* 6(3): 369–391 doi: 10.1080/1461674042000235573.

2 CONCEPTUAL ABANDONMENT OF PATRIARCHAL LABOUR EXPLOITATION

The main concern of this book is to investigate the ways in which the short-comings of social theory prevent effective feminist strategies sustaining the paradox of a resilient feminist opposition coupled with persistent patriar-chal injustices. In this regard, the previous chapter critically assessed influ-ential theories on socio-economic transformation. In this chapter, I analyse the ways in which the lack of attention to patriarchal labour exploitation within the cis-gender heterosexual family weakens feminist strategies by either reducing the dynamics of gendered oppression to the capitalist sys-tem or obscuring the causes of gender inequality.

Feminist research has largely dropped analysis of patriarchal labour exploitation from their theoretical framework and has instead followed a number of alternative approaches. Two of those approaches appear to be very influential in shaping feminist strategies: one identifies the capitalist system as the key determinant of uneven gender relations, and another conceptualises the multi-faced structure of gender inequality. The former subordinates the distinguishing dynamics of the patriarchal property and labour relations to the capitalist system, whereas, the latter conceals the cau-sality by obscuring the nexus between the exploitation of labour and social inequalities. The chapter starts with a brief assessment of the early theories on patriarchal exploitation (Section 2.1). Then I explain how abandoning the concept of patriarchal labour exploitation leads the social reproduction approach to a position of capitalism-based reductionism (Section 2.2) and limits varieties of gender regime theories to analysis of the aspects of gender inequality (Section 2.3).

2.1 The initial accounts of patriarchal exploitation

Early theories of the second wave feminist movement provide a detailed account of how male dominance is produced, maintained and changed. For example, Susan Brownmiller (1975) claims that rape is the main mechanism that sustains male supremacy by keeping women in subjection, whereas, Catharine A. MacKinnon (1982) suggests that men exert power over women through sexual violence, including sexual harassment, rape, pornography

DOI: 10.4324/9781003054511-4

and prostitution. Kate Millett (1977) argues that men oppress women in every aspect of life including family, economy, religion, sexuality and psychology, and as such patriarchy is considered as a particular mode of power relations and domination which cross cuts class and spatial differences. These various approaches are however, limited to examining the dynamics of unequal power relations and tend to portray men as an oppressor group in and of themselves. In this way, the reasons why men dominate women are overlooked. Nevertheless, the initial theories of patriarchal exploitation provide a detailed analysis of causality by exploring the connections between gender-based exploitation, oppression and inequality. These studies are differentiated by their analysis of what patriarchal exploitation comprises: (i) men's exploitation of women as a whole, or (ii) women's reproductive work or (iii) women's domestic labour (including care labour) within the home.

2.1.1 Men exploit women as a whole

The studies of Andrea Dworkin and Colette Guillaumin provide a detailed account of the patriarchal exploitation of women. While, Dworkin (1983) suggests that gender inequality is derived from men's exploitation of women's bodies and sexuality, Guillaumin (1995) argues that men appropriate women's time and sexuality, the products of their body (children) as well as women's care labour for sick, elderly and disabled male members of society. In her investigation of the powers of patriarchal exploitation, Dworkin proposes that rape, battery, economic exploitation and reproductive exploitation keep women at the bottom of the sex hierarchy. Meanwhile, Guillaumin proposes that *the means of patriarchal exploitation* include (i) the labour market which does not allow women to establish an independent life from men, (ii) direct force, i.e. male violence against women, (iii) sexuality-based constraints, (iv) the arsenal of the law and customary rights and (v) spatial confinement meaning that men in their position as husbands have the right to determine women's place of residence.

Furthermore, these scholars examine the contradictions surrounding patriarchal exploitation. Guillaumin, for example, identifies two kinds of contradictions – one is the contradiction between the *private* and the *collective* appropriation of women and another is the contradiction between the patriarchal bondage and the capitalist labour market. Drawing a distinction between private and collective appropriation of women by men, she describes collective appropriation as the generalised relationship between men and women, and argues that private appropriation derives from some men's appropriation of some women within the domestic sphere. According to her, marriage restricts other men's (e.g. fathers, brothers, religious men) usage of this particular woman by giving this usage to a single individual man. Private appropriation is therefore a particular and restricted form of collective appropriation:

[Women] are appropriated as a group (and not only as individuals bound by personal ties). And it is known that *this appropriation is collective*: it is not limited to the private appropriation of some of us, by the husband (or concubine-keeper) when one is a wife. But every man (and not only fathers and husbands) has rights over all women, and these rights are *lessened* only by the private appropriation of a woman by a particular man. And finally no woman, even if she has escaped private appropriation, has ownership of herself

(Guillaumin 1995: 240, my emphasis)

Guillaumin identifies another contradiction between the patriarchal appropriation of women and the fact that women can sell their labour power:

A second contradiction takes place between the appropriation of women, whether it be collective or private, and their re-appropriation by themselves, their objective existence as social subjects – in other words, the possibility of their selling on their own authority their labour power on the classical open market

(Guillaumin 1995: 194)

In French, *esclavage* means slavery and *servage* means serfdom. By coining the term *sexage*, Guillaumin establishes a conceptual link between the systems of slavery and patriarchy. In slavery and feudalism, bondage is the main relationship between the appropriators (masters and feudal lords) and direct producers (slaves and serfs) whereas there is no bondage in capitalism, meaning labourers are "free" to sell their labour power. She highlights that women are not free labourers but rather *bounded* to men. *Sexage*, therefore, refers to a system derived from men's collective appropriation of women. Capitalism shifts the status of women to labourers who are free to sell their labour, leading to a contradiction between the patriarchal bondage of *sexage* and "free" capitalist wage labour (Juteau-Lee 1995; Guillaumin 1995).

Dworkin, on the other hand, develops concept of the *sex-class system*, in which women constitute a gender-based class and share a common condition that is "subordinate to men, sexually colonised in a sexual system of dominance and submission, denied rights on the basis of sex, historically chattel, generally considered biologically inferior, confined to sex and reproduction" (Dworkin 1983: 221). She distinguishes two major forms of the sex-class system: *the farming model* and *the brothel model*. In the farming model, single men control single women's domestic labour and reproductive abilities through child-birth. The male-headed marriage and motherhood are thus the necessary conditions of the farming model. The brothel model is based on the sexual use of women as women are collected to serve many men:

In the brothel model, several women belong to one man... the brothel suggests a wealth of women available to the man, it means he is rich in

having so many women in one place for him, it means he chooses abso-
lutely and his will is done by whomever he chooses

(Dworkin 1983: 178–79)

Dworkin points out that these models are on a continuum, arguing that
they represent a set of forms for the "mass use of whole class" (1983: 185).
The distinction and opposition between the farming and brothel models,
she argues, is in fact superficial since they are two sides of the same coin.
For Dworkin then, the farming and brothel models are the trajectories of
patriarchal exploitation.

Although, the earlier mentioned frameworks provide a valuable account
of the powers of patriarchal exploitation, they do have some limitations.
First, the products of labour appropriated by the dominant sections of society need to be distinguished from the aspects of this exploitation. To a certain extent, all forms of exploitation of labour – in patriarchy, capitalism,
feudalism or slavery – encompass labourers' time and bodily energy necessary for production, but appropriation of time and bodily energy are aspects
of labour exploitation. Second, considering Guillaumin's emphasis on the
patriarchal exploitation of the products of women's body (i.e. children), I
argue that fathers' appropriation of children's labour is different from patriarchal exploitation. Children are children for a limited time period, yet men
exploit women for their entire life. In addition, children's labour is not necessarily unpaid. In some cases, fathers do provide payment to their sons
through inheritance, and to their daughters through dowry. Third, powers
necessary to sustain the exploitation of labour are different to the products
of labour appropriated by the dominant sections of society. In case of patriarchy, for example, men utilise compulsory heterosexuality to sustain their
patriarchal exploitation of labour within the cis-gender heterosexual family,
yet do not exploit women's sexuality.

Fourth, Guillaumin identifies a contradiction between men as individuals and men as the collective group, but Dworkin emphasises the nexus
between the collective and individual exploitation throughout the farmer
and brothel models. I suggest that exploitation of labour occurs both at
individual and collective levels which tends to raise the appropriators' consciousness at both individual and collective levels. I do not deny that there
may be tensions amongst different groups of appropriators. For example,
a landowning male peasant who benefits from his daughter's labour on the
land, loses this unpaid labourer to another man following his daughter's
marriage. The father, the groom and other male peasants in the village,
however, know that sustaining the (cis-gender) heterosexual family is a precondition for their exploitation of women's labour, so the father does not
prevent his daughter's marriage. Like other appropriators, their collective
consciousness maintains men's overall interest as the appropriators.

Finally, Guillaumin identifies a contradiction between the patriarchal
and capitalist exploitations of labour but at the same time points out that

gendered patterns in the labour market maintain women's dependency on the heterosexual family structure. Rather than a contradiction, I argue that this is a tension, which can be resolved through establishing women's double burden of paid and unpaid labour. As Carol Brown (1981) describes, women handle domestic goods and services produced within the home but at the same time get involved in paid employment in the non-agricultural sectors. Under such conditions, I suggest, the sustainability of women's double burden is guaranteed by the state. The contradiction described by Guillaumin, therefore, appears to be a tension that requires state regulation.

2.1.2 Men exploit women's reproductive abilities and labour

Stressing the equal significance of the patriarchal and capitalist relations of labour, these scholars propose that patriarchal exploitation derives from men's appropriation of women's reproductive abilities and labour. For example, Maureen Mackintosh (1977; 1984) suggests that the subordination of women to men is embedded in the sexual division of labour in agricultural and non-agricultural household based activities. Mackintosh defines patriarchy as men's control of the means of reproduction, including women's fertility, bodies and sexual preferences. She investigates the connections between the social relations of human reproduction and the dominant mode of production, arguing against the notion that the dynamics of women's reproductive roles are subordinate to the capitalist system. Instead, Mackintosh proposes that the mutual determinations between the capitalist mode of production and the patriarchal relations of reproduction need to be examined.

In her research, Lourdes Beneria (1979) investigates how far reproductive obligations limit women's mobility, and suggests that women's role within the reproduction sphere is the key dynamic which shapes the conditions of their subordination and access to the labour market, as well as the gendered division of labour. Nancy Folbre (1983, 1982), furthermore, elaborates on the connections between men's control over women's reproductive labour within the family and women's access to paid employment in the labour market. She suggests that men keep women busy within the home by refusing to share care work. This strategy, in turn, disadvantages women in the labour market, increases men's bargaining power within the family as well as maintaining women's dependency on men. Folbre (1987) also argues that in capitalism men continue to benefit from children as unpaid family workers within small production units and establish some degree of control over their children's future income.

To summarise, these scholars emphasise that the patriarchal relations of reproduction are as significant as the capitalist relations of production for socio-economic transformation. Moreover, their approach reveals the extent to which men benefit from women's reproductive work and thereby enables an assessment of the causality of persistent gendered oppression and inequality. However, they tend to neglect the complicated structure of the patriarchal exploitation of labour by limiting men's appropriation of women's labour to the reproductive labour associated with childbearing and thus assume that women's unpaid labour within the family is limited to the provision of non-market goods and services. This assumption, in turn, prevents a detailed investigation of the complicated structure of patriarchal relations of production. Furthermore, the conceptual division between production and reproduction does not explain the conditions of patriarchal labour exploitation. As Stephanie Coontz and Peta Henderson (1986) highlights, it is not male control over the women's reproductive capacities but the control of her labour power and of her potential to produce a surplus within a determinate set of production relations and division of labour that explains the condition of women. Next, I, elaborate on the scholarship that emphasises the continuity between the patriarchal exploitation of labour within the reproductive and productive spheres.

2.1.3 Men exploit women's labour within the family

Christine Delphy develops one of the most comprehensive theories concerning the patriarchal exploitation of women's labour by identifying two modes of production available within contemporary industrialised societies: domestic and capitalist modes of production. The domestic mode of production gives rise to patriarchal exploitation whereas, the capitalist mode gives rise to capitalist exploitation (Delphy 1977). Accordingly, she identifies gender inequality as "the system of subordination of women to men in contemporary industrial societies" and argues that "this system has an economic base, and that this base is the domestic mode of production" (1984: 18). In the domestic mode of production, marriage constitutes a contractual relationship between men and women, whereby men exploit women's domestic labour within the home. Women's work at home does not only include economically or practically productive work, but also comprises cultural, emotional, sexual and reproductive work (Delphy 1992). A single task can involve more than one form of work and these forms are not necessarily limited to the domestic sphere, for example childcare can extend beyond the domestic sphere.

Drawing on her research on patriarchal property and labour relations in peasant families, Delphy (2003; 1977) also argues that women's unpaid family labour does not only produce use value, but also produces exchange value. She, therefore, suggests that the division between production and reproduction is inaccurate. Moreover, according to Delphy (1984), the positions of men and women in the domestic mode of production refer to different class positions in conflict. Rejecting the argument that women's oppression derives almost entirely from ideological, cultural and/or psychological factors, Delphy (1992) proposes that women's material oppression maintains the ideological or psychological power of men as the oppressors, though further research is necessary to provide a satisfactory account of the relationship between patriarchy and the domestic mode of production.

In her recent studies, Delphy (2014; 2004) suggests that the Marxist theory of surplus value constitutes a barrier to investigating the co-existence of multiple forms of exploitation, obscuring that patriarchy, as well as feudalism and slavery, are pertinent along with capitalism. Developing the concept of *extortion of labour*, she emphasises that capitalist labour exploitation is one form of labour extortion, but not the only form. Slaves, serfs, peons and wives are also exploited within contemporary societies. In order to address the articulations between the capitalist, domestic, slave and serfdom modes of production, Delphy proposes that a general theory of exploitation needs to be developed based on the concept of labour extortion.

The studies of Delphy are powerful and influential and this book is intended to be a companion to them. Nevertheless, her original interpretation of historical materialism has some limitations that I wish to go beyond. First, Delphy provides a critical assessment of Marxist reductionism yet, as I will discuss in Chapter 8, the Althusserian base/superstructure approach remains influential in her analysis. Subsequently, her lack of attention to the Hegelian principle of unity of the material and social leads to the separation of the material base of gendered oppression and inequality (i.e. the domestic mode of production) from the patriarchal system. In turn, this confounds the workings of the material base and creates some ambiguity with regard to the constitution of the patriarchal system.

Second, Marx's theory of surplus value is crucial in understanding the distinguishing features of capitalist labour exploitation but not all varieties of labour exploitation need to comply with such theory. As Folbre suggests, "patriarchal exploitation can be defined in the same way Marxists have always defined exploitation in non-capitalist modes of production such as feudalism: in terms of surplus labour time, or the difference between the amount of time individuals work and the amount of time embodied in the goods they themselves consume" (1987: 331). Needless to say, all forms of labour exploitation different to capitalist exploitation of labour need to be recognised. However, here the concern is that a general theory of exploitation conceals the distinguishing ways in which exploitation of labour is mediated under patriarchy, capitalism or modern slavery. An example of this problem is when Delphy (2004) fails to distinguish the patriarchal relations of agrarian production and labour exploitation from feudalism in Pakistan.

Third, Delphy insists on focusing on patriarchy rather than examining the interconnections between patriarchy and capitalism (or racism) (Jackson 1996). While I agree that analysis of the patriarchal system cannot be reduced to the ways capitalism necessitates patriarchy, in order to provide a detailed account of any system of exploitation one must assess its relationship with other systems. For example, as argued previously, a dismissal of patriarchy prevents the classical and Marxist political economists from adequately describing the determinants of capitalist transformation. Likewise, the mutually shaping relationship between patriarchal and capitalist systems of exploitation and the racist regimes of oppression reveals the key characteristics of patriarchy and therefore cannot be ignored.

Finally, in her analysis of multiple forms of exploitation, Delphy does not seem to differentiate the main characteristics of labour exploitation in modern slavery. History witnessed a particular form of slavery which drew on the naturalisation processes, whereby some skins were socially marked as symbols of being a slave (Guillaumin 1995). The exploitative system of slavery still exists but its contemporary forms do not draw on the same naturalisation process. Rather, the race-based system of slavery is being replaced with contemporary forms of slavery whereby, the enslaved people's condition is not naturalised. As Emily Kenway (2021) argues, poverty in conjunction with the immigration and border control policies are the key enablers of modern slavery. These contemporary forms of labour exploitation do not necessarily give rise to racism in the same way as the historical transatlantic slave trade and, at the same time, the contemporary varieties of racist regimes are not limited to anti-Black racism, but also include anti-indigenous, anti-migrant, anti-Jewish, anti-Palestinian, anti-caste, anti-Alevi or anti-Kurdish racisms. Thus, I argue that feminist theories need to differentiate the naturalisation process of race-based slavery from contemporary forms of slavery. In the former, certain skins are socially marked as a symbol of being a slave and, as such, lead to anti-Black racism, whereas, the latter is derived from exploitation of unfree labour but is not necessarily associated with such a naturalisation process.

Thus far, I have assessed the key theories of patriarchal exploitation based on their account of what such exploitation comprises: (i) men exploit women as a whole, (ii) men exploit women's reproductive work or (iii) men exploit women's domestic labour (including care labour) within the family. Despite their differences, these scholars all conceptualise the role of patriarchal exploitation in reproducing gendered oppression and inequality. The initial debate on the patriarchal exploitation of labour has, however, been interrupted leading to neglect of the importance of gendered patterns of labour exploitation. This interruption has multiple origins, including the argument that gender relations are fragmented on the basis of, for example, class, race, ethnicity and age differences, and as such do not have a systemic characteristic (Patil 2013; Pollert 1996; Barrett 1980). At the same time, theories on patriarchal labour exploitation are portrayed as economically deterministic (Barrett and McIntosh 1979). These critical interventions into the debate have initiated a shift from "how the subordination of women is produced, maintained, and changed" towards "how gender is involved in processes and structures" (Acker 1989: 238). Rather than revealing the dynamics sustaining gender inequality, feminist theories have increasingly focused on the ways that gender relations are produced in certain processes or organisations (e.g. science, military, labour market) (Harding 1986; Hacker and Hacker 1987; Acker 1988).

Consequently, the initial discussion on the connections between gendered patterns of labour exploitation and gendered oppression and inequality is interrupted. Although, research on the gender gaps in time spent on housework (including care work) continue to reveal a sharp gender-based division of labour and inequality across class, race-ethnicity and geography differences (Kongar and Memiş 2017; Öneş, Memiş, and Kızılırmak 2013; Gershuny and Harms 2016; Ringhofer 2015), such imbalance is perceived as one of the aspects of patriarchal norms and attitudes. Dismissing the significance of patriarchal labour exploitation within the cis-gender heterosexual family leads to the adoption of different feminist approaches. The next section assesses two of those approaches, namely the social reproduction approach (Section 2.2) and theories on varieties of gender regimes (Section 2.3).

2.2 Causality reduced to capitalism: The social reproduction approach

The social reproduction approach derives from the domestic labour debate (1970s–1980s) which focused on the role of women's domestic/unpaid labour within the home in *subsidising* capitalist wages (Dalla Costa and James 1973; Harrison 1973; Benston 1969), or being *necessary* for daily life maintenance and the reproduction of labour power (Himmelweit and Mohun 1977; Gardiner 1975; Morton 1971). This initial debate has since been developed by further research. Drawing on their analysis of primitive accumulation, Maria Mies, Veronika Bennholdt-Thomsen, and Claudia von Werlhof (1988), for example, contribute to the social reproduction approach by arguing that capitalism not only relies on wage labour but also requires various forms of non-wage labour. According to these scholars, capitalism is in fact characterised by the non-wage relations of subsistence reproducers. No labourers would be free to sell their labour power without women's unwaged labour within the home. Considering that women's domestic labour is the most important form of non-wage labour, these scholars claim that the super-exploitation of women, colonies and nature is a prerequisite for the primitive accumulation required by contemporary capitalism. They further develop the concept of housewifisation in referring to the housewifisation of women and of labour. In the former, women are confined to the home since domestic labour is a prerequisite for capital accumulation. In the latter, a particular category of labourers (i.e. precariat) replaces the proletariat who are too expensive and not productive enough (Mies 1998 [1986]; Mies, Bennholdt-Thomsen, and Werlhof 1988).

Feminist theories on social reproduction also focus on the separation between the spheres of production of value and reproduction of labour power during the capitalist transition. As Tithi Bhattacharya states, "the activities to reproduce life (unwaged) and the activities to produce commodities (waged) grew to be strictly separated and the latter began to *determine* the former" (Bhattacharya 2017: 18, my emphasis). The dynamics of commodity production therefore determines the reproduction of labour power.

An example of such an approach is the original work of Silvia Federici. Federici (2004) argues that women's reproductive labour within the home is a precondition for the capitalist exploitation of wage labour. Capitalism, she argues, sustained women's reproductive labour by establishing a new sexual division of labour. This sexual division of labour required a new patriarchal order which excluded women from free wage labour and subordinated women to men. Subsequently, the European ruling class arranged paid employment to maintain women's subordination to men and "appropriation of their [women's] labour by male workers" (Federici 2004: 98). Federici further claims that capitalism benefits from the "power-difference" between men and women in many ways (2004: 115). For instance, capitalists manage to increase the unpaid part of the working day by sustaining women's reproductive labour and, in so doing, accumulate women's labour. According to Federici, the capitalist classes also replace class antagonism with an antagonism between men and women, male workers therefore did not gain but lost from women's subordination:

> the power that men have imposed on women by virtue of their access to wage-labour and their recognised contribution to capitalist accumulation has been paid at the price of self-alienation, and the 'primitive disaccumulation' of their own individual and collective powers
>
> (Federici 2004: 115)

Drawing on this approach, Adrienne Roberts suggests that as gender difference is a precondition for capitalism and its reproduction, "violent and coercive forms of primitive accumulation", including capitalist utilisation of the law and welfare policies, have established a gender-based division of labour and sustained the control of capital and the state over women and social reproduction (Roberts 2017: 5). Likewise, Cinzia Arruzza attributes "a determining role to class exploitation", whereas, Martha Gimenez argues that as the dominant mode of production, capitalism determines human reproduction or mode of reproduction, therefore, the subordination of reproduction to production is common to all capitalist societies (Giménez 2018; Arruzza 2016: 15). In explaining the roots of women's oppression, others investigate "capital's dependence upon biological processes specific to women – pregnancy, childbirth, lactation – to secure the reproduction of the working-class" (Ferguson and McNally 2014: 29). The labouring body is therefore at the core of the social reproduction approach (Ferguson 2008). Others, furthermore, focus on the intensified privatisation and re-privatisation of social reproduction, and its increased integration with the global neoliberal governance (Bakker and Silvey 2008; Bakker 2007; Bakker and Gill 2003; Luxton and Bezanson 2006; Katz 2001).

Analysing the ways in which household production is embedded in global value chains, other scholars, however, reject the notion of an analytical divide between production and reproduction (Sen 2019; Dunaway 2014;

O'Laughlin 2012; Naz and Bögenhold 2020). Calling for a more holistic understanding of socio-economic activity, Wilma Dunaway suggests that "the productive and reproductive spheres are inextricably linked and over-lapping" (2014: 5). Jamie Winders and Barbara E. Smith (2019), furthermore, claim that early debates on social reproduction are based on the experience of US, Canadian, British and Italian women in white working class families in industrial cities. Other historical and geographical contexts, they suggest, point to different theoretical directions to the social reproduction approach. In addition, they argue that the wider scope recently adopted serves to shed light on the roles of neoliberalism, the state, and global governance but, at the same time, loses a focus on the patriarchal character of the household (Winders and Smith 2019).

Delphy's critique addresses an important methodological problem associated with the social reproduction approach. She argues that in the analysis of social reproduction, the capitalist system of production is positioned as the key determinant of social change. This positioning means the dynamics of social reproduction are subordinated to capitalist production and gendered oppression is understood as a consequence of capitalism (Delphy 1984) thereby obscuring patriarchal relations of production and reproduction. Theories on social reproduction, Delphy states, remain gender blind by failing to explain why it is almost exclusively women who are responsible for social reproduction (Delphy and Leonard 1992). Building on Delphy's critique, Stevi Jackson (1999) argues that this approach tends to sustain biological essentialism by reducing the dynamics of a gendered division of labour to women's reproductive abilities. Michèle Barrett (1984) also scrutinises the assumption that the gender-based division of labour is determined by childbirth and lactation; instead she argues that the matters perceived as biological, including lactation, are in fact social matters.

Moreover, those scholars' understanding of capitalism appears to be derived from the assumption that the locus of capitalism is an unequal exchange in the market. Alternatively, in their assessment of the Dependency and the World-System theories, Robert Brenner (1977) and Ellen Meiksins Wood (2002, 1999) criticise such a market based Neo-Smithian approach and emphasise the significance of the transformation of production relations for the transition to capitalism. Drawing on their approach, I argue that Mies neglects the distinctive characteristics of capitalist labour exploitation and suggests there is a transition from wage labour to non-wage labour, and at the same time, as others state, transition to capitalism is absent during the period when Federici argues for the role of capitalism in establishing the gender-based division of labour (Leach 2019; Folbre 2021).

Overall, the social reproduction approach appears to have three major limitations. First is the assumption of a one-sided deterministic relationship in which capitalist relations of labour (in production) dictate patriarchal labour relations (in reproduction) which overlooks the significance of patriarchal exploitation of labour for socio-economic transformation. As Delphy argues, these scholars subordinate the distinguishing dynamics of patriarchal labour relations to capitalist relations of labour. In doing so, they fail to explain the dynamics of the gendered division of labour. This first limitation gives rise to the second problem: in order to explain the roots of the gender-based division of labour within the home, the social reproduction approach draws on biologically determinist accounts of gender inequality. The third limitation is the assumption that the Western trajectory is the only possible trajectory for socio-economic transformation. The conditions of increasing wage dependency and dispossession (of labourers from means of production, including land) are assumed to be the case everywhere.

There is an alternative perspective within the social reproduction approach whereby the equal significance of patriarchal reproduction and capitalist production is stressed. Drawing on the initial theories on patriarchal exploitation of women's reproductive labour (see Section 2.1.2), these scholars propose a mutually shaping relationship between capitalist production and patriarchal reproduction. For example, Folbre (2009b) argues that not only class interests but also gender interests shape human behaviour. According to her, production is based on a capitalist labour market, whereas reproduction relies on a patriarchal family in which "men try to minimize their responsibility for the care of dependents to protect their bargaining power within family" (Folbre 2009b: 207). By emphasising the role of men in confining women to reproductive activities, Folbre therefore avoids both the capitalism and biology based reductionisms. Drawing on evidence that shows a transition from family to market with respect to care work, she further concludes that the intersection between capitalist production and patriarchal reproduction generates conflicting pressures and unstable coalitions. In this concern, early capitalism did not eliminate but weakened some forms of patriarchal control over women (Folbre 2009a). Although women gained new rights and opportunities with capitalist transformation, "their continued specialisation in the care of dependents often left them with little bargaining power, dependent on support from fathers of their children" (Folbre 2014: xxvi).[1] Similarly, Heidi Gottfried (2009), Gülnur Acar-Savran (2019; 2020) and Melda Yaman (2020) avoid subordinating the dynamics of patriarchal reproduction to capitalist production. Instead, those scholars emphasise that there is a mutual interaction, the systemic linkages and tensions between the relations of production and reproduction, establishing a dialectic unity of patriarchy and capitalism.

These alternative accounts, however, rest upon the same assumption that capitalist transformation separates all direct producers from the means of production (including the peasantry from land). In addition, their conceptual division between the spheres of production and reproduction tends to limit patriarchal relations of labour to non-market goods and services, particularly care work. This, in turn, impedes recognition of the importance of patriarchal labour exploitation in commodity production.

This book rejects the assumption that the dynamics of capitalist trans-formation are the only determinant of social change and suggests instead that the distinguishing characteristics of gender or class based dispossession and labour exploitation give rise to *the patriarchal* or *capitalist systems,* whereas the race-ethnicity based subordination maintains *the racist regimes of oppression.* Conceptualising a mutually shaping relationship between the patriarchal and capitalist systems and the racist regimes, I investigate the ways in which the patriarchal relations of labour result in diverse capital accumulation strategies. Drawing on the case of Turkey, I assess the extent to which men, in their roles as both household heads and small producers, exchange the agrarian surplus produced by women's unpaid family labour thereby forcing women to produce for the market. I also examine whether the products of women's unpaid labour are limited to non-market goods and services or if they are circulated based on capitalist relations of exchange within the market. Furthermore, I argue that the gendered division of labour is not related to pregnancy, childbirth, lactation or any other biological process. Instead, the family-mediated powers of patriarchal exploitation, including gender-based dispossession, shape gendered patterns of production by establishing a strong division of labour. This, in turn, sustains the dominance of small-medium scale family farms and women's unpaid family labour thereby preventing the development of large-scale capitalist farms and wage labour.

2.3 Obscured causality: Theories on varieties of gender regime

While the social reproduction approach perceives the capitalist system as the key determinant of gendered oppression and inequality, theories on varieties of gender regime focus on the forms and degrees of inequality within the domains of economy, polity, civil society and violence. Arguing that there is no single origin of patriarchy, Sylvia Walby conceptualises the multi-faced structure of the patriarchal system. She initially constructs three levels of abstraction. At the most abstract level, patriarchy is "a system of social structures, and practices whereby men dominate, oppress and exploit women" (Walby 1989: 214). At the next level, patriarchy is composed of six relatively autonomous structures having causal affects upon each other: the patriarchal mode of production; male violence; patriarchal relations in paid work; in the state; in sexuality and in cultural institutions (e.g. religion, media and education) (Walby 1986). By identifying these autonomous structures, she aims to replace a single origin-based explanation with a multiple origins focused analysis. Finally, at the least abstract level, there is a set of patriarchal practices located within each of the above structures (Walby 1990).

In her recent studies, Walby extends her initial typology by developing four crosscutting levels of abstraction (2020b, 2009, 2007, 1997): at the most abstract level, there are class, gender, and ethnicity based regimes of inequality. The gender regime, she argues, is "a system of gender relations which is analytically separate from other regimes of inequality" (2009: 259). At the second level of abstraction, the gender regime takes different forms: domestic and public. The public form of gender regime has two further forms: neoliberal and social-democratic (Walby 2009). The third level includes four institutional domains: economy, polity, violence and civil society. In brief: economy includes both the market and household production; polity contains states, nations, organised religions, empires, hegemons and global political institutions; civil society comprises social movements, sexuality and intimacy and knowledge-institutions; and state violence, armies, militias, interpersonal and intergroup violence, and gendered violence together constitute the domain of violence. All the regimes of inequality – based on class, gender and ethnicity – operate in each and every institutional domain and "there is no single privileged domain" (Walby 2009: 260). The meso and micro levels of gender relations are at the fourth and the least abstract level. Gender relations are embedded within social practices ranging from gender-based occupational segregation to the production of self.

Walby, further argues that the dominance of gender-based exclusionary strategies within those four domains is associated with a domestic gender regime, and gender-based segregationist strategies with the neoliberal or social-democratic forms of public gender regime. For example, when the domestic gender regime dominates the economy, women are excluded from free wage labour and household production becomes the primary place where women's labour is organised. However, in the economy of the public gender regime, "[t]here has been *a reduction* in household production as a result of the purchase of substitute goods and services from the national and global marketplace" which thus leads to a transition away from household production to market production (Walby 2009: 111, my emphasis).

Rejecting universal and unidirectional trajectories of social change, Walby (2020b) uses the term uneven and combined development to conceptualise the transformation of varieties of patriarchy. She argues that there is combined and uneven development of the domestic and public forms of patriarchy. While some institutional domains remain under the predominance of domestic patriarchy, others can shift to the neoliberal or social-democratic forms of public patriarchy. Her approach further enables an alternative understanding of modernity. While existing accounts place the concept at a macro-societal level, she applies the concept of modernity at the lower level abstraction of institutional domains. By identifying "the modern with the public [forms of patriarchy] and the premodern with the domestic [patriarchy]", she investigates the extent to which each institutional domain (i.e. economy, polity, violence and civil society) has shifted from premodern to modern (Walby 2020b: 419). Therefore, it is possible for premodern social formations to exist with modern social formations. In her analysis of the non-linear processes of social change, Walby (2009) also develops the concepts of catalysts and dampeners. While catalysts (e.g. the feminist movement and women's non-agricultural employment) promote changes in the systems, dampeners (e.g. war) counter those changes.

Theories on varieties of gender regime provide a suitable context for examining historically and geographically diversified forms of patriarchal transformation. For example, the notion of combined and uneven development of patriarchy along with the concepts of catalysts and dampeners enables an assessment of the unilinear trajectories of social change thereby shedding light on effective feminist strategies. Walby's differentiation of two major forms of patriarchal domination – the gender-based exclusion and the gender-based segregation and subordination – allows for a detailed analysis of changes within the different institutional domains. In turn, this conceptualisation allows for an assessment of the dominant form of gender regime within particular historical and geographical contexts thereby revealing women's diverse experiences.

Despite the earlier mentioned strengths, varieties of gender regime theories do have some limitations that I wish to go beyond. For example, proponents tend to focus on changes within forms of public patriarchy at the expense of varieties of domestic patriarchy. Considering the significance of the gender-based exclusionary strategies in the global South, I argue that varieties of domestic patriarchy require detailed investigation. Furthermore, Walby portrays patriarchal relations of labour in household production as one of the multiple aspects of gender. Attempting to avoid "the tendency to reduce or conflate the multiple *aspects* of gender into the concept of family", she aims to "dispers[e] the practices traditionally associated with the concept of the family across" four domains, e.g. care work in the economy, sexuality in civil society, the governance of reproduction in the polity and domestic violence in violence (Walby 2020b: 418, my emphasis). In doing so, Walby reduces the role of the patriarchal exploitation of labour within the family to one of the many outcomes of gendered oppression and inequality. This approach does not only ignore the nexus between relations of labour exploitation and social inequalities, but also obscures the causality sustaining gender gaps within the institutional domains. Her lack of attention to patriarchal exploitation of labour within the cis-gender heterosexual family, I argue, gives rise to further limitations, as discussed later.

First, women's time spent on housework (including care work) and the total number of full-time homemakers may well decrease in some countries over time (Folbre and Nelson 2000); however, the gender-based division of labour and the gender gaps in time spent on housework (including care work) within the family persist across class and race-ethnicity differences as well as various geographies, cultures and religions. Heidi Hartmann explains that capitalism has shifted the direct personal system of patriarchal control towards the indirect, impersonal system which is mediated by society-wide institutions, especially the labour market (Hartmann 1979).

With the development of capitalism, she argues, men "are more likely to exercise control in public domains" (Hartmann 1983: 36), but the family is still significant for men's control over women's labour. Drawing on Hartmann's approach, I suggest that the neoliberal and social-democratic forms of public patriarchy may draw on gender-based segregationist strategies to sustain women's double burden of paid and unpaid labour, but the gendered division of labour and patriarchal labour exploitation within the family remain strong.

Second, assuming patriarchal relations of labour constitute one of the many consequences of gendered oppression and inequality, Walby disperses the various gender gaps occurring within the family to four institutional domains (see above). Drawing on evidence from Germany, Japan, and the Middle East and North Africa, Karen Shire and Kumiko Nemoto (2020) and Valentine Moghadam (2020), however, find that family has a central role within policy frameworks, and should be perceived as another institutional domain (Moghadam 2020). I agree that the heterosexual family remains significant under the public forms of patriarchy. However, both Walby and her critics neglect the role of family in obscuring the patriarchal exploitation of labour. In this book, I examine how far the cis-gender heterosexual family *mediates* the relationship between male appropriators and female direct producers and, as such, whether it constitutes one of the most complex mediating categories of the patriarchal system. Therefore, considering the family-mediated powers of labour exploitation, I argue that the role of the family cannot be reduced to an institutional domain or dispersed across four institutional domains.

Third, the assumption that patriarchal labour exploitation within the family is one aspect of gendered oppression and inequality conceals the dynamics of a shift from domestic to public forms of patriarchy. Considering that the premodern is identified with domestic patriarchy whereas the modern with forms of public patriarchy, Walby (2009) provides a detailed analysis of what constitutes the premodern or the modern within the domains of economy, polity, civil society and violence. For example, increased female employment in non-agricultural sectors, the market or the state led substitution of household production, depth of democracy, state-led monopoly of legitimate violence and sexual autonomy are some of the key indicators pointing to a shift away from domestic patriarchy. However, I argue that this modernisation-based assessment gives rise to two undesirable outcomes that Walby herself is critical of: one pointing to capitalist transformation as the main driver of change, and another focusing on varieties of modernity in establishing different forms of public patriarchy. To a certain extent, both of those approaches are adopted by proponents of varieties of gender regime theories. While Moghadam (2020; 2021) proposes that underdevelopment or peripheral capitalism establishes neopatriarchal or conservative-corporatist forms of public patriarchy in the Middle East and North

Africa, Shire (2020; 2021) suggests that conservative modernisations shape varieties of patriarchy in ways different to democratic modernisations leading to the conservative-authoritarian or conservative-democratic gender regimes.

While, I do not deny the significance of capitalist transformation for varieties of patriarchy, my analysis focuses on the collective acting capacity of men, examining the ways in which labourers' dispossession and wage dependency reinforces changes in the key strategies of patriarchal domination. Therefore, I suggest that a shift from domestic to public forms of patriarchy should be assessed by looking at changes in the forms of patriarchal oppression and labour exploitation. According to my conceptual framework, the predominance of gender-based segregationist strategies along with a shift towards women's double burden of paid and unpaid labour signals the transition to the neoliberal or social-democratic forms of public patriarchy, whereas, the predominance of gender-based exclusionary strategies and women's unpaid family labour imply the hegemony of domestic patriarchy.

Fourth, the framework of institutional domains provides a suitable context for analysing how gender inequality occurs but, at the same time, it tends to obscure causality. Once the patriarchal exploitation of labour is repositioned as one of the aspects of gendered oppression and inequality, the collective acting capacity of men as a socially constructed dominant group of society tends to get lost. Despite her initial account of patriarchy as "a system of social structures, and practices whereby men dominate, oppress and exploit women" (1989: 214), Walby does not theorise the interdependence and solidarity among individual members of the dominant groups of society. Rather, she emphasises that systems, including gender regime, are self-reproducing and thus do not require additional input for their reproduction (Walby 2020a). This shift in her approach prevents a detailed assessment of the collective agency of men in establishing and reproducing the gender regime from which they benefit.

Finally, Walby's concept of regimes of inequalities neglects the significance of labour exploitation in maintaining certain forms of inequalities differently to oppression-based inequalities. She (2009) initially suggests that gender, class, ethnic, disability and sexuality regimes establish various forms of social inequalities, but more recently, identifies three regimes of inequalities based on class, gender and ethnicity (Walby 2020b, a). I argue that the inequalities derived from regimes of oppression are sustained in ways different to those inequalities concerning relations of labour exploitation. All forms of exploitation are maintained through relations of domination and subordination, but not every kind of oppression is associated with exploitation. Therefore, I propose that it is necessary to differentiate exploitation-based systems from the oppression-based regimes to identify the distinctive features of gender, class and race-ethnicity based inequalities.

2.4 Conclusion

Feminist theories have largely dropped the analysis of patriarchal labour relations from their conceptual framework. Unlike the early theories of male domination which neglect why men dominate women and what they gain from it, the initial analyses of patriarchal exploitation shed light on what men gain by oppressing women in every aspect of life. Despite their differences, these studies all attempted to identify the causality of women's subordination and gender inequality by providing a detailed account of patriarchal exploitation. However, this undertaking has been interrupted and has been supplanted by different approaches. Critically engaging with two of those approaches, the social reproduction approach and theories on varieties of gender regimes, I propose that the dismissal of patriarchal labour exploitation leads to reductionism and/or obscures causality within the context of gendered oppression and inequality. In light of this discussion, the following chapter details the political implications and introduces the key concepts of my theoretical framework.

Note

1   In her recent theoretical framework, Folbre develops the intersectional political economy perspective (for details see Folbre 2021).

Reference

Acar-Savran, Gülnur. 2019. "%99 İçin Feminizm Manifestosu üzerine." *Çatlak Zemin.*

Acar-Savran, Gülnür. 2020. "Bakım/toplumsal yeniden üretim krizi ve ötesi." *Çatlak Zemin.*

Acker, Joan. 1988. "Class, Gender, and the Relations of Distribution." *Signs* 13 (3):473–497. doi: 10.1086/494429

Acker, Joan. 1989. "The Problem with Patriarchy." *Sociology* 23 (2):235–240.

Arruzza, Cinzia. 2016. "Functionalist, Determinist, Reductionist: Social Reproduction Feminism and its Critics." *Science and Society* 80 (1):9–30. doi: 10.1521/siso.2016.80.1.9.

Bakker, Isabella. 2007. "Social Reproduction and the Constitution of Gendered Political Economy." *New Political Economy* 12 (4): 541–556.

Bakker, Isabella, and Stephen Gill. 2003. *Power, Production, and Social reproduction.* Basingstoke: Palgrave Macmillan.

Bakker, Isabella, and Rachel Silvey. 2008. *Beyond States and Markets: The Challenges of Social Reproduction, RIPE Series in Global Political Economy.* London: Routledge.

Barrett, Michele, and Mary McIntosh. 1979. "Christine Delphy: Towards a Materialist Feminism?" *Feminist Review* 1 (1):95–106. doi: 10.1057/fr.1979.8.

Barrett, Michèle. 1980. *Women's Opression Today.* London: Verso.

Barrett, Michèle. 1984. "Rethinking Women's Oppression: A Reply to Brenner and Ramas." *New Left Review* (146):123.

Beneria, Lourdes. 1979. "Reproduction, Production and the Sexual Division of Labour." *Cambridge Journal of Economics* 3:203–225.

Benston, Margaret. 1969. "The Political Economy of Women's Liberation." *Monthly Review* 21 (September):13–27.

Bhattacharya, Tithi. 2017. "Introduction." In *Social Reproduction Theory: Remapping Class, Recentering Oppression*, edited by T. Bhattacharya. London, New York: Pluto Press. doi: 10.2307/j.ctt1vz494j.5

Brenner, Robert P. 1977. "On the Origins of Capitalist Development: A Critique of Neo-Smithian Marxism." *New Left Review* 104:25–92.

Brown, Carol. 1981. "Mothers, fathers and children: From private to public patriarchy." In *Women and Revolution: A Discussion of the Unhappy Marriage of Marxism and Feminism*, edited by L. Sargent. New York: Pluto Press.

Brownmiller, Susan. 1975. *Against Our Will: Men, Women, and Rape*. New York: Simon and Schuster.

Coontz, Stephanie, and Peta Henderson. 1986. *Women's Work, Men's Property: The Origins of Gender and Class*. London: Verso.

Dalla Costa, Mariarosa, and Selma James. 1973. *The Power of Women and the Subversion of the Community*. 2d ed. Bristol: Falling Wall Press.

Delphy, Christine. 2003. "Par où Attaquer le « Partage Inégal » du « Travail Ménager »?" *Nouvelles Questions Féministes* 22 (3):47–72.

Delphy, Christine. 2004. "For a General Theory of Exploitation, Part Two: Get Off to a Good Start." *Movements* 1 (31):97–106

Delphy, Christine. 1977. *The Main Enemy: A Materialist Analysis of Women's Oppression*. Vol. 3, *Explorations in Feminism*. London: Women's Research and Resources Centre Publications.

Delphy, Christine. 1984. *Close to Home: A Materialist Analysis of Women's Oppression*, New York: The University of Massachusetts Press.

Delphy, Christine. 1992. *Familiar Exploitation: A New Analysis of Marriage in Contemporary Western Societies*, Cambridge, Massachusetts: Polity Press.

Delphy, Christine. 2014. "Feminist Economics." *Perspectives on the Economy*. 15 (2): 29–41

Dunaway, Wilma. 2014. "Introduction." In *Gendered Commodity Chains: Seeing Women's Work and Households in Global Production*, edited by W. Dunaway. Stanford, California: Stanford University Press.

Dworkin, Andrea. 1983. *Right-Wing Women: The Politics of Domesticated Females*. London: Women's Press.

Federici, Silvia. 2004. *Caliban and the Witch: Women, the Body and Primitive Accumulation*. Brooklyn: Autonomedia.

Ferguson, Susan. 2008. "Canadian Contributions to Social Reproduction Feminism, Race and Embodied Labor." *Race, Gender & Class* 15 (1–2):42–57.

Ferguson, Susan, and David McNally. 2014. "Capital, labour-power, and gender-relations: Introduction to the historical materialism edition of marxism and the oppression of women." In *Marxism and the Oppression of Women: Toward a Unitary Theory* edited by L. Vogel. London: Haymarket Books.

Folbre, Nancy. 1982. "Exploitation Comes Home: A Critique of the Marxian Theory of Family Labor." *Cambridge Journal of Economics* 6 (4):317–329.

Folbre, Nancy. 1983. "Of Patriarchy Born: The Political Economy of Fertility Decisions." *Feminist Studies* 9 (2):261–284.

Folbre, Nancy. 1987. "A patriarchal mode of production." In *Alternatives to Economic Orthodoxy: Reader in Political Economy*, edited by R. Albelda, C. Gunn and W. Waller. New York, London: M.E. Sharpe Inc.

Folbre, Nancy. 2009a. *Greed, Lust and Gender: A History of Economic Ideas*. Oxford: Oxford University Press.

Folbre, Nancy. 2009b. "Varieties of Patriarchal Capitalism." *Social Politics* 16 (2): 204–209.

Folbre, Nancy. 2014. "The Care Economy in Africa: Subsistence Production and Unpaid Care." *Journal of African Economies* 23 (suppl1):i128–i156. doi: 10.1093/jae/ejt026.

Folbre, Nancy. 2021. *The Rise and Decline of Patriarchal Systems: An Intersectional Political Economy*. London, New York: Verso.

Folbre, Nancy, and Julie A. Nelson. 2000. "For Love or Money or Both?" *Journal of Economic Perspectives* 14 (4, Fall):123–140.

Gardiner, Jean. 1975. "Women's Domestic Labor." *New Left Review* 89 (January, February):47–58.

Gershuny, Jonathan, and Teresa Harms. 2016. "Housework Now Takes Much Less Time: 85 Years of US Rural Women's Time Use." *Social Forces* 95 (2):503–524.

Giménez, Martha E. 2018. *Marx, Women, and Capitalist Social Reproduction: Marxist-Feminist Essays* Vol. 169, *Historical Materialism Book Series*: Brill.

Gottfried, Heidi. 2009. "Japan: the reproductive bargain and the making of precarious employment." In *Gender and the Contours of Precarious Employment*, edited by L. F. Vosko, M. MacDonald, and I. Campbell. London, New York: Routledge

Guillaumin, Colette. 1995. *Racism, Sexism, Power and Ideology*. London, New York: Routledge.

Hacker, Barton C., and Sally L. Hacker. 1987. "Military Institutions and the Labour Process: Noneconomic Sources of Technological Change, Women's Subordination and the Organisation of Work." *Technology and Culture* 28 (4): 743–775.

Harding, Sandra. 1986. *The Science Question in Feminism*. London, New York: Cornell University Press.

Harrison, John. 1973. "The political economy of housework." *Bulletin of the conference of socialist economists* Winter.

Hartmann, Heidi I. 1983. "Capitalism and patriarchy: an overview." In *Capitalism and Patriarchy: Report From a Seminar at Aalborg University Centre*, edited by M. Brink Aalborg: Aalborg University press.

Hartmann, Heidi I. 1979. "Capitalism, patriarchy and job segregation by sex." In *Capitalist Patriarchy and the Case for Socialist Feminism*, edited by Z. Eisenstein. New York, London: Monthly Review Press.

Himmelweit, Susan, and Simon Mohun. 1977. "Domestic Labor and Capital." *Cambridge Journal of Economics* 1 (1, March):15–31.

Jackson, Stevi. 1996. *Christine Delphy*. London, Delhi: Sage publications.

Jackson, Stevi. 1999. "Marxism and feminism." In *Marxism and Social Science*, edited by A. Gamble, D. Marsh and T. Tant. London: MacMillan.

Juteau-Lee, Danielle. 1995. "Introduction: (Re)constructing the categories of 'race' and 'sex': the work of a precursor " In *Racism, Sexism, Power and Ideology*, edited by C. Guillaumin. London, New York: Routledge.

Katz, Cindi. 2001. "Vagabond Capitalism and the Necessity of Social Reproduction." *Antipode* 33 (4):709–728. doi: 10.1111/1467-8330.00207.

Kenway, Emily. 2021. *The Truth About Modern Slavery.* London, NY: Pluto Press.

Kongar, Ebru, and Emel Memiş. 2017. "Gendered Patterns of Time Use Over the Life Cycle in Turkey." In *Gender and Time Use in a Global Context: The Economics of Employment and Unpaid Labor*, edited by R. Connelly and E. Kongar. London, New York: Palgrave Macmillan

Leach, Nicole. 2019. "Rethinking the rules of reproduction and the transition to capitalism: reading federici and brenner together." In *Case Studies in the Origins of Capitalism*, edited by X. Lafrance and C. Post. London, New York: Palgrave Macmillan. doi: doi.org/10.1007/978-3-319-95657-2_13

Luxton, Meg, and Kate Bezanson. 2006. *Social Reproduction: Feminist Political Economy Challenges Neo-liberalism.* Montreal: McGill-Queen's University Press.

MacKinnon, Catharine. A. 1982. "Feminism, marxism, method and the state: An agenda for theory." In *A Feminist Theory: A Critique of Ideology*, edited by N. O. Keohane, M. Z. Rosaldo and B. C. Gelpi. Brighton: Harvester Press.

Mackintosh, Maureen. 1977. "Reproduction and Patriarchy: A Critique of Claude Meillassoux." *Capital and Class* 2 (Summer):120–127.

Mackintosh, Maureen. 1984. "Gender and economics: The sexual division of labour and the subordination of women." In *Of Marriage and the Market: Women's Subordination Internationally and Its Lessons*, edited by K. Young, C. Wolkowitz and R. McCullagh. London, Boston, Melbourne, Henley: Routledge.

Mies, Maria. 1998 [1986]. *Patriarchy and Accumulation on a World Scale: Women in the International Division of Labour.* London, New York: Zed Books.

Mies, Maria, Veronika Bennholdt-Thomsen, and Claudia von Werlhof. 1988. *Women: The Last Colony.* London; Atlantic Highlands: Zed Books.

Millett, Kate. 1977. *Sexual Politics.* London: Virago.

Moghadam, Valentine M. 2021. "Gender Regimes, Polities, and the World-System." Global Dialogue, The International Sociological Association, 12 (1):26–27.

Moghadam, Valentine M. 2020. "Gender Regimes in the Middle East and North Africa: The Power of Feminist Movements." *Social Politics* 27 (3):467–485. doi: 10.1093/sp/jxaa019.

Morton, Peggy. 1971. "Women's work is never done!" In *The Politics of Housework*, edited by E. Altbach. Cheltenham: New Clarion Press.

Naz, Farah, and Dieter Bögenhold. 2020. *Unheard Voices: Women, Work and Political Economy of Global Production.* London: Palgrave Macmillan.

O'Laughlin, Bridget. 2012. "Gender justice, land and the agrarian question in Southern Africa." In *Peasants and Globalization*, edited by A. Akram-Lodhi and C. Kay. London, New York: Routledge.

Öneş, Umut, Emel Memiş, and Burca Kızılırmak. 2013. "Poverty and Intra-Household Distribution of Work Time in Turkey: Analysis and Some Policy Implications." *Women's Studies International Forum* 41 (1):55–64. doi: 10.1016/j.wsif.2013.01.004

Patil, Vrushali. 2013. "From Patriarchy to Intersectionality: A Transnational Feminist Assessment of How Far We've Really Come." *Signs* 38 (4):847–867. doi: 10.1086/669560.

Pollert, Anna. 1996. "Gender and Class Revisited; or, the Poverty of 'Patriarchy'." *Sociology* 30 (4):639–660.

Ringhofer, Lisa. 2015. "Time, Labour, and the Household: Measuring "Time Poverty" Through a Gender Lens." *Development in Practice* 25 (3):321–332.

Roberts, Adrienne. 2017. *Gendered States of Punishment and Welfare: Feminist Political Economy, Primitive Accumulation and the Law.* London: Routledge

Sen, Samita. 2019. "The problem of reproduction: waged and unwaged domestic work." In *'Capital' in the East: Reflections on Marx,* edited by A. Chakraborty, A. Chakrabarti, B. Dasgupta and S. Sen. Singapore: Springer Singapore.

Shire, Karen. 2021. "All in the Family: Conservative Gender Regimes." Global Dialogue, The International Sociological Association, 12 (1):20–21.

Shire, Karen A., and Kumiko Nemoto. 2020. "The Origins and Transformations of Conservative Gender Regimes in Germany and Japan." *Social Politics* 27 (3): 432–448. doi: 10.1093/sp/jxaa017.

Walby, Sylvia. 1989. "Theorising Patriarchy." *Sociology* 23 (2):213–234.

Walby, Sylvia. 1986. *Patriarchy at Work.* Minneapolis: University of Minnesota Press.

Walby, Sylvia. 1990. *Theorizing Patriarchy.* Oxford, Cambridge: Basil Blackwell.

Walby, Sylvia. 1997. *Gender Transformations.* London, New York: Routledge.

Walby, Sylvia. 2007. *Gendering the Knowledge Economy: Comparative Perspectives.* Basingstoke: Palgrave Macmillan.

Walby, Sylvia. 2009. *Globalisation and Inequalities: Complexity and Contested Modernities.* London: Sage Publications Ltd.

Walby, Sylvia. 2020a. "Developing the Concept of Society: Institutional Domains, Regimes of Inequalities and Complex Systems in a Global Era." *Current Sociology.* doi: 10.1177/0011392120932940.

Walby, Sylvia. 2020b. "Varieties of Gender Regimes." *Social Politics* 27 (3):414–431. doi: 10.1093/sp/jxaa018.

Winders, Jamie, and Barbara E. Smith. 2019. "Social Reproduction and Capitalist Production: A Genealogy of Dominant Imaginaries." *Progress in Human Geography* xx (x):1–19. doi: 10.1177/0309132518791730.

Wood, Ellen M. 1999. *The Origin of Capitalism.* New York: Monthly Review Press.

Wood, Ellen M. 2002. "The Question of Market Dependence." *Journal of Agrarian Change* 2 (1): 50–87.

Yaman, Melda. 2020. "Toplumsal Yeniden üretim, Birleşik Bir Feminist Teori?" *Praksis* (53): 9–38.

3 THEORISING THE PATRIARCHAL SYSTEM OF EXPLOITATION

The theoretical shortcomings discussed previously have an impact on the transformative capacity of feminist strategies. This chapter starts with a discussion of the political implications of neglecting patriarchal labour exploitation (Section 3.1). In light of this discussion, I introduce the key concepts in my theoretical framework, including the relations of labour exploitation (Section 3.2), political collective subject (Section 3.3), as well as differentiating the systems of exploitation from the regimes of oppression (Section 3.4). I further conceptualise changes within the patriarchal character of the state and distinguish the premodern and modern forms of domestic patriarchy (Sections 3.5 and 3.6).

3.1 Political implications of theoretical shortcomings

The lack of attention to patriarchal labour exploitation by feminist scholars has several political implications. *First*, it limits feminist analysis to a focus on gender gaps in, for example, the economy, politics, law, citizenship, education and culture and religion, at the expense of looking closely at the reasons which explain these gaps. In turn, this leads to a simplistic account of the dynamics sustaining gender inequalities. For example, in her popular book where a feminist journalist, Caroline Criado-Perez, details different forms of gender inequalities across the global North and the global South, she points to unintentional male bias as the cause of gender inequality. Increased representation of women in science, technology, economy and politics is therefore proposed as a solution (Criado-Perez 2019: 318).

Second, the shift away from the causes and towards the aspects of gender inequality replaces the feminist goal of women's liberation *from* the patriarchal system by women's empowerment *within* the patriarchal system. One example of such a shift is the focus on the public provisioning of domestic goods and services, particularly childcare. While these services are important for women, they ultimately tend to sustain women's double burden of paid and unpaid work instead of eliminating the gender gaps within this double burden. As the recent Covid-19 pandemic has revealed, such strategies do not lead to transformative changes and can easily be disrupted

DOI: 10.4324/9781003054511-5

(İlkkaracan and Memiş 2021). Rather than focusing on work/family reconciliation policies, as Delphy (2014; 2003) suggests, it is necessary to target the gender-based division of labour within household production (including care work). Transformative strategies are required which, in the short term, destabilise patriarchal dynamics and in the long term, abolish the patriarchal system.

Third, once the causality of gendered oppression and inequality is concealed, feminist strategies become distorted by interpreting certain biological differences in particular ways in order to explain the origins of gender inequality. The assumption that biological differences – utilised either by capitalism or by men – sustain women's oppression (i) assigns meaning to certain differences thereby naturalising gendered oppression and inequality, (ii) attacks other women, particularly women with transitioning experience and (iii) sabotages the strategic alliance with the LGBTQ+ movements.

Fourth, feminist theories do not pay enough attention to the respective roles of the dominant gender in maintaining the patriarchal exploitation of labour. The neglect of the collective acting capacity of men, in their position as heads of household and small producers, misdirects the strategies of feminist movement by, for example, pointing to unintentional male bias as the cause of gendered oppression and inequality. At the same time, this neglect leads to the assumption that equalises men's and women's losses within the patriarchal system. One of the consequences of following this erroneous path is the viewpoint that patriarchal attitudes can be reversed with increased awareness. The United Nations global solidarity movement for gender equality, *#HeForShe*, is an example of a campaign which adopts this viewpoint and thereby conceals the ways in which men benefit from the patriarchal system (The UN 2014).

Finally, positing an one-sidedly deterministic relationship whereby capitalism shapes patriarchy leads to the assumption that capitalist relations of labour are superior to patriarchal labour relations in shaping social transformation. This, in turn, prevents feminist strategies from distinguishing the dynamics of the patriarchal system and, at the same time, upholds the view that, depending on its requirements, capitalism either maintains or destabilises the patriarchal arrangements within society.

The political implications that I have investigated thus far suggest that a theoretical re-positioning of patriarchal labour exploitation supports feminist strategies in terms of: (i) going beyond the aspects of the patriarchal system, (ii) shedding light on the dynamics which sustain gendered oppression and inequality thereby targeting women's liberation from the patriarchal system rather than women's empowerment within it, (iii) investigating the ways in which men in their position as the dominant gender sustain the system of gender-based exploitation, (iv) avoiding biological essentialism and (v) capitalism-based reductionism. In theorising the patriarchal system, I use the concepts of exploitation of labour and collective subject. These concepts are discussed next.

3.2 Patriarchal exploitation of labour

In my theoretical framework, I perceive exploitation of labour as purely a social relationship in which the dominating sections of society appropriate the surplus produced by the subordinated sections (Roamer 2014). Surplus occurs when the subordinated section of society is made to work for longer than that required by their own needs (Shaikh 1990a). Under such conditions, the subordinated section become (direct) producers, whereas the dominating section become appropriators. By utilising various powers of oppression, appropriators get producers "to work beyond the time necessary to produce their own means of consumption, for it is this surplus labour time which creates the requisite surplus product" (Shaikh 1990b: 346).

Throughout history, there have always been appropriators who establish strong control over the surplus produced by the subordinated groups which has thus led to systems of exploitation. Systems are differentiated by who comprises the appropriators and producers, how the surplus is produced and appropriated, and which powers of exploitation are utilised. In feudalism, for example, the feudal lords maintained their control over the land predominantly by utilising direct coercive forces (extra-economic forces) to appropriate the agrarian surplus produced by peasants. As well as direct coercive forces, as Guillaumin (1995) explains, the social systems of marking sustained the enslavement of Black people by marking certain skins as the symbols of being a slave. In both of those systems of exploitation, the ties of the bondage – of the serf to the lord or of the slave to the master – reinforced relations of labour exploitation. In capitalism, however, the relations of labour exploitation are non-coercive. During production "capitalists buy workers' labour power at a wage equal to its value, but being in control of production, extract labour greater than the equivalent of that wage" (Himmelweit 1983: 158). Wage workers therefore 'voluntarily' join such unequal process of exchange.

Drawing on time use surveys and research on gender gaps in time spent on housework (including care work), I suggest that gendered oppression and inequality derive from the relations of labour exploitation thereby establishing the patriarchal system of exploitation. Evidence demonstrates a sharp gender-based division of labour and large gender gaps in time spent on housework across class, race-ethnicity and geography (Kongar and Memiş 2017; Öneş, Memiş, and Kızılırmak 2013; Gershuny and Harms 2016; Ringhofer 2015). On average, women spend two to ten times more time on unpaid care work than men, and as such, this is associated with significant gender gaps in all forms of unpaid work. Neither education nor economic growth appear to be effective in closing those gender gaps (Ferrant and Thim 2019; Ferrant, Pesando, and Nowacka 2014; OECD.Stat 2020). At the same time, there seems to be greater intra-household equality for same-sex couples in comparison to different-sex couples (Giddings et al. 2014; Leppel 2009; Black, Sanders, and Taylor 2007; Becker 1993). These findings suggest that the cis-gender heterosexual family is significant for the patriarchal exploitation of labour. While the market and/or state led substitution might decrease the total time spent on housework, it does not abolish the gender-based division of labour and the patriarchal labour exploitation within household production, including care work. Therefore, the patriarchal or capitalist exploitation of labour refers to a causal element sustaining those systems of exploitation, and cannot be reduced to a domain of economy, or separated from political struggle and the collective acting capacity of gender or class based dominant groups of society.

3.2.1 Distinctiveness of patriarchal labour exploitation

The patriarchal exploitation of labour is different to other forms of labour exploitation, such as capitalist, feudal or exploitation of labour within slavery. In patriarchal labour exploitation, the dominating section of society is constructed based on gender. This means that appropriators force certain tasks on producers by sustaining the binary sex/gender system and uneven gender relations within society. The enforcement of these tasks through the categories of sex and gender is accompanied by the reinforcement of inequalities, violence, discrimination, segregation and also certain cultural and religious values, meanings, affect and other psychological patterns. Bodies are interpreted in ways which justify the gender-based division of labour. The categories of male sex and female sex, in turn, maintain patriarchal domination and exploitation regardless of class, race-ethnicity and geography. The patriarchal exploitation of labour is, therefore, veiled by naturalisation. Since the enslavement of Black people, patriarchy remains the only system in which producers are themselves essentially naturalised.

Moreover, the surplus produced by women's unpaid family labour has a complicated composition obscuring its visibility. The products of women's unpaid family labour include both the material and non-material necessities of life (e.g. emotional, psychological, spiritual) and cannot be reduced to only the daily or weekly activities of cooking, cleaning, laundry, and shopping. For example, men's self-esteem and confidence is sustained through patriarchal love and intimacy. As Simone de Beauvoir argues in *The Second Sex*, "[w]oman has often been compared to water, in part because it is the mirror where the male Narcissus contemplates himself" (1997 [1969]: 239). Eva Illouz (2012) further argues that while men's demands from their intimate relationships with women have been complicated throughout various psychological processes, women continue to satisfy men's demands (for a detailed assessment of patriarchal love and intimacy see also Gunnarsson 2015, 2014, 2013; Jónasdóttir and Ferguson 2013; Jónasdóttir 1994; Coontz 2006).

In addition, the products and services produced by women's unpaid labour vary depending on the extent to which men and women experience class and race-ethnicity based inequalities within society. For example, in some families, the material necessities of life are the main proportion of household production, yet for others, the educational, emotional and/or psychological necessities are the main parts. Nonetheless, patriarchal exploitation of labour still exists in working class families and in families from the subordinated race-ethnicity. Depending on their class and race-ethnicity as well as organisational capacity, men utilise different subsets of powers of oppression to varying degrees as well as appropriating different forms of surplus.

Furthermore, household production is not limited to use value or non-market goods and services as the social reproduction approach suggests. Under certain conditions, men in their position as heads of household control women's labour power and women's potential to produce a surplus within small units of production in agriculture, manufacturing or service sectors (e.g. textile ateliers, hotels, restaurants, shops). This means that men control women's labour for the production of exchange value and, at the same time, family-mediated powers of exploitation are required to maintain men's appropriation of women's labour. To summarise, powers of patriarchal labour exploitation have different characteristics to other systems of exploitation, e.g. capitalism, and the surplus produced by women has a dynamic and complex structure obscuring its recognition.

3.2.2 Exploitation or not?

In order to differentiate the dynamics sustaining the patriarchal system of exploitation, it is important to distinguish what refers to exploitation of labour and what does not. As argued earlier, exploitation of labour occurs when a group of people do not work but force others to work for them. Producers, given the circumstances of exploitation, produce the needs of themselves yet continue to work for an extra amount of time to provide the surplus for appropriators. However, exploitation of labour does not occur if producers only work for a time period necessary to reproduce the labourers themselves. In this case, they consume the products of their labour and surplus is not produced. Here, one should also consider cases in which the products of labour are *unequally* distributed amongst producers. Children, elderly or sick members of the community consume without equally participating in production. Those members of producers, however, temporarily keep their positions meaning their status is not fixed as an appropriator. Elderly members have already worked as producers and children and sick members occupy their position for limited time period. Those temporary inequalities amongst producers do not refer to exploitation of labour.

As argued previously, the feudal, capitalist or patriarchal labour exploitation as well as labour exploitation in slavery are differentiated based on who the appropriators and producers are and in which ways labour exploitation is maintained. Drawing on the distinguishing features of each and every form of labour exploitation, I argue that the unequal distribution of tasks amongst producers does not refer to labour exploitation. For instance, within a capitalist unit of production, a foreman is certainly exploited less than other workers as well as holding a powerful position. Likewise, within extended households, a mother-in-law holding a greater degree of power is likely to transfer the heavy tasks of household production to younger women, especially daughters in law. The position of the mother-in-law in this case becomes similar to that of foreman. The unequal power relations amongst producers are not derived from relations of labour exploitation. While the foreman upholds a relatively powerful position, the mother-in-law draws on her son's power. Furthermore, she once was a daughter in law and so did not spend her entire life in an authoritative position, and to a certain degree, she is still involved in household production, including childcare, despite the privileges of her role. It is only her husband and/or son(s) who do not participate in household production and force women to work for their needs. Therefore, I propose that patriarchal exploitation of labour does not occur amongst women within extended families.

Patriarchal labour exploitation also needs to be differentiated from the capitalist labour exploitation occurring amongst women. In the case of male or female domestic workers, who are paid for their domestic work including care work, the male household head and/or the housewife (or single woman) hold the position of appropriator and exploit the domestic workers' labour. In this concern, the appropriated products include, but are not limited to the domestic goods and services, including care work, produced within the home. Employers often establish strong control over those domestic workers' involvement in household production. However, the market-mediated power of labour exploitation is the key dynamic which determines domestic workers' decision to work or quit, rather than the control established by these female or male employers.[1] Considering that the family-mediated powers of patriarchal labour exploitation are different to market-mediated powers of capitalist labour exploitation, I argue that domestic workers' labour is exploited through the relations of capitalism but not patriarchy.

In my investigation of the case of Turkey, I focus on a particular case in which men in their positions as heads of household and small producers have sustained a strong gender-based division of labour and appropriated the product of women's unpaid family labour in small-medium scale farms. My analysis further allows for an examination of how far the patriarchal exploitation of labour in agriculture constitutes a factor shaping the terms and conditions of capitalist labour exploitation in the country.

3.3 Patriarchal collective subject

A theory of a patriarchal collective subject is necessary to understand the persistence of the system of gender-based exploitation. As argued earlier, in patriarchal exploitation, the dominating section of society is constructed based on gender. Contrary to the notion of a harmony of interest, i.e. the assumption that men and women equally lose in a patriarchal society,

Raewyn Connell emphasises the significance of the "battle of the sexes" for the configuration of masculinity as a collective practice amongst men (2005: 82). She argues that hegemonic masculinity guarantees the global dominance of men over women (Connell 2005). Engaging with her argument, I argue that gender conflict is one of the main drivers of social change. Gender-based socially constructed groups pursue different interests, i.e. the ability of the dominating group to achieve its goals inhibits the ability of members of the subordinated group to achieve their goals. Subsequently, the system of gender-based exploitation occurs "as a set of social relations between men, which have a material base, and which, through hierarchical, establish or create interdependence and solidarity among men that enable them to dominate women" (Hartmann 1979: 18). Therefore, I identify a continuum between an individual and the collective subject. At the individual level, appropriators benefit from the patriarchal exploitation and at the same time, are aware of the significance of their solidarity and collectively act for their individual benefits. Cis-gender men, as a gender-based socially constructed group, therefore, constitute a patriarchal collective subject.

Nonetheless, I acknowledge that some groups of men have the potential to threaten the collective strength of a patriarchal subject. In such conditions, solidarity and punishment are two sides of the same coin; as well as solidarity between individual members of the dominant group, the punishment of betrayers is necessary to sustain systems of exploitation. In her theory of subordinated masculinities, Connell (2005, 2003) does not pay enough attention to the significance of the patriarchal exploitation of labour. Therefore, I develop the concept of betrayers to theorise the role of men who handle the tasks allocated to women within household production (e.g. gay men, stay-at-home fathers, as well as male wageworkers and peasants lacking means to sustain the gendered division of labour within their households). Betrayers threaten the patriarchal collective subject in the system of gender-based exploitation and are thus punished in different ways.

Feminist theories highlight the role of male household heads (Delphy 2016; Folbre 2009, 1994) and wageworkers (Cockburn 1991, 1985; Adkins 1995; Walby 1986) in sustaining patriarchal relations of labour within the home and at work. In the following chapters, I start to detail how far men, in their position as rural and urban small-producers, also constitute a patriarchal collective subject by excluding women from the ownership of a means of production (land) and subsistence (wage or other forms of income) thereby sustaining patriarchal exploitation of labour within rural and urban households.

3.4 Systems of exploitation and regimes of oppression

Oppression is a prerequisite for any form of exploitation of labour, but not every kind of oppression is associated with exploitation. Erik Olin Wright (1997) differentiates non-exploitative economic oppression from exploitation. In the latter, he argues, the exploiters depend on the labour of exploited therefore need the exploited, whereas in the former, the non-exploitative oppressors benefit from the material deprivations of the oppressed, but do not depend on the oppressed thus prefer the oppressed to be disappeared. For this reason, the resistance of the oppressed is more likely to escalate mass killings, massacres or genocides.

Feudal, capitalist and patriarchal, including exploitation in slavery, all forms of labour exploitation are maintained through relations of domination and subordination. However, contemporary forms of race-ethnicity based inequalities do not derive from the relations of labour exploitation meaning that the dominant race and/or ethnicity do not exploit labour of the subordinated race or ethnicity. This does not mean that varieties of race-ethnicity based oppressions are less harmful than the patriarchal or capitalist labour exploitation. Contemporary history is marked with a number of massacres of religious and ethnic minorities and indigenous people. Further, state-led direct violence targets Black people and, in some contexts, speaking the language of ethnic minority group in public can lead to lynching. Being killed is undoubtedly more harmful than being exploited. The key point is that the mediating-powers of race-ethnicity based oppression have different consequences to those of labour exploitation. While the former functions in ways which eliminate social and, in some cases, physical existence of the oppressed, the latter has to secure a partial consent of the exploited to maintain the relations of labour exploitation.

Drawing on the earlier distinction between exploitation and oppression, I develop concepts of systems and regimes. Systems of exploitation comprise class or gender based exploitation of labour as well as contemporary forms of slavery, whereas, regimes of oppression include the race-ethnicity, religion and caste based oppression. My conceptual framework allows for an assessment of *varieties of racist regimes* which vary according to historical and geographical contexts. Anti-Black racism represents one particular variety of racism, other varieties such as anti-indigenous, anti-Jewish, anti-Muslim, anti-Palestinian, anti-lower caste or anti-Kurdish racisms occur across the global North and global South. The main concern of this book is not varieties of racist regimes of oppression, but in drawing on the case of Turkey, I do examine how far anti-Alevi and anti-Kurdish racisms provide a suitable context for men to increase their bargaining capacity and diversify women's experiences.

3.5 The state

In contrast to the ungendered accounts of the state, addressed in Chapter 1, I suggest that the patriarchal and capitalist systems of exploitation and the racist regimes of oppression impose their agendas on the state thereby shaping its formation. In other words, depending on the political struggle and the collective acting capacity of (gender, class or race-ethnicity based) dominant groups of society, there is an interplay between the patriarchal, capitalist as well as racist agendas of the state which is significant for state formation. The focus of this book is the dynamics of, and changes in the patriarchal character of the state.

In her investigation of changes within patriarchal domination, as argued previously in Chapter 2, Walby states that the predominance of gender-based exclusionary strategies refers to domestic patriarchy, whereas, the gender-based segregation and subordination are linked to the neo-liberal or social-democratic forms of public patriarchy. Furthermore, she proposes that the polity domain both shapes and is shaped by the patriarchal, capitalist and racist inequality regimes (Walby 2020, 2009). Building on her framework, I propose that *the domestic patriarchal state* confines women's labour to household production (including care work) by sustaining gender-based exclusionary strategies, whereas, *the public patriarchal state* utilises various degrees of commodification and decommodification (of goods and services produced by women within the home) to uphold women's double burden of paid and unpaid labour. The domestic patriarchal state, therefore, sustains (i) large gender gaps in paid employment, (ii) poor provision of publicly provided domestic services, (iii) social policy that reinforces women's dependency on the cis-gender heterosexual marriage, (iv) compulsory heterosexuality and (v) preserves gender-based violence in both the domestic and the public spheres. The public patriarchal state, on the other hand, shapes the terms and conditions of women's double burden. A predominance of commodification refers to the neoliberal form of public patriarchy, whereas, decommodification points to the social-democratic form.

In order to assess the connections between the state and the collective bargaining capacity of men, I further engage with the concept of *the patriarchal gender contract* originally developed by Moghadam (1998). Moghadam provides a detailed account of the ways in which a social agreement is established between the state and the patriarchal collective subject in the oil and mixed oil economies. She explains that oil-based income has allowed for relatively high urban wages and emergence of a patriarchal gender contract (Karshenas 2001; Karshenas and Moghadam 2001). Moghadam uses the term to refer to a social agreement in which men are the breadwinners and women are the homemakers, mothers and caregivers. According to her (2003), this contract further gives rise to the neopatriarchal state which reinforces the role of women as full-time homemakers largely by using Muslim family laws. I argue that the establishment of such social contract does not depend on oil revenues, but the bargaining capacity of the patriarchal collective subject and women's struggle.

In Part II of this book, I investigate how far the interplay between the racist and capitalist agendas of the Turkish state has provided a suitable context for men to increase their collective bargaining capacity thereby sustaining the domestic patriarchal character of the state and the patriarchal gender contract through gender-based exclusionary strategies. In order to do so,

I examine the determinants of the initial patriarchal gender contract established during the early Republican period (1923–1940s). Despite changes in the racist and capitalist agendas of the state, I also assess the extent to which the contemporary patriarchal gender contract (the 2000s- current) continues to be associated with gender-based exclusionary strategies which signal the strength of a domestic patriarchal state.

3.6   Theorising gender regimes in the global South

Differentiating varieties of patriarchy is necessary to analyse women's diverse experiences and to develop effective strategies for achieving greater gender equality. Identifying different forms of domestic patriarchy is particularly important in the global South where gender-based exclusionary strategies play an important role in shaping state formation, capitalist development, civil society and culture and religion. Existing theories of gender regimes, however, tend to focus on the neoliberal or social-democratic forms of public patriarchy to the neglect of domestic patriarchy; at the same time, theories of capitalist development tend to neglect the significance of the patriarchal peasantry and the gendered patterns of agriculture (see Chapters 1 and 2). I argue that the patriarchal path of agrarian transformation not only diversifies trajectories of capitalist development, but also allows men to establish strong control over women's labour power and produce a surplus within small agricultural production units. It is this form of patriarchy that needs to be addressed when considering varieties of patriarchy in the global South.

Existing research on rural arrangements of gendered oppression and inequality sheds light on this particular form of patriarchy in various ways by examining: the integration of patriarchal relations of agrarian production with the capitalist market; implications for proletarianisation; strategies of resistance adopted by female peasants; polarisation between rural and urban gender regimes; as well as investigating the connections between women's exclusion from the means of production (e.g. land) and higher levels of gender inequality. In the following section, I assess the key arguments in this research.

3.6.1   Debate on rural forms of patriarchy

John Caldwell conceptualises *a familial mode of production* in North Africa, Southwest and South Asia by examining intra-household relations and fertility behaviours (1982, 1978). He suggests that the familial mode of production is exploitative and usually found in the context of subsistence production in agriculture. It is associated with a high stable fertility rate, relies on kinship and provides material advantages to male authority. Caldwell further analyses the relationship between familial and capitalist modes of production, arguing that the familial mode can adapt "for at least a time to the market economy without fully succumbing to the rules of the market and, indeed, while allowing that market to operate in a highly specialised way. Thus, the economic and demographic structure of the familial mode of production may dominate in a society with a limited market economy" (Caldwell 1982: 159).

According to Hisham Sharabi (1988), patriarchy was the main feature of pre-capitalist social formations in Europe and Asia. While it has been dissolved with the development of capitalism in Europe, neopatriarchy in the Arab world has been sustained and taken a specific and distinctive form due to two main forces. First, peripheral capitalism has prevented development of the domestic bourgeoisie and the proletariat. Therefore, such "distorted, dependent capitalism" has supported the petty bourgeoisie in controlling social and political life through Islamic fundamentalism (Sharabi 1988: 5). Secondly, subsistence farming has prevented emergence of proletariat-culture. Given the conditions of subsistence farming, Sharabi suggests, semi-employed male peasants tended to migrate to urban areas which, in turn, prevented female labour force participation.

Bina Agarwal (2016) goes beyond the limitations of such a culture-based analysis and examines the implications of gendered property and labour relations in agriculture for the proletarianisation process. Elaborating on the connections between the "slow, uneven, and highly gendered" agrarian transformation in India and the gendered patterns of agriculture, she argues that women's domestic work and lower levels of education serve to limit their access to paid employment thereby leading to gender gaps in the shift of labour from agriculture to non-agricultural sectors (Agarwal 2003: 191).

In her ethnographic study, Germaine Tillion (1983 [1966]) investigates gender relations in the two shores of the Mediterranean region and their hinterlands and develops the concept of the *republic of cousins*. She suggests that the republic of cousins derives from agriculture and upholds male dominance over women through marriages between first cousins. As men are responsible for relatives from their fathers' side, the marriage is usually between the children of two brothers. It therefore prevents foreign people from taking the villagers' daughters and so the land.

Deniz Kandiyoti investigates rural forms of patriarchy "through an analysis of women's strategies in dealing with them" (1988: 275). Drawing upon her concept of patriarchal bargain, she defines two forms of male domination: the sub-Saharan African pattern and classic patriarchy. While the former derives from women's resistance to unequal relations in household production, the latter arises from "women's strategies and coping mechanisms" within the extended family household and small peasantry based agrarian societies in North Africa, the Muslim Middle East and South and East Asia (Kandiyoti 1988: 285). She claims that in classic patriarchy, senior women adopt particular strategies to increase their security by establishing patriarchal control over younger women. Kandiyoti, furthermore, acknowledges that the small peasantry based extended family household is the material base of classic patriarchy as well as observing "the complete appropriation by the patrilineage of the girl's production and reproduction" (1984: 18). Recognising that patriarchal control of women in rural areas is an implicit part of traditional male privilege, she underlines the significance of a "dynamic interplay between economic change and traditional gender-role systems" for rural transformation (1984: 19). But at the same time she concludes that "[t]he material bases of classic patriarchy crumble under the impact of new market forces, capital penetration in rural areas, or processes of chronic immiseration" (Kandiyoti 1988: 282).

In her research, exploring the reasons for the persistence of patriarchy in the Middle East and North Africa, Moghadam conceptualises two forms of patriarchy. Assuming that patriarchal society is "a pre-capitalist social formation that has historically existed in varying forms in Europe and Asia in which property, resistance, and descent proceed through the male line", Moghadam focuses on the respective roles of periphery capitalism in sustaining *neopatriarchy* in oil-rich countries and *classic patriarchy* in countries with a significant rural population (2004: 141). According to her, oil-dependent capitalism has maintained neopatriarchal society in both the oil economies (Kuwait, Libya, Oman, Qatar, Saudi Arabia and the United Arab Emirates) and the mixed oil economies (Algeria, Egypt, Iran, Iraq, Syria and Tunisia) (Moghadam 2004; 2003). In these countries, oil-based income has increased the level of wages which, in turn, limited the supply of women's labour by reinforcing the patriarchal gender contract. At the same time, the structure of rural life and the nature of production relations have sustained classic patriarchy in countries with a considerably large rural population (e.g. Northern India, Pakistan, Afghanistan, Turkey, Iran, Yemen, Sudan and rural China). While pre-capitalist forms of social organisations can be found in Afghanistan, Sudan and Yemen, she suggests that Turkey has a "split between a highly patriarchal countryside and an urban context where gender and family relations are more egalitarian" (2003: 123). In her recent work where she considers the authoritarian states, oil economies, corporatism and restrictions of neoliberalism, Moghadam (2020) conceptualises two forms of public gender regime in the Middle East and North Africa region: neopatriarchal and conservative-corporatist.

> *In the neopatriarchal form*, aspects of private/domestic patriarchy prevail, in terms of the retention of conservative family law, a rentier or dependent form of capitalism that limits female economic participation, restraints on civil society that impede sustained feminist organizing, and inadequate or non-existent legislation on violence against women. *The emerging conservative-corporatist form* is most evident in Tunisia, Morocco, and Algeria, countries characterized by strong feminist movements, the visibility of women in the professions (especially the judiciary), and reformed family law
>
> (Moghadam 2020: 468, my emphasis)

Moghadam also considers the significance of the feminist movement and transnational feminist networks in challenging these varieties of patriarchy in the Middle East and North Africa (Moghadam 2020; 2013, 2005).

Feminist research on the gender gaps in landownership further provides a detailed account of the ways in which greater access to landownership increases women's economic empowerment, wellbeing, intra-household bargaining power and reduces health risks and poverty, as well as being a marker of status and identity and serving as a prevention against domestic violence (Doss et al. 2015; Deere and Doss 2006; Agarwal 2016; Rao 2018; Panda and Agarwal 2005; Deere, Alvarado, and Twyman 2012; O'Laughlin 2012). In their analyses of the causes of gender gaps in landownership, those scholars develop different approaches. Assuming that the productive use of land requires mutuality and interdependence between male and female peasants, some scholars point to the needs of capital (i.e. commodification of nature) and the implications for ethnicity-based oppression as the main reasons for gendered landownership (Mitra and Rao 2019; Rao 2005). Critically engaging with the assumption that the family is a unit of harmonious interests and preferences, others consider the significance of gendered oppression and inequality within the peasant family. In doing so, these scholars emphasise the role of landowning male peasants in excluding women from landownership by, for example, discriminating against women in land inheritance, limiting women's access to resources and utilising violence (Deere, Alvarado, and Twyman 2012; Deere 2001; Agarwal 2016).

These theories on the rural arrangements of gendered oppression and inequality provide a detailed analysis of the key characteristics of patriarchal transformation in countries with a relatively large rural population. Challenging the assumption that capitalist transformation dominates agrarian change, Caldwell points to an integration between patriarchal relations of production in agriculture and capitalist relations of exchange within the market. While Caldwell and Kandiyoti investigate the material benefits that male peasants gain from appropriating female peasants' labour, Sharabi and Agarwal elaborate on the implications of patriarchal control over women's agricultural labour for proletarianization. Moreover, Moghadam's differentiation of neopatriarchy in oil-rich countries and classic patriarchy in countries with a large rural population sheds light on the differences between rural and urban forms of patriarchy and divisions amongst women. Although Kandiyoti tends to dismiss female peasants' struggle in Muslim contexts, Moghadam acknowledges the role of women's struggle in changing patriarchal settings. Furthermore, feminist research on the gendered patterns of landownership contributes to an assessment of the connections between gendered dispossession, oppression and inequalities.

The capitalism-based reductionist approach nevertheless appears influential in these accounts, leading scholars to explain the persistence of patriarchy by focusing on capitalism. It is assumed that peripheral capitalism, the oil-based economy, or the pre-capitalist forms of agrarian social organisation maintain patriarchy (Sharabi 1988; Moghadam 2003), or it is seen as only a matter of time before capitalism destroys the material base of classic patriarchy (Kandiyoti 1988). Reducing the dynamics of gendered landownership either to capitalism or masculinities shaped by capitalism and ethnicity-based oppression, the first approach developed by feminist research on gendered landownership (Mitra and Rao 2019; Rao 2005) also fails to clarify why the commodification of nature results in various gendered outcomes in different countries or why peasants of the dominant ethnic background experience gendered patterns of agriculture. While invaluable in revealing the determinants of gendered landownership and the implications for gender inequality, the second approach tends to overlook the significance of patriarchal property and labour relations in agriculture for the proletarianization process, thereby obscuring the nexus between rural and urban gender regimes (Agarwal 2016; Deere, Alvarado, and Twyman 2012; Deere 2001). Although an early study of Agarwal (2003) represents an exception, she adopts the widely accepted assumption that the key determinant of proletarianisation is the capitalist sectors' capacity to absorb the surplus labour in agriculture which limits her account to the gendered barriers preventing such absorption.

In light of the assessment provided thus far, I argue that under the conditions in which women's exclusion from landownership is associated with the predominance of small landownership, a particular form of patriarchy is established which effectively shapes socio-economic transformation, including proletarianisation.

3.6.2 The premodern and modern forms of domestic patriarchy

Considering the conditions of dispossession and wage dependency, feminist research elaborates on the ways in which *women's exclusion from a means of subsistence* (e.g. wage, salary, rent or other forms of income) supports male household heads in maintaining their control over women's labour in household production (see Chapter 2). My research examines the extent to which *women's exclusion from a means of production* (e.g. land) increases the capacity of male small producers to exploit women's unpaid family labour. Subsequently, I differentiate two forms of gender-based exclusionary strategies:

1 *Gender-based exclusion in ownership of land*: The demands of landownership by dominant sections of society establish a division of labour and appropriation of agrarian surplus. Gendered landownership gives rise to a gender-based division of labour within agriculture and patriarchal exploitation of women's labour. Women's exclusion from landownership is therefore an important form of gender-based exclusion which sustains patriarchal exploitation of labour in rural households.

2 *Gender-based exclusion in income generating activities:* Under conditions of labourers' dispossession and increasing wage dependency, women's

exclusion from paid employment or other forms of income generating activities (e.g. ownership of a house or shop which either generates rental income or prevents rental payments) becomes a particular form of gender-based exclusionary strategy that shapes varieties of domestic patriarchy.

The outcomes of the earlier arrangements depend on the conditions of dispossession and increasing wage dependency. For example, women's exclusion from landownership has different gendered outcomes according to whether there is a predominance of capitalist farms and wage labour in agriculture or largely small landownership and unpaid family labour. Moreover, increasing wage dependency transforms the means of subsistence thereby compelling the patriarchal collective subject to adopt new strategies to maintain their control over women's labour. In order to highlight the importance of wage dependency and dispossession, I use the concepts of modern and premodern in referring to two forms of domestic patriarchy: in *premodern domestic patriarchy*, men sustain their exploitation of women's labour in rural households by excluding women from landownership in a context of predominantly small landownership. In *modern domestic patriarchy*, under the conditions of increasing wage dependency, men maintain their exploitation of women's labour within urban households by excluding women from paid employment. To summarise, my theoretical framework uses the concepts of the premodern and modern forms of domestic patriarchy along with the neoliberal and social-democratic forms of public patriarchy.

As discussed previously, theories on varieties of gender regime reject universal and unilinear perceptions of social change and instead adopt the notion of the uneven and combined development of socio-economic transformation. Building on this approach, I argue that the development of neoliberal or social-democratic public patriarchies can take place alongside premodern and modern domestic patriarchies. This means that the public and domestic forms of patriarchy coexist and together shape gendered patterns of economy, polity, civil society and violence. Drawing on my analysis that patriarchal exploitation of labour within the family persists under the neoliberal or social-democratic forms of public patriarchy, I argue that a shift away from women's unpaid labour within household production towards women's double burden of paid and unpaid labour is a prerequisite of the transition away from domestic forms of patriarchy. In the global South today, the question of what factors maintain the hegemony of premodern and modern domestic patriarchies remains important. Drawing on the case of Turkey, Part II of this book sheds light on some of those factors.

3.7 Conclusion

The theoretical dismissal of patriarchal exploitation of labour within the heterosexual family limits the scope of feminist strategies to a focus on gender inequalities. Analyses become restricted to revealing various forms of gender inequalities which, in turn, impedes development of transformative strategies to liberate women from the patriarchal system. Moreover, the shortcomings of social theory tend to provide fertile ground for a resurgence of biological essentialism. When the causal element of gender inequality is concealed, a biology-based rationale increases its influence over feminist strategies. Biologically determinist accounts do not only deny the womanhood of certain groups women (e.g. those who have transitioning experience) but also sabotage the strategic alliance with the LGBTQ+ movement. Dismissing the importance of the patriarchal collective subject also upholds the misleading assumption that men and women equally lose out within the patriarchal system. Finally, the belief that the capitalist system is the main dynamic sustaining women's oppression and gender inequality prevents feminist strategies from engaging with the distinguishing characteristics of the patriarchal system.

In light of those political implications, I suggest that it is necessary to put an analysis of the gendered patterns of labour exploitation back into feminist theory. The distinctive features of this particular form of labour exploitation need to be acknowledged and, at the same time, the question of what constitutes labour exploitation requires attention. I draw a conceptual distinction between the patriarchal or capitalist systems of exploitation and the racist regimes of oppression by exploring the connections between exploitation and oppression. While gender and class inequalities are derived from the relations of labour exploitation, race-ethnicity inequalities are linked to relations of domination. Furthermore, varieties of racisms are not limited to anti-Black racism, but extend to other forms, including anti-Alevi and anti-Kurdish racist regimes of oppression within the context of Turkey.

In my theory of the patriarchal system, I investigate the role of the patriarchal collective subject in maintaining the gender-based exploitation of labour. I consider the collective acting capacity of men as the gender-based dominant group of society. The patriarchal collective subject negotiates with the state which leads to a patriarchal gender contract. Depending on the collective bargaining capacity of men, women's struggle and the interplay between the multiple agendas of the state, the patriarchal gender contract is established on the grounds of gender-based exclusionary or segregationist strategies. Differentiating the domestic patriarchal state from the public patriarchal state, I argue that the former confines the majority of women's labour to household production whereas the latter guarantees the sustainability of women's double burden of paid and unpaid labour.

Moreover, I suggest that the contexts of the global South require a detailed investigation of the rural forms of patriarchy. My theoretical framework refers to two forms of domestic patriarchy: premodern and modern. Women's exclusion from agricultural landownership, in conjunction with a pattern of small landownership, leads to patriarchal exploitation of labour in rural households and, as such, creates premodern domestic patriarchy. Under the conditions of dispossession and increasing wage dependency, women's exclusion from paid employment sustains patriarchal exploitation within urban households, thereby establishing modern domestic patriarchy.

Drawing on the case of Turkey, Part II presents my data analysis which differentiates the causes and consequences of the premodern form of domestic patriarchy from those of the modern form within historical context (Chapter 4). In Chapter 5, I investigate how far the post-2000s' emergence of neoliberal public patriarchy has challenged the hegemony of the premodern and modern forms of domestic patriarchy. I then examine the uneven and combined development of premodern and modern domestic and neoliberal public patriarchies in the country (Chapter 6), as well as assessing the ways premodern domestic patriarchy has effectively shaped capital accumulation strategies, state formation and the cultural and religious conditions in Turkey (Chapter 7).

Note

1 The case I examine here does not include the condition of enslaved domestic workers who are not free to leave the family they work for.

Reference

Adkins, Lisa. 1995. *Gendered Work: Sexuality, Family and the Labour Market.* Buckingham; Bristol: Open University Press.

Agarwal, Bina. 2003. "Gender and Land Rights Revisited: Exploring New Prospects via the State, Family and Market." *Journal of Agrarian Change* 3 (1/2):184–225. doi: 10.1111/1471-0366.00054.

Agarwal, Bina. 2016. *Gender Challenges (Vol 1, 2 and 3).* India: Oxford University Press.

Beauvoir, Simone de. 1997 [1969]. *The Second Sex.* Vintage Classics.

Becker, Gary S. 1993. *A Treatise on the Family.* Cambridge, Mass.; London: Harvard University Press.

Black, Dan A., Seth G. Sanders, and Lowell J. Taylor. 2007. "The Economics of Lesbian and Gay Families." *Journal of Economic Perspectives* 21 (2):53–70. doi: 10.1257/jep.21.2.53.

Caldwell, John. 1978. "A Theory of Fertility: From High Plateau to Destabilization." *Population and Development Review* 4 (4):553–577.

Caldwell, John. 1982. *Theory of Fertility Decline.* London, New York: Academic Press Inc.

Cockburn, Cynthia. 1985. *Machinery of Dominance: Women, Men, and Technical know-how.* London: Pluto Press.

Cockburn, Cynthia. 1991. *Brothers: Male Dominance and Technological Change.* London: Pluto Press.

Connell, Raewyn. 2003. *Gender and Power: Society, the Person, and Sexual Politics.* Cambridge: Polity Press.

Connell, Raewyn. 2005. *Masculinities.* Berkeley, CA: University of California Press.

Coontz, S. 2006. *Marriage, A History: From Obedience to Intimacy or How Love Conquered Marriage.* London, New York: Penguin Group.

Criado-Perez, Caroline. 2019. *Invisible Women: Exposing Data Bias in a World Designed for Men*: Chatto & Windus.

Deere, Carmen, Gina E. Alvarado, and Jennifer Twyman. 2012. "Gender Inequality in Asset Ownership in Latin America: Female Owners vs Household Heads." *Development and Change* 43 (2):505–530. doi: 10.1111/j.1467-7660.2012.01764.x.

Deere, Carmen Diana. 2001. *Empowering Women: Land and Property Rights in Latin America*. Pittsburgh: University of Pittsburgh Press.

Deere, Carmen Diana, and Cheryl R. Doss. 2006. "The Gender Asset Gap: What Do We Know and Why Does it Matter?" *Feminist Economics* 12 (1–2):1–50. doi: 10.1080/13545700500508056.

Delphy, Christine. 2003. "Par où Attaquer le « Partage Inégal » du « Travail Ménager »?" *Nouvelles Questions Féministes* 22 (3):47–72.

Delphy, Christine. 2014. "Feminist Economics." *Perspectives On The Economy*. 15 (2): 29–41.

Delphy, Christine. 2016. *Close to Home: A Materialist Analysis of Women's Oppression*. London, Brooklyn: Verso.

Doss, Cheryl, Chiara Kovarik, Amber Peterman, Agnes Quisumbing, and Mara Van den Bold. 2015. "Gender Inequalities in Ownership and Control of Land in Africa: Myth and Reality." *Agricultural Economics* 46 (3):403–435.

Ferrant, Gaelle, and Annelise Thim. 2019. Measuring Women's Economic eEmpowerment: Time Use Data and Gender Inequality. *OECD Development Policy Papers*, No. 16, OECD Publishing, Paris, https://doi.org/10.1787/02e538fc-en

Ferrant, Gaëlle, Luca Maria Pesando, and Keiko Nowacka. 2014. *Unpaid Care Work: The Missing Link in the Analysis of Gender Gaps in Labour Outcomes*. OECD Development Centre.

Folbre, Nancy. 1994. *Who Pays for the Kids? Gender and the Structures of Constraint, Economics as Social Theory*. London, New York: Routledge.

Folbre, Nancy. 2009. "Varieties of Patriarchal Capitalism." *Social Politics* 16 (2):204–209.

Gershuny, Jonathan, and Teresa Harms. 2016. "Housework Now Takes Much Less Time: 85 Years of US Rural Women's Time Use." *Social Forces* 95 (2):503–524.

Giddings, Lisa, John M. Nunley, Alyssa Schneebaum, and Joachim Zietz. 2014. "Birth Cohort and the Specialization Gap between Same-Sex and Different-Sex Couples." *Demography* 51 (2):1–26. doi: 10.1007/s13524-013-0267-4.

Guillaumin, Colette. 1995. *Racism, Sexism, Power and Ideology*. London, New York: Routledge.

Gunnarsson, Lena. 2013. "Loving him for who he is: The microsociology of power." In *Love: A Question for Feminism in the Twenty-First Century*, edited by A. G. Jónasdóttir, and A. Ferguson. London, New York: Routledge

Gunnarsson, Lena. 2014. *The Contradictions of Love: Towards a Feminist-realist Ontology of Sociosexuality*. London, New York: Routledge.

Gunnarsson, Lena. 2015. "Nature, Love and the Limits of Male Power." *Journal of Critical Realism* 14 (3):325–332. doi: 10.1179/1476743015Z.00000000071.

Hartmann, Heidi I. 1979. "The Unhappy Marriage of Marxism and Feminism: Towards a More Progressive Union." *Capital and Class* 8 (Summer):1–33.

Himmelweit, Susan. 1983. Exploitation. In *A Dictionary of Marxist Thought*, edited by T. B. Bottomore. Massachusetts: Basil Blackwell.

Illouz, Eva. 2012. *Why Love Hurts? A Sociological Explanation*. Cambridge, Malden: Polity Press.

İlkkaracan, İpek, and Emel Memiş. 2021. "Transformations in the Gender Gaps in Paid and Unpaid Work During the COVID-19 Pandemic: Findings from Turkey." *Feminist Economics* 27 (1–2):288–309. doi: 10.1080/13545701.2020.1849764.

Jónasdóttir, Anna G. 1994. *Why Women Are Oppressed.* Philadelphia: Temple University Press.

Jónasdóttir, Anna G., and Ann Ferguson. 2013. *Love: A Question for Feminism in the Twenty-first Century.* London, New York: Routledge

Kandiyoti, Deniz. 1988. "Bargaining with Patriarchy." *Gender and Society* 2 (3):274–290.

Kandiyoti, Deniz. 1984. "Rural transformation in turkey and its implications for women's status." In *Women on the Move: Contemporary Changes in Family and Society.* UNESCO.

Karshenas, Massoud. 2001. "Economic liberation, competitiveness, and women's employment in the middle east and north Africa." In *Labour and Human Capital in the Middle East,* edited by D. Salehi-Ishfahani. Reading: Ithaca Press.

Karshenas, Massoud, and Valentine M. Moghadam. 2001. "Female labour force participation and economic adjustment in the middle east north Africa region." In *The Economics of Women and Work in the Middle East and North Africa,* edited by M. Çınar. JAI Press

Kongar, Ebru, and Emel Memiş. 2017. "Gendered patterns of time use over the life cycle in Turkey." In *Gender and Time Use in A Global Context: The Economics of Employment and Unpaid Labor,* edited by R. Connelly and E. Kongar. London, New York: Palgrave Macmillan

Leppel, Karen. 2009. "Labour Force Status and Sexual Orientation." *Economica* 76 (301):197–207. doi: 10.1111/j.1468-0335.2007.00676.x.

Mitra, Amit, and Nitya Rao. 2019. "Contract Farming, Ecological Change and the Transformations of Reciprocal Gendered Social Relations in Eastern India." *The Journal of Peasant Studies.* 48 (2): 436–457. doi: 10.1080/03066150.2019.1683000.

Moghadam, Valentine M. 2004. "Patriarchy in Transition: Women and the Changing Family in the Middle East." *Journal of Comparative Family Studies* 35 (2):137–162.

Moghadam, Valentine M. 2005. *Globalising Women: Transnational Feminist Networks.* Baltimore, London: The John Hopkins University Press.

Moghadam, Valentine M. 2013. *Globalisation and Social Movements: Islamism, Feminism, and the Global Justice Movement.* Lanham, Boulder, New York, Toronto, Plymouth: Rowman & Littlefield Publishers.

Moghadam, Valentine M. 1998. *Women, Work and Economic Reform in the Middle East and North Africa.* London, New York: Lynne Rienner.

Moghadam, Valentine M. 2003. *Modernising Women: Gender and Social Change in the Middle East.* London: Lynne Reinner.

Moghadam, Valentine M. 2020. "Gender Regimes in the Middle East and North Africa: The Power of Feminist Movements." *Social Politics* 27 (3):467–485. doi: 10.1093/sp/jxaa019.

OECD.Stat. 2020. Time use survey. edited by OECD.

O'Laughlin, Bridget. 2012. "Gender justice, land and the agrarian question in southern Africa." In *Peasants and Globalization,* edited by A. Akram-Lodhi and C. Kay. London, New York: Routledge.

Öneş, Umut, Emel Memiş, and Burca Kızılırmak. 2013. "Poverty and Intra-Household Distribution of Work Time in Turkey: Analysis and Some Policy Implications." *Women's Studies International Forum* 41 (1): 55–64. doi: 10.1016/j.wsif.2013.01.004

Panda, Pradeep, and Bina Agarwal. 2005. "Marital Violence, Human Development and Women's Property Status in India." *World Development* 33 (5):823–850. doi: 10.1016/j.worlddev.2005.01.009.

Rao, Nitya. 2005. "Questioning Women's Solidarity: The Case of Land Rights, Santal Parganas, Jharkhand, India." *The Journal of Development Studies* 41 (3):353–375. doi: 10.1080/0022038042000313282.

Rao, Nitya. 2018. *'Good Women Do Not Inherit land': Politics of Land and Gender in India*: London, New York: Routledge.

Ringhofer, Lisa. 2015. "Time, Labour, and the Household: Measuring "Time Poverty" Through a Gender Lens." *Development in Practice* 25 (3):321–332.

Roamer, John. 2014. *A General Theory of Exploitation and Class*: Harvard University Press.

Shaikh, Anwar. 1990a. "Exploitation." In *Marxian Economics*, edited by J. Eatwell, M. Milgate and P. Newman. London: MacMillan.

Shaikh, Anwar. 1990b. "Surplus value." In *Marxian Economics*, edited by J. Eatwell, M. Milgate and P. Newman. London: MacMillan.

Sharabi, Hisham. 1988. *Neopatriarchy: A Theory of Distorted Change in Arab Society*. New York: Oxford University Press.

The UN. 2014. "#HeForShe." The United Nations, accessed 02.03.2021. https://www.heforshe.org/en.

Tillion, Germain. 1983 [1966]. *The Republic of Cousins: Women's Oppression in Mediterranean Society*. London: Al Saqi Books.

Walby, Sylvia. 1986. *Patriarchy at Work*. Minneapolis: University of Minnesota Press.

Walby, Sylvia. 2009. *Globalisation and Inequalities: Complexity and Contested Modernities*. London: Sage Publications Ltd.

Walby, Sylvia. 2020. "Developing the Concept of Society: Institutional Domains, Regimes of Inequalities and Complex Systems in a Global Era." *Current Sociology*. doi: 10.1177/0011392120932940.

Wright, Erik Olin. 1997. *Class Counts: Comparative Studies in Class Analysis*. Cambridge: Cambridge University Press.

PART II

VARIETIES OF PATRIARCHY AND IMPLICATIONS FOR CAPITALIST DEVELOPMENT: THE CASE OF TURKEY

4 NEW VARIETIES OF PATRIARCHY

THE EARLY REPUBLICAN PERIOD

Drawing on the case of Turkey, this chapter distinguishes new varieties of domestic patriarchy within historical context. My analysis also allows investigation of how far men, in their position as rural and urban small producers, constitute a patriarchal collective subject by excluding women from the ownership of means of production (e.g. land) and subsistence (e.g. income generating activities, including paid employment) thereby sustaining patriarchal labour exploitation within the family. In this chapter, I further assess the ways in which the domestic patriarchal character of the Turkish state plays a significant role in sustaining the gender-based exclusionary strategies and thus premodern and modern forms of domestic patriarchy.

I use a historical sociology-based case study method to differentiate the causes and consequences of the premodern form of domestic patriarchy from those of the modern form. The period considered is from the late Ottoman Empire until the early Republican period (1923–1940s). The selected time period allows for a detailed investigation of the extent to which men in their position as household heads and small producers shaped the patriarchal character of the Republican state. Considering this period also enables an analysis of how far changing forms of a patriarchal domination divided rural and urban women as well as revealing the possible reasons for the lack of alignment between their separate agendas and strategies. The evidence includes work which has drawn on the Ottoman and Republican state archives, including the Independence Tribunal (*İstiklal Mahkemeleri*) and the Republican archives (*Cumhuriyet arşivleri*), and other archival materials such as the Imperial code, sharia court records, land inheritance laws and regulations and petitions and complaints.

I begin by distinguishing the causes of the premodern form of domestic patriarchy from those of the modern form (Sections 4.1 and 4.2), followed by investigation of the respective roles of the capitalist and racist agendas of the state in terms of increasing the bargaining power of male small producers and establishing a patriarchal gender contract (Section 4.3). I then assess the reasons for the failure of the first wave feminist movement to maintain their influence over the Turkish state as well as investigate the divisions amongst women (Sections 4.4 and 4.5).

DOI: 10.4324/9781003054511-7

4.1 The premodern form of domestic patriarchy

Both the Ottoman and the Republican legal frameworks treated agricultural land differently to other forms of property. The Sultan symbolised the owner of the entire land in the Empire – except the private and *awqaf* lands – called the *miri* land. The *miri* land was distributed to tax-farmers who had a lifetime contract *without* hereditary rights. Peasants, however, had hereditary rights on the land; upon the death of a peasant, the *miri* land automatically passed to the son(s). Other than a son, anyone who wished to cultivate the land, called outsiders, had to pay an entrance fee, called *tapu-tax* (Imber 2010). During the Ottoman period, the main struggle between male and female peasants was whether daughters, sisters and mothers constituted outsiders and were eligible to pay *tapu-tax*.

Daughters were accepted as outsiders for the first time in 1568, followed by mothers and sisters in the early seventeenth century. According to existing accounts, Ottoman women's landownership rights were attributable either to the decline in the male population due to wars and rebellion (Imber 2010, 2012) or to the development of capitalism (Aytekin 2009). These accounts, however, neglect the significance of women's struggle. As argued elsewhere, Ottoman women were relatively successful in utilising the Hanefi School of Islamic Law and the local sharia courts to gain property and landownership rights thereby gaining property ownership and inheritance rights much earlier than women in European feudal kingdoms (Kocabıçak 2018).

Having attained the status of outsiders, female peasants tried to delay payment of *tapu-tax* since immediate access to financial resources was rare, especially for women. Analysis of the local sharia courts' archives demonstrates that in many cases courts postponed the deadline of the *tapu-tax* payment in favour of women and, as such, supported female peasants (Imber 2010; Gerber 1980). Male peasants, however, did not accept female peasants' increased control over the *miri* land. They organised various petitions and written complaints to the Ottoman state which led the state to impose time restrictions for *tapu-tax* payment (Imber 2010). Court cases demonstrate that local sharia courts played a significant role in the struggle for landownership; male peasants often utilised these courts to claim ownership of land that was under female peasants' control (Jennings 1975).

The Nizamiye court system (1860–1923) also limited women's access to legal powers of property relations in the following ways (Agmon 2006, 2003; Rubin 2012): (i) since women were not allowed to be professional attorneys, replacing self-representation with professional attorneys increased women's dependency on male attorneys. (ii) The Hanefi School's appointment of *kadıs* as protectors of women against men's abuses was undermined and autonomy restricted by the imposition of increased obligations to local and central authorities. (iii) The legal costs associated with Nizamiye courts required significant financial resources. (iv) Increased legal terminology and replacing witnesses' verbal statements with documented evidence required professional support which increased the legal costs and, given women's limited financial assets, undermined their access to justice. The Nizamiye court system thus gradually limited female peasants' access to legal powers which supported male peasants' control over women's land, but it was not until the 1926 civil code that female peasants almost entirely lost their control over landownership.

The Turkish civil code (1926–2002) discriminated against women in inheritance of agricultural land. The code regulated the inheritance of small-scale land differently to large-scale land and passed land under a certain scale[1] directly to the son:

> Article 598: On his death, *only if none of his sons want* to take the responsibility of the [agrarian] holding, under the condition in which his daughters or the husbands of his daughters are eligible, his daughters or the husbands of his daughters can demand the transfer of the holding to themselves.
>
> (Velidedeoğlu 1970: 324, my emphasis)

The earlier article meant that a woman could inherit her father's land *only if* none of her brothers wanted it *and* if she *or* her husband were eligible to cultivate the land, manage the agrarian holding *and* demanded to do so. A new civil code in 2002 removed the previous discriminatory article but introduced an ambiguous criterion of eligibility which was not addressed until 2015. In December 2014, the Ministry of Agriculture announced an eligibility formula which remains slightly problematic but nevertheless represents the most gender-equal law female peasants have witnessed for centuries. Legal discrimination against women in land inheritance has, therefore, sustained gendered dispossession of agricultural land across the Ottoman and the Republican periods (1923– 2015).

Such gendered discrimination certainly allowed the state to protect land from dispersing through the generations thereby maintaining agricultural productivity under conditions of increased commercialisation. However, this justification does not explain why the state in Turkey waited for almost 90 years before introducing a gender-equitable formula for selecting an heir (as many other states did in the first place). Given such discrimination, I argue that domestic patriarchal character of the state persisted into the Republican period.

Assessing the character of the Turkish state needs to take into account the conditions under which the peasantry was capable of negotiating to protect small landownership against the market-led powers of dispossession. Research shows that peasant revolts, protests and petitions during the Ottoman Empire and early Republican period (Aytekin 2013, 2012; Quataert 1991; Faroqhi 1992; Saraçoğlu 2007; Pinson 1975; Orhan 2012), as well as electoral pressure through the ballot box in the early Republican (Karaömerlioğlu 2008; Pamuk 1991) and also the Justice and Development

Party period (2002– current) (Gürel, Küçük, and Taş 2019) comprise the key mechanisms for peasants to bargain with the state. The early decades of the Republic witnessed significant revolts against the state, for example, the *Seikh Said* rebellion (1925) and the *Dersim* revolt (1930–1939). The former relied on a strong alliance between elites and peasants in the Kurdish provinces and, in the latter, peasants refused rural taxation, compulsory military service and the state's disarmament policy, but were ultimately defeated by the massacre of thousands. During the Republican period, the parliamentary system has increasingly become a significant means of negotiation between the state and peasants; the opposition parties had considerable support in rural areas which led to party closures (in 1925 and 1930). Furthermore, in 1950, peasants' "vote of protest" ended the single party regime in Turkey (Pamuk 1991: 138). Peasants were therefore successful in negotiating with the state and securing small production.

As a result, the 1926 civil code legalised peasants' claims over the (*miri*) land and allowed official occupation of Greek and Armenian peasants' land. Land re-distribution continued with the Land and Settlement Laws (1930 and 1934) and the Law of Giving Land to the Farmers (1945). The state also drove agrarian commercialisation in ways that protected small-medium scale farms from market-led dispossession of land. The pressure from the peasantry did not allow the state to allocate a greater proportion of surplus through rural taxation (Pamuk 1991). State-led incentives further supported the peasantry in allocating a relatively significant proportion of surplus.

Male domination is not inherent to the state form, rather male small producers in rural areas were able to negotiate with the state to retain power. As well as providing economic incentives to peasants, the state utilised the gender-based exclusionary strategies to gain male peasants' support for the overall regime. The state, therefore, maintained the dominance of small-landownership and legal discrimination against women in land inheritance and, at the same time, intensified the gendered division of labour and patriarchal control over women in agriculture through policies and regulations. As a result, the domestic patriarchal character of the Turkish state has been retained.

Gendered dispossession in these conditions has had significant consequences. Qualitative research shows that women's exclusion from land-ownership leads to a strong gender-based division of labour in agriculture thereby sustaining patriarchal exploitation of labour (Karkiner 2009, 2006; Hoşgör-Gündüz and Smits 2007; Onaran-İncirlioğlu 1999; Kandiyoti 1990; Sirman 1988; Morvaridi 1993, 1992; GDSW 2000; Ecevit 1993). Men tend to handle commercial and bureaucratic tasks, whereas, women are responsible for the heaviest and most labour-intensive and repetitive tasks. Male peasants further use control over the agrarian surplus to their advantage by, for example, spending more time and money on leisure, eating more and having more nutritious food than women and having greater luxury consumption (Kandiyoti 1990). Rural women's dispossession sustains the patriarchal exploitation of labour in rural households and thereby establishes premodern domestic patriarchy. As I will argue in the following chapters, premodern domestic patriarchy has significant implications for the key dynamics of the overall gender regime and the trajectories of capitalist development in Turkey.

4.2 The modern form of domestic patriarchy

Here, I investigate the extent to which male small producers in urban areas sustained their influence over the patriarchal character of the state and, in so doing, limited women's access to income generating activities (including paid employment). Historical research shows that Ottoman guilds were key institutions in allowing male small producers to utilise their collective acting capacity. These associations set prices and salaries, regulated production quality, organised the buying and flow of raw materials and goods, decided on production quotas and supervised selling and were therefore significant in shaping the socio-economic life of the Empire (Chalcraft 2015; Yi 2004; Quataert 1994, 1993; Gerber 1976). Guilds further established strong control over Ottoman urban labour; indeed, some argue that no workers existed outside of these structures (Quataert 2001). Analysis of the Ottoman archives demonstrates that male small producers limited women's access to income generating activities by excluding women from guilds, organising petitions and complaints against female artisans and labourers, utilising courts and sustaining the myth that goods made by women were of inferior quality (Shatzmiller 1988; Zarinebaf 2001; Gerber 1980, 1976; Kal'a 1997).

Ottoman archival materials, further, show that the imperial orders supported guilds in sustaining those gender-based exclusionary strategies. The state repeatedly banned women from establishing their own guilds, opening shops and selling products of their labour (Kal'a 1997). In addition, legal discrimination against women in inheritance was a significant barrier to women's access to small production. Although inheritance from their fathers (*hisse*) supported women in pursuing an occupation, female small producers were not allowed to pass their occupation to descendants (Gerber 1980). Moreover, in the seventeenth and the eighteenth centuries, merchants started to deliver raw materials to female producers to decrease production costs which allowed women to work in the home. In response, male producers and their guilds wrote many petitions and complaints to secure state intervention to limit women's access to such income (Zarinebaf 2001; Kal'a 1997).

Why did the state adopt male small producers' discriminatory approach towards women? Male small producers in urban areas appeared to yield influence over the state by utilising their collective bargaining capacity under the guild system. Guilds held considerable power with respect to regulating socio-economic life, as well as being the main resource of urban taxation. Furthermore, they played an important role in times of war by paying army-tax and providing goods and services to the Ottoman army (Yi 2004; Quataert 2001, 1994, 1993; Gerber 1976; Shatzmiller 1988). Historical research demonstrates the significance of petitions, complaints, uprisings and the justice system in maintaining the bargaining power of the guildsmen (Yi 2004). In doing so, they enjoyed not only a monopoly guaranteed by customary rights, but also managed to sustain the domestic patriarchal character of the state. In comparison to colonial regions (e.g. North Africa), Turkey's guild system was therefore protected against the market-led powers of dispossession for a longer period of time (Chalcraft 2015; Quataert 1994, 1993; Clancy-Smith 2018) which meant gender-based exclusion in income generating activities was sustained.

The male-dominated urban labour market was not challenged until the late nineteenth century when women's access to income generating activities increased. Women of elite households began to manage their property and invest in trading and manufacturing, particularly textiles, by providing capital and entering partnerships with men (Zarinebaf 2001, 2010; Fay 1998, 2010; Jennings 1975; Gerber 1980). The 1927 industrial survey suggests around a quarter of manufacturers were non-Muslim women, and around a quarter of industrial workers were women and girls (Makal 2010). However, the domestic patriarchal character of the state was reconstructed during the early decades of the Republican period (1923–1940). As Quataert (2001) suggests, guilds remained important and sustained their influence on workplace culture, including labour unions and syndicates.

In addition, as I will argue later, the first wave of the feminist movement in Turkey failed to challenge the resurgence of the patriarchal state. As the domestic patriarchal character of the state was preserved without facing significant challenge, subsequent decades saw various forms of gender-based exclusionary strategies in paid employment. These strategies included: (i) gender-based discriminatory laws and regulations, including the prohibitions relating to women's employment in certain jobs and patriarchal rights being granted to husbands to restrict their wives' employment, (ii) lack of preventative measures targeting sexual harassment at work, (iii) the patriarchal character of the Turkish welfare regime, which assumes men are the single-breadwinners and women are the homemakers, and consequently, (iv) the lack of public provisioning of childcare.

To summarise, male peasants have utilised legal discrimination against women in land inheritance and, in so doing, sustained patriarchal exploitation of labour in rural households. At the same time, male small producers, as well as male household heads played a considerable role in excluding women from income generating activities (including paid employment) which, in turn, maintained patriarchal exploitation of labour within urban households. I therefore, identify the premodern and modern forms of domestic patriarchy by distinguishing two main arrangements of gender-based exclusionary strategies. Women's exclusion from agricultural landownership, in conjunction with the predominance of small landownership, leads to patriarchal exploitation of labour in rural households and as such, constructs premodern domestic patriarchy. Under the conditions of dispossession and increasing wage dependency, women's exclusion from paid employment and income generating activities sustains patriarchal exploitation of labour within urban households, thereby, establishing modern domestic patriarchy.

4.3 The patriarchal gender contract in the early Republican period

In light of the evidence examined thus far, I suggest that men, in their position as rural and urban small producers, constitute a patriarchal collective subject that is mediated by the state. Through such mediation, gender-based exclusion in property ownership is represented as unintentional, traditional or as an aspect of culture or religion. However, as I have shown, this appearance is misleading; male small producers in rural and urban areas were relatively successful in negotiating with the state and, in so doing, secured small scale production as well as the exclusion of women from ownership of the means of production (e.g. land) and subsistence (e.g. income generating activities, including paid employment). In this section, I investigate the ways in which the interplay between the racist and capitalist agendas of the Republican state provided a suitable context for men to increase their bargaining power and led to a patriarchal gender contract on the grounds of gender-based exclusionary strategies.

Since the establishment of the Republic in 1923, the Turkish state has been characterised by a racist national agenda which, in many respects, provided a suitable context for male household heads and small producers to increase their influence over the patriarchal character of the state. For example, a nation-building process was accelerated on the grounds of Turkishness and Sunni-Muslimness thereby initiating a large scale expulsion of the non-Muslim population, including Armenian, Greek and Jewish artisans, peasants, merchants and also manufacturers (Ekmekcioğlu 2014; İçduygu, Toktas and Ali Soner 2008; Kadıoğlu 2007; Kuyucu 2005; Yıldız 2001). With the Population Exchange Agreement, approximately 60% of Anatolian Greeks left the country (1923–1927). The non-Muslim population was 15% of total population in 1919, but this figure dropped to 2% in 1927, 1,3% in 1950, and 0,8% in 1961 (İçduygu, Toktas, and Ali Soner 2008). The emigration of the non-Muslim population continued until the mid-1960s, and required Turkish Muslim citizens to take over rural and urban production.

Moreover, a strong military was intrinsic to the state's racist agenda for several reasons: (i) the Turkish nation-building process was initially accentuated by the Young Turk military coup of 1908. With the War of Independence (1919–1923), the Turkish army negotiated and succeeded in establishing the Republic, with its high-ranking officers occupying parliamentary duties

(Rustow 1959). (ii) In addition, during the early decades of the Republic, the army was transformed into a protective force which remained loyal to the Kemalist nationalism (Harris 1965). The army was, therefore, rebuilt not only as an effective fighting force, but also as a protector of the Kemalist regime (Gürsoy 2014; Hale 2011; 1994). The initial symbolic character of this military guardianship (1924–1960) later transformed into an assertive guardianship (Sarigil 2014). (iii) Furthermore, the army served as an instrument of nation-building which taught discipline, cleanliness, tidiness, reading and writing to young men of the nation (Hale 2011; Kral 1937).

As the army was a constitutional component of its Turkish Muslim agenda, the state introduced a compulsory military service. All young men were required to perform military service lasting between 18 months and 3 years. The military recruitment of male peasants was crucial since the majority of the population lived in rural areas. Furthermore, as Düzgün (2018) investigates, during the Ottoman Empire the peasants' role as soldiers was of equal importance to their role as taxpayers. I suggest that the Republican state adopted this previously established army of peasant proprietors and thus relied upon landowning-male peasants to safeguard its strong military.

However, military conscription was not welcomed in rural areas. As well as organising a number of revolts and uprisings (Orhan 2012; Yelbasi 2019), the peasantry avoided official marriage and registration of new-borns thereby postponing young men's compulsory military service (Timur 1957; Stirling 1957). The Independence Tribunal archives also show that rural men ignored the declaration of mobilisations, did not come back after their leave, escaped from combat and frequently ran away from their troops, sometimes leading to armed revolts in the villages (Independence Tribunal 1920–1927).

While the racist agenda entailed expulsion of non-Muslim populations and military conscription, the capitalist agenda necessitated a workforce in agrarian and non-agrarian production. The state needed to motivate the Turkish Muslim peasants to cultivate the land that had been abandoned by non-Muslim peasants and, at the same time, persuade urban small producers to take over the occupations of non-Muslim craftsmen and merchants. In rural areas, the 1926 civil code legally transformed the status of the entire *miri* land to *private* land and allowed Muslim Turkish and Kurdish peasants' official occupation of Greek and Armenian peasants' land. As noted above, land allocation continued with the Land and Settlement Laws (1930 and 1934) and the Law of Giving Land to the Farmers (1945). In this way, the state: prevented peasants from leaving their villages; increased the number of landowning peasants; attempted to mobilise peasants' support for the regime; and prevented the peasantry from developing radical demands (Karaömerlioğlu 2008). The Muslim settlers, whom the Population Exchange Agreement had forced to migrate to Turkey, were assigned to various regions and jobs depending on their occupation (The Republican

State Archives 1923–1960). These Muslim settlers, in part, compensated the loss of the workforce; yet the ethnicity-based occupational segregation in the cities meant that it was not easy for them to take over occupations. Thus, occupational training was crucial to raising Turkish Muslim crafts-men and, subsequently the state took immediate action to improve those occupational courses.

As well as securing the workforce necessary for rural and urban produc-tion, the capitalist agenda required a national industrialisation strategy. The key principles of this strategy were developed in the 1923 İzmir Economy Congress and included an immediate enhancement of transportation (rail-ways) and the establishment of a national bank to invest in those sectors which the Turkish Muslim bourgeoisie considered too risky (Yerasimos 2005; Boratav 2011). As one of the first nation-based independent coun-tries in the global South, the Turkish Republic needed initial accumula-tion in order to apply its national industrialisation strategy but the Great Depression of the 1930s and the Second World War (1939–1945) prevented direct foreign investments. Agriculture thus remained the primary source of the initial accumulation necessary for early industrialisation (until the 1970s). The state, therefore, drove agrarian commercialisation to transfer the surplus into industry which necessitated a social contract between the peasantry and the state.

The Republican state required support from the peasantry and urban small producers in order to fulfil the requirements of its racist and capitalist agendas. However, the domestic patriarchal character of the state was not a precondition for achieving these agendas. The Turkish state could have suc-cessfully implemented these agendas by adopting a public patriarchal char-acter meaning that, in addition to their domestic roles and duties, Turkish Sunni-Muslim women could have been mobilised as rural and urban small producers and soldiers to fulfil the racist and capitalist agendas. Indeed, historical research demonstrates that there were attempts to challenge the domestic patriarchal state and, to a certain extent, the Republican state did abolish gender-based exclusionary laws and regulations, focused on wom-en's emancipation and narrowed the gender gaps in citizenship and the nation-building process (Arat 2010; Kandiyoti 1989, 1991, 1995; Abadan-Unat 1981; Tekeli 1981). Nevertheless, those attempts were defeated, and the initial steps towards the public patriarchal state were rapidly supplanted by the resurgence of its domestic patriarchal character.

The negotiation between the Turkish state and male small producers was driven not only by the agendas of the state, but also by the collective act-ing capacity of male small producers. The interplay between the racist and capitalist agendas of the Republican state allowed male small producers to sustain the domestic patriarchal character of the state while women failed to maintain their influence. The negotiation between the state and male small producers, therefore, achieved a patriarchal gender contract on the grounds of gender-based exclusionary strategies. Subsequently, women's role was rapidly re-defined as the bearers of the Turkish Sunni-Muslim nation. Their access to education and paid employment which had hitherto been increasing was interrupted, the domesticity of women was promoted, and women's control over their bodies was restricted, culminating in the introduction of pro-natalist policies (Arat 1994; 1999a; Ertürk 1995; Navaro-Yasin 2000; Maksudyan 2015). The discourse of 'women as citizens' was swiftly transformed into one of women as 'wives and mothers' (Gümüşoğlu 1998). The domestic patriarchal state, furthermore, initiated direct attacks on the key organisations of the first wave feminist movement (see later). The state, therefore, played a significant role in confining women's labour to household production by sustaining gender-based exclusionary strategies which, in turn, led to the dominance of the premodern and modern forms of domestic patriarchy.

While men, in their position as small producers and head of households, have managed to sustain the domestic patriarchal character of the state, women have failed to maintain their influence over the state. In the next section, I investigate the factors that appear to underlie this weakening of women's collective acting capacity.

4.4 The first wave feminist movement

Initial studies on first wave feminism in Turkey tend to neglect the significance of the movement by claiming that women's rights functioned to support the Republican regime in achieving its strategic goals, including modernisation, nation building and detaching from the Ottoman Islamic past (Kandiyoti 1989, 1991, 1995, 1997; Tekeli 1981, 1982). Engaging with this approach, Kandiyoti (1989) compares the women's movement in the early Republican period with Western suffragist movements and concludes that women's rights in Turkey were not obtained through the women's movement but granted by male modernist reformists and "male feminism" (Kandiyoti 1997: 121). Nevertheless, recent research suggests that during the late Ottoman and early Republican periods the first wave did represent an important political actor that put pressure on the state (Durakbaşa and İlyasoğlu 2001; Durakbaşa 1988, 1998; Os 2000; Demirdirek 1999; Çakır 1994; Tekeli 1990a, 1998).[2]

The relatively unique character of the first wave feminist movement in Turkey seems to prevent acknowledgement of its significance. For example, the Ottoman Empire did not have a strong tradition of the parliamentary system and the Turkish Republic had a single party regime until 1950. Women therefore strategically prioritised education and employment rights while demands for full suffrage came later with the Women's Federation plans and attempts to organise a rally (in 1930). The first wave also discussed their demands within an Islamic framework until political modernisation at the end of the nineteenth and beginning of the twentieth century (Demirdirek 1999).

Historical research shows that the movement achieved significant organisational strength and constructed a robust, cohesive and dynamic social movement during the late Ottoman and early Republican periods. Organisations explicitly committed to women's rights followed the initial forms of women's religious charity organisations (Os 2000). Serpil Çakır (1994) estimates there were over 40 women's organisations between the mid-nineteenth century and 1923, while Nicole Van Os (2000) suggests approximately one hundred. Women's organisations were also consulted by various journals including *Şükufezar* (in 1886), *Hanımlara Mahsus Gazete* (in 1895), *Demet* (in 1908), *Mehasin* (between 1908 and 1909), *Kadın* (Selanik 1908–1909), *Kadın* (Istanbul 1911–1912), *Kadınlar Dünyası* (1913–1914 and 1918–1921) and *Kadınlık* (in 1914). The first wave in Turkey further established strong connections with the feminist movement in Western Europe. The Turkish Women's Federation organised the twelfth Congress of the International Federation of Women (in 1935) with the participation of British, American and French women.

Furthermore, the first wave feminist movement developed strategies to challenge women's exclusion from income generating activities, particularly paid employment. The organisational strength of the movement brought considerable achievements regarding the demands for education and employment. For example, the first teacher training school for girls was opened (in 1863), the American college for girls was established (in 1875) and the first university opened their doors to women in 1914. A lack of male wageworkers during the First World War extended women's access to paid employment, but women's struggle was also a significant force. The first wave had a considerable role in founding the Women's Islamic Working Union (*Kadınların Çalışma Cemiyet-i İslamiyesi*) (in 1916) and pressurising the Istanbul municipality to provide training to support women's employment as housekeepers (Altınbaş 2014). The movement also demanded a change in the Islamic dress code, protested against police surveillance and refused to wear the face veil in public (Adak 2022; Altınbaş 2014; Kandiyoti 1989). The Ottoman state later prohibited the wearing of *niqab* that covers the entire face (in 1881). The first wave further pressed the state and gained some rights to initiate divorce under certain conditions (in 1917). These achievements suggest the first wave feminist movement in Turkey was a significant political force between the mid-nineteenth and early twentieth centuries.

However, the feminist movement did not sustain its influence and thereby failed to challenge the resurgence of the domestic patriarchal character of the Republican state. I identify three possible factors that weakened the movement. *First*, the Republican state had closed key first wave organisations, suppressed the movement's leaders and banned women's demonstrations by the mid-1940s (Tekeli 1998). For example, the attempt to establish a women's political party upon formation of the Turkish Republic (in 1923) failed since the state refused to authorise it (Arat 1997). The Turkish

Women's Federation (in 1924) was established as an alternative but the federation was depoliticised through enforced change of its board members (in 1928) (Zihnioğlu 2003). Although the federation continued to push for further rights and attempted to organise a rally for women's full suffrage (in 1930), the leadership of the ruling Republican People's Party stopped the rally (Tekeli 1990b). The state later closed the Federation just after the Congress of the International Federation of Women (in 1935) (Os 2000). These attacks by the Republican state on the first wave were certainly a barrier to wielding influence.

Second, Şirin Tekeli states that achievements of the first wave feminist movement created an "illusion" that gender equality was reached in the West as well as in Turkey (1998: 338). The Republican regime, she argues, strengthened the illusion to recruit women to the regime. Establishing this illusion required a multifaceted strategy; construing Ottoman women as passive victims of Islamic patriarchal society (Os 2000; Tekeli 1998) thereby, dismissing the achievements of Ottoman women's struggle, as well as portraying female peasants as ignorant people who did not know what was best for themselves (Arat 1999b; Onaran-İncirlioğlu 1999). I use the terminology of 'equality manipulation' rather than 'illusion' to emphasise the active role taken by the state in creating this context. I argue that equality manipulation led by the state tended to increase the division between urban and rural women and, at the same time, depicted the Republican state as the guardian of gender equality within society. The suppression of key organisations and thinkers in the movement probably laid the groundwork for manipulating the actual conditions of gender equality. Over the ensuing decades, the Republican state was successful in increasing its influence over urban women and portraying itself as the protector of gender equality.

Third, the first wave of the feminist movement almost exclusively comprised urban women. Urban women needed to achieve education, paid employment, electoral and mobility rights given their increasing wage dependency, whereas, female peasants were still living under the conditions of male dominance in landownership, working as unpaid family labourers on small to medium scale farms, and experiencing limited mobility. In the next section, I investigate how far this division between rural and urban women weakened the overall capacity of the first wave to challenge the domestic patriarchal character of the Turkish state.

4.5 Division of rural and urban women

In the Ottoman Empire, property ownership and inheritance rights were significant and relevant to the lives of female peasants, artisans and women of the elite households, thereby, uniting women's agendas and strategies. While female peasants fought for ownership and inheritance of the land and forms of property on the land, women of the elite households defended their access to money, jewellery, urban commercial and residential properties, land and other forms of rural property (Fay 2010, 1998; Zarinebaf 2010, 2001; Doxiadis 2010, 2011). As noted previously, inheritance rights were also significant for female artisans and small producers who were generally excluded from the guilds and thus prohibited from working. The Hanefi School of Islamic law and the local sharia courts were accessible to women and relevant to their lives. As a result, despite the limits of the patriarchal legal framework, Ottoman women were relatively successful in utilising the Hanefi School of Islamic Law and the local sharia courts to gain property rights.

During the late nineteenth and the early twentieth centuries, increasing wage dependency and male dominance in paid employment had significant implications for urban women. Having access to a wage and/or any kind of income generating activity was significant to their lives. Female wageworkers and small producers as well as manufacturers, all supported an increase in women's access to paid employment. Therefore, demanding access to education and paid employment was important for all women in urban areas, crosscutting class and ethnicity differences. The first wave of the feminist movement was relatively successful in addressing such demands. Nevertheless, female peasants were subjected to the conditions of male dominance in landownership thus focusing on their rights to property and land ownership.

Given the gender discriminatory legal framework, which limited rural women's access to land and other forms of rural property, female peasants did not have many alternatives to defend their rights other than insisting on the Islamic legal framework. They were already familiar with the Hanefi School of Islamic law and local sharia courts. During the Ottoman period, female peasants went to court predominantly for property related issues such as sale or usage without consent and in many cases the transfer of property was cancelled. They also sought justice concerning matters such as male violence, bride wealth[3], forced marriage, humiliation, allowance in the case of husbands' disappearance and loans (Jennings 1975). Therefore, female peasants insisted on the Islamic legal framework in order to defend their property rights.

Existing research shows that in response to the 1926 civil code, people in Turkey developed a new hybrid system by combining the Islamic premodern and modern laws which, in turn, allowed them to manipulate both legal frameworks (Yılmaz 2003). In his research analysing Turkish villages between 1949 and 1952, Stirling also finds that villagers developed a set of ad hoc arrangements to resolve civil disputes (Stirling 1965, 1957). I argue that women, not only men, also participated in the development of this hybrid legal system by using the practice of unofficial marriage in rural areas.

Although the 1926 civil code outlawed Islamic marriages and introduced obligatory official marriages, the number of official marriages during the 1950s was approximately less than half of the total marriages (Timur 1957). Unofficial Islamic marriages, predominantly in rural areas (Velidedeoğlu 1944a; Stirling 1957), comprised the majority until the 1970s, despite the penalty of up to six months imprisonment (Özsu 2010). In 1997, the state was still campaigning to reduce the proportion of unofficial marriages in Turkey (The Ministry of Women and Family 1997). Hıfzı Timur (1957) and Paul Stirling (1957) argue that peasants' avoidance of official marriages was due to several factors. Male peasants using polygamy to access women as unpaid family workers wanted to retain the opportunity to easily divorce a childless wife, and if they officially got married, governmental clerks' daughters lost access to their fathers' retirement pension. These commentators also hold that religious marriage was more appealing to Muslim peasants. It avoided the 1926 civil code age limitation and supported males in postponing compulsory military service and avoiding certain taxes. The obligatory health check constituted another barrier to official marriage due to the lack of doctors and hospitals. Furthermore, most individuals did not have the required birth certificates.

However, the earlier arguments are either inaccurate or dismiss female peasants' role in sustaining unofficial marriages thereby perceiving female peasants as passive victims of patriarchal rural society. Many practical barriers to official marriage could have been resolved in the years following the (religious) marriage and, if religion was significant, Muslim peasants could have had both a religious ceremony and an official marriage, as many people still do. Governmental clerks' daughters lived in urban areas and their avoidance of official marriage does not explain peasants' preference for unofficial Islamic marriage in villages. There is some truth in the idea that divorce in Islamic marriage was easier than it was in official marriages. Hıfzı Velidedeoğlu (1944b, a) argues that the 1926 civil code created extra barriers to divorce by (i) asking couples to join a moderated peace negotiation (*Sulh mahkemesi*) before applying to the court, (ii) appointing judges as the single decision makers regarding the divorce case and (iii) assigning the divorce case to the court that was in the residence of husband since the law perceived a wife's residence to be the same as that of her husband. However, neither polygamy, nor the opportunity to divorce a childless wife easily, explains the prolonged nature of unofficial marriages in rural areas. Polygamy was in fact limited to a few elite households in Istanbul rather than being prevalent in rural areas (Duben and Behar 2002) and, irrespective of the number (or gender) of their children, marriages of the majority of rural women remained unofficial.

I argue that the role of female peasants in developing a new hybrid system of laws through the practice of unofficial marriage was important; discrimination against female peasants in the 1926 civil code meant the legitimisation of marriage brought loss of their land, bride-wealth and other properties on the land (e.g. bride-wealth, and machinery, tools, animals, mills and water wheels on the land). It may be that female peasants attempted to defend their rights through unofficial Islamic marriage and thereby sustained Islamic property law in rural areas. Historical research demonstrates that female peasants claimed some rights by manipulating unofficial Islamic law (Stirling 1957; Belgesay 1944). Although the modern civil code discriminated against women in inheriting land and other forms of property on the land, Stirling (1965) finds that villagers followed the Islamic inheritance law and accepted that a daughter's share is half of a son's, relying on Quran Sura 4, aya 7. This "universal recognition of [women's] inheritance rights in the village" did not bring an equal distribution of land but did provide the opportunity for women to negotiate their share (Stirling 1965: 131). There were cases where brothers had a large outstanding debt to their sisters for their share of the land, exchanged animals and tools on the land with their sisters and where female peasants received their bride-wealth (Belgesay 1944; Stirling 1965, 1957; Morvaridi 1993).

> ... the abolition of any formal sanctions which might fill the gaps in the existing Islamic informal marriage system, has opened the door to a relaxing of the rules, and even to malpractices. For example, though the villagers know that a Muslim woman who has lost her husband through death or divorce should wait for the *iddet*, a period of some three months, women are frequently remarried to widowers within this period... even more striking, women are sometimes remarried when their husbands have not divorced them at all... the new law has left the village informal system totally unsupported, with no means of plugging the gaps at its weak points. Hence the system which the new laws were intended to abolish continues, but in a less orderly form.
>
> (Stirling 1957: 31)

Therefore, women, not only men, played an important part in the development of a new hybrid legal system. Rural women lived under the conditions of male dominance in landownership rather than increasing wage dependency. The demands of ownership of land and other forms of rural property were significant in their lives; women defended their access to rural forms of property by utilising Islamic law.

Mary Lou O'Neil and Şule Toktaş demonstrate that legal pluralism is still one of the ways in which women in Turkey defend their rights. Their research provides a contemporary account of how far women negotiate their property rights by using a complex and intertwined combination of different legal sources (O'Neil and Toktaş 2014; Toktaş and O'Neil 2015). Rural women, therefore, benefited from the legal pluralism regarding their access to rural forms of property. But, at the same time, unofficial marriages restricted women's access to education and eliminated their legal person-hood (Ertürk 1995; Hoşgör-Gündüz and Smits 2007; Akşit 2008) and, as such, these negative implications of unofficial marriages increased the division between rural and urban women.

To recapitulate, women's exclusion from the ownership of means of production (e.g. land) and subsistence (e.g. income generating activities) differentiated their demands and strategies thereby dividing rural and urban women. Urban women increasingly focused on their education and employment rights as well as demanding access to the public sphere given their exclusion from income generating activities, including paid employment. Meanwhile, rural women insisted on their property and inheritance rights under the conditions of male dominance in landownership. While rural women strategically utilised an Islamic framework, urban women increasingly drew on political modernisation. Urban and rural women were not directly opposed but their separate agendas and strategies did not align and their overall capacity to challenge the domestic patriarchal character of the Turkish state was weakened.

Although the first wave of the feminist movement achieved greater strength in the late Ottoman and early Republican periods, it was organised by urban women for urban women as well as weakened by state attacks and equality manipulation. Those factors, in turn, prevented the feminist movement from aligning the diverse strategies and demands of rural and urban women. Women's failure to maintain their collective acting capacity and power over the state, in turn, led to the resurgence of the domestic patriarchal state during the early Republican period (1923–1940). While the racist and the capitalist agendas of the state required small producers' recruitment to the regime, men, in their position as household heads and rural and urban small producers, increased their collective bargaining power and shaped the patriarchal character of the Republican state.

4.6 Conclusion

Women's exclusion from the ownership of a means of production (e.g. land) and subsistence (e.g. income generating activities, including paid employment) are significant for varieties of domestic patriarchy. During the early Republican period, male peasants utilised legal discrimination against women in land inheritance and, in so doing, sustained patriarchal exploitation of labour in rural households. At the same time, male household heads and male small producers played an important part in excluding women from income generating activities which, in turn, maintained patriarchal exploitation of labour within urban households. I therefore identify the premodern and modern forms of domestic patriarchy by distinguishing two main arrangements of gender-based exclusionary strategies. Women's exclusion from agricultural landownership, in conjunction with the dominance of small landownership, leads to patriarchal exploitation of labour in rural households establishing the premodern form of domestic patriarchy. Women's exclusion from paid employment and income generating activities under the conditions of dispossession and wage dependency sustains patriarchal exploitation of labour within urban households, thereby maintaining modern domestic patriarchy.

Men, as heads of households as well as in their role as rural and urban small producers, constitute a patriarchal collective subject. At the same time, the patriarchal collective subject is mediated by the state. My analysis thereby reveals an enduring bond between the domestic patriarchal character of the Turkish state and the patriarchal collective subject. Male small producers have been relatively successful in negotiating with the state and have thus not only protected urban and rural small production from market-led powers of dispossession but also excluded women from landownership and income generating activities to sustain gender-based dispossession. At the same time, the state secured its racist and capitalist agendas by recruiting the patriarchal collective subject to the regime.

Meanwhile, the gender-based exclusionary strategies in landownership and income generating activities gave rise to differences in women's demands and strategies which effectively divided rural and urban women. Urban women focused on various rights relating to the conditions of male dominance in paid employment, whereas, rural women were concerned with their land inheritance rights given their exclusion from landownership. Urban and rural women did not fight against each other, but the separate agendas and strategies did not help their cause. As well as the division of women, state attacks and equality manipulation prevented the first wave feminist movement from aligning the separate demands and strategies and, as such, weakened women's overall capacity to challenge the domestic patriarchal state. As a result, the domestic patriarchal character of the Republican state sustained gender-based exclusionary strategies in the ownership of means of production and subsistence thereby preserving the patriarchal gender contract.

Notes

1 According to the 2017 regulation of the Ministry of Agriculture (no 2768754), approximately 35% of total agricultural holdings are under the category of indivisible unity.
2 Şirin Tekeli later admits she (not only other scholars) was "unfair and wrong" in refusing the significance of the first wave in Turkey (1998: 345)
3 Women were granted a certain amount of wealth in marriage, bride-wealth (*Sadāḳ*), which is distinct from bride-price (*mahr*) in that the former is an integral element of Muslim marriage whereas the latter is not (for details see Kocabıçak 2018)

Reference

Abadan-Unat, Nermin. 1981. "Social change and Turkish women." In *Women in Turkish Society*, edited by N. Abadan-Unat. Leiden: E. J. Brill.

Adak, Sevgi. 2022. *Anti-Veiling Campaigns in Turkey: State, Society and Gender in the Early Republic: I.B. Tauris.*

Agmon, Iris. 2003. "Text, court, and family in the late-nineteenth century Palestine." In *Family History in the Middle East: Household, Property and Gender*, edited by B. Doumani. New York: State University of New York Press.

Agmon, Iris. 2006. *Family and Court: Legal Culture and Modernity in Late Ottoman Palestine.* Syracuse, New York: Syracuse University Press.

Akşit, Elif E. 2008. "Halk Eğitiminin Başarı ve Başarısızlığı." *Türkiye Araştırmaları Literatür Dergisi* 6 (12):587–614.

Altınbaş, Nihan. 2014. "Marriage and Divorce in the Late Ottoman Empire: Social Upheaval, Women's Rights, and the Need for New Family Law." *Journal of Family History* 39 (2):114–125.

Arat, Yeşim. 1997. "The project of modernity and women in Turkey." In *Rethinking Modernity and Rational Identity in Turkey*, edited by R. Kasaba and S. Bozdoğan. Seattle. London: University of Washington.

Arat, Yeşim. 2010. "Religion, Politics and Gender Equality in Turkey: Implications of a Democratic Paradox?" *Third World Quarterly* 31 (6):869–884.

Arat, Zehra F. 1994. "Kemalism and Turkish Women." *Women and Politics* 14 (4):57–80. doi: 10.1300/J014v14n04_05.

Arat, Zehra. 1999a. "Educating the daughters of the Republic." In *Deconstructing Images of 'the Turkish Women'*, edited by Z. Arat. New York: Palgrave Macmillan US.

Arat, Zehra. 1999b. "Introduction: Politics of representation and identity." In *Deconstructing Images of 'the Turkish Women'*, edited by Zehra Arat. New York: Palgrave Macmillan US.

Aytekin, Attila E. 2009. "Agrarian Relations, Property and Law: An Analysis of the Land Code of 1858 in the Ottoman Empire." *Middle Eastern Studies* 45 (6):935–951.

Aytekin, Attila E. 2012. "Peasant Protest in the Late Ottoman Empire: Moral Economy, Revolt and the Tanzimat Reforms." *International Review of Social History* 57 (2):191–227.

Aytekin, Attila E. 2013. "Tax Revolts During The Tanzimat Period (1839-1876) and Before The Young Turk Revolution (1904–1908): Popular Protest and State Formation in the Late Ottoman Empire." *Journal of Policy History* 25 (3):308–333.

Belgesay, Mustafa R. 1944. "Karı-koca arasında karşılıklı vazifeler." In *Medeni Kanunun XV. Yıl Dönümü İçin.* Ankara: Ankara University.

Boratav, Korkut. 2011. *Türkiye İktisat Tarihi (1908- 2009).* Ankara: İmge Kitabevi.

Chalcraft, John. 2015. "Out of the frying pan into the fire: protest, the state, and the end of the guilds in Egypt." In *Bread from the Lion's Mouth: Artisans Struggling for A Livelihood in Ottoman Cities*, edited by S. Faroqhi. Oxford: Berghahn Books.

Clancy-Smith, Julia. 2018. "A woman without her distaff: Gender, work, and hand-icraft production in Colonial North Africa." In *A Social History of Women and Gender in the Modern Middle East*, edited by M. Meriwether and J. E. Tucker. New York: Routledge.

Çakır, Serpil. 1994. *Osmanlı Kadın Hareketi.* İstanbul: Metis Yayınları.

Demirdirek, Aynur. 1999. "In pursuit of the Ottoman women's movement." In *Deconstructing Images of 'the Turkish Women'*, edited by Z. Arat. New York: Palgrave Macmillan US.

Doxiadis, Evdoxios. 2010. "Property and Morality: Women in the Communal Courts of Late Ottoman Greece." *Byzantine and Modern Greek Studies* 34 (1):61–80.

Doxiadis, Evdoxios. 2011. "Legal Trickery: Men, Women, and Justice in Late Ottoman Greece." *Past and Present* February (210):129–153.

Duben, Alan, and Cem Behar. 2002. *Istanbul Households: Marriage, Family and Fertility, 1880- 1940, Cambridge Studies in Population, Economy and Society in Past Time.* Cambridge: Cambridge University Press.

Durakbaşa, Ayşe. 1988. "Kemalist kadin kimliğinin oluşumu." *Tarih ve Toplum* March, 51:39–43.

Durakbaşa, Ayşe. 1998. "Cumhuriyet Döneminde Modern kadin ve erkek kimliklerinin oluşumu: Kemalist kadin kimliği ve münevver erkekler." In *75 Yılda Kadınlar ve Erkekler*, edited by A. Berktay-Hacımirzaoğlu. Istanbul: Türkiye Ekonomik ve Toplumsal Tarih Vakfı yayınları.

Durakbaşa, Ayşe, and Aynur İlyasoğlu. 2001. "Formation of Gender Identities in Republican Turkey and Women's Narratives as Transmitters of 'Herstory' of Modernization." *Journal of Social History* 35 (1):195–203.

Düzgün, Eren. 2018. "Capitalism, Jacobinism and International Relations: Re-Interpreting the Ottoman Path to Modernity." *Review of International Studies* 44 (2):252–278. doi: 10.1017/S0260210517000468.

Ecevit, M. 1993. "Rural Women and the Small Peasant Economy." *Turkish Public Administration Annual* 17–19: 87–89.

Ekmekcioğlu, Lerna. 2014. "Republic of Paradox: The League of Nations Minority Protection Regime and the New Turkey's Step-Citizens." *International Journal of Middle East Studies*, 46 (4):657–679. doi: 10.1017/S0020743814001007

Ertürk, Yakın. 1995. "Rural women and modernisation in Southeastern Anatolia." In *Women in Modern Turkish Society: A reader*, edited by Ş. Tekeli. London, New Jersey: Zed Books.

Faroqhi, Suraiya. 1992. "Political Activity among Ottoman Taxpayers and the Problem of Sultanic Legitimation (1570–1650)." *Journal of the Economic and Social History of the Orient* 35 (1):1–39.

Fay, Mary A. 1998. "From Concubines to Capitalists: Women, Property and Power in Eighteenth-Century Cairo." *Journal of Women's History* 10 (3):118–140.

Fay, Mary A. 2010. "Counting on Kin: Women and property in eighteenth-century Cairo." In *Across the Religious Divide: Women, Property, and Law in the Wider Mediterranean (ca. 1300-1800)*, edited by J. G. Sperling and S. K. Wray. New York, London: Routledge.

GDSW. 2000. *Kırsal Alan Kadınının İstihdama Katkısı.* Ankara: Head Quarter of Women's Problems and Status.

Gerber, Haim. 1976. "Guilds in Seventeenth-Century Anatolian Bursa." *Asian and African Studies* XI (1):59–83.

Gerber, Haim. 1980. "Social and Economic Position of Women in an Ottoman City, Bursa, 1600–1700." *International Journal of Middle East Studies* 12:231–244.

Gümüşoğlu, Firdevs. 1998. "Cumhuriyet döneminin ders kitaplarinda cinsiyet rolleri (1928- 1998)." In *75 Yılda Kadınlar ve Erkekler*, edited by A. Berktay-Hacımirzaoğlu. İstanbul: Türkiye Ekonomik ve Toplumsal Tarih Vakfı yayınları.

Gürel, Burak, Bermal Küçük, and Sercan Taş. 2019. "The Rural Roots of the Rise of the Justice and Development Party in Turkey." *The Journal of Peasant Studies* 1–23. doi: 10.1080/03066150.2018.1552264.

Gürsoy, Yaprak. 2014. "From tutelary powers and interventions to civilian control: an overview of Turkish civil–military relations since the 1920s." In *Turkey's Democratization Process*, edited by C. Rodriguez, A. Avalos, H. Yılmaz and A. I. Planet. London: Routledge.

Hale, William. 2011. "The Turkish Republic and its Army, 1923–1960." *Turkish Studies: Civil-Military Relations in Turkey* 12 (2):191–201. doi: 10.1080/14683849.2011.572628.

Hale, William M. 1994. *Turkish Politics and the Military.* London, New York: Routledge.

Harris, George. 1965. "The Role of the Military in Turkish Politics, Part I." *Middle East Journal* 19 (1):54.

Hoşgör-Gündüz, Ayşe, and Jeroen Smits. 2007. "The status of rural women in Turkey: What is the role of regional differences?" In *From patriarchy to empowerment women's participation, movements, and rights in the Middle East, North Africa, and South Asia*, edited by V. M. Moghadam. Syracuse, New York: Syracuse University Press.

Imber, Colin. 2010. "Women as outsiders: The inheritance of agricultural land in the Ottoman Empire." In *Across the Religious Divide: Women, Property, and Law in the Wider Mediterranean (ca. 1300-1800)*, edited by J. G. Sperling and S. K. Wray. New York, London: Routledge.

Imber, Colin. 2012. "The law of the land." In *The Ottoman World*, edited by C. Woodhead. London. New York: Routledge.

Independence Tribunal. 1920-1927. *Independence Tribunal archives (1920–1927) addressing Ankara, Eskişehir, Kastamonu, Konya, Isparta, Pozantı, Yozgat, Amasya, Elcezire, İstanbul, and Şark.*

İçduygu, Ahmet, Şule Toktas, and B. Ali Soner. 2008. "The Politics of Population in a Nation-Building Process: Emigration of Non-Muslims from Turkey." *Ethnic and Racial Studies* 31 (2):358–389. doi: 10.1080/01419870701491937

Jennings, Ronald C. 1975. "Women in the Early Seventeenth Century Ottoman Judicial Records – The Sharia Court of Anatolian Kayseri." *Journal of the Economic and Social History of the Orient* 18 (1):53–114.

Kadıoğlu, Ayse. 2007. "Denationalization of Citizenship? The Turkish Experience." *Citizenship Studies* 11 (3):283–299. doi: 10.1080/17450100701381839.

Kal'a, Ahmet. 1997. *İstanbul Külliyatı: Ahkam Defterleri, Esnaf Tarihi*. İstanbul: İstanbul Araştırmaları Merkezi.

Kandiyoti, Deniz. 1989. "Women and the Turkish state: Political actors or symbolic Pawns?" In *Woman- Nation- State*, edited by N. Yuval-davis and F. Anthias. London: Macmillan.

Kandiyoti, Deniz. 1990. "Rural transformation in Turkey ad its implications for women's status." In *Women, Family, and Social Change in Turkey*, edited by F. Özbay. Bangkok: UNESCO.

Kandiyoti, Deniz. 1991. "End of Empire: Islam, nationalism, and Women in Turkey." In *Women, Islam and the State*, edited by D. Kandiyoti. London, New York: MacMillan.

Kandiyoti, Deniz. 1995. "Patterns of patriarchy: Notes for an analysis of male dominance in Turkish Society." In *Women in Modern Turkish Society: A Reader*, edited by Ş. Tekeli. London, New Jersey: Zed Books.

Kandiyoti, Deniz. 1997. "Gendering the modern: On missing dimensions in the study of Turkish modernity." In *Rethinking Modernity and National Identity in Turkey*, edited by R. Kasaba and S. Bozdoğan. Seattle, London: University of Washington Press.

Karaömerlioğlu, Asım M. 2008. "Elite Perceptions of Land Reform in Early Republican Turkey." *The Journal of Peasant Studies* 27 (3):115–141.

Karkiner, Nadide. 2006. "Tarımda Kadın ve Bazı Yapısal İlişkiler." *Iktisat Dergisi* 469:24–30.

Karkiner, Nadide. 2009. *Feminist Analysis of Rural Woman in a Village of Turkey: Feminist Theory, Method, Research*: LAP Lambert Academic Publishing.

Kocabıçak, Ece. 2018. "What Excludes Women from Landownership in Turkey? Implications for Feminist Strategies." *Women's Studies International Forum* 69 (July–August):115–125. doi: 10.1016/j.wsif.2018.06.005.

Kral, August von. 1937. *Das Land Kamâl Atatürks: Der Werdegang der modernen Türkei.* Wien, Leipzig: Braumüller.

Kuyucu, Ali T. 2005. "Ethno-religious 'Unmixing' of 'Turkey': 6–7 September Riots as a Case in Turkish Nationalism." *Nations and Nationalism* 11 (3):361–380. doi: 10.1111/j.1354-5078.2005.00209.x.

Makal, Ahmet. 2010. "Türkiye'de erken Cumhuriyet Döneminde Kadın Emeği." *Çalışma ve Toplum* 2:12–39.

Maksudyan, Nazan. 2015. "Control Over Life, Control Over Body: Female Suicide in Early Republican Turkey." *Women's History Review* 24 (6):861–880. doi: 10.1080/09612025.2014.994858.

Morvaridi, Behrooz. 1992. "Gender Relations in Agriculture: Women in Turkey." *Economic Development and Cultural Change* 40 (3):567–586.

Morvaridi, Behrooz. 1993. "Gender and household resource management in agriculture: Cash crops in Kars." In *Culture and Economy: Changes in Turkish Villages,* edited by P. Stirling. London: Eothen Press.

Navaro-Yasin, Yael. 2000. "Cumhuriyetin İlk Yıllarında Ev Işinin Rasyonelleşmesi (The Rationalisation of Housework During the First Years of Turkish Republic)." *Toplum ve Bilim* 84 (Bahar):51–74.

O'Neil, Mary Lou, and Şule Toktaş. 2014. "Women's Property Rights in Turkey." *Turkish Studies* 15 (1):29–44.

Onaran-İncirlioğlu, Emine. 1999. "Images of village women in Turkey: Models and anomalies." In *Deconstructing Images of 'the Turkish Women',* edited by Z. Arat. New York: Palgrave Macmillan US.

Orhan, Mehmet. 2012. "Kurdish Rebellions and Conflict Groups in Turkey During the 1920s and 1930s." *Journal of Muslim Minority Affairs* 32 (3):339–358.

Os, Nicole van. 2000. "Ottoman Women's Organisations: Source of the Past, Sources for the Future." *Islam and Christian- Muslim Relations* 11 (3): 369–383 doi: 10.1080/713670331.

Özsu, Umut. 2010. "'Receiving' the Swiss Civil Code: Translating Authority in Early Republican Turkey." *International Journal of Law in Context* 6 (1): 63–89.

Pamuk, Şevket. 1991. "War, state economic policies and resistance by agricultural producers in Turkey, 1939–1945." In *Peasants and Politics in the Modern Middle East,* edited by F. Kazemi and J. Waterbury. Miami: Florida International University Press.

Pinson, Mark. 1975. "Ottoman Bulgaria in the First Tanzimat Period- the Revolts in Nish (1841) and Vidin (1850)." *Middle Eastern Studies* 11 (2):103–146.

Quataert, Donald. 1991. "Rural unrest in the Ottoman Empire, 1830–1914." In *Peasants and Politics in the Modern Middle East,* edited by F. Kazemi and J. Waterbury. Miami: Florida International University Press.

Quataert, Donald. 1993. *Ottoman Manufacturing in the Age of the Industrial Revolution.* Cambridge: Cambridge University Press.

Quataert, Donald. 1994. "Ottoman workers and the state 1826–1914." In *Workers and Working Classes in the Middle East: Struggles, Histories, Historiographies,* edited by Z. Lockman. Albany: State University of New York Press.

Quataert, Donald. 2001. "Labor History and the Ottoman Empire, c. 1700-1922." *International Labor and Working-Class History* (60): 93–109.

Rubin, Avi. 2012. "From Legal Representation to Advocacy: Attorneys and Clients in the Ottoman Nizamiye Courts." *International Journal of Middle East Studies* 44 (1): 111–127.

Rustow, Dankwart A. 1959. "The Army and The Founding of the Turkish Republic." *World Politics* 11 (4):513–552. doi: 10.2307/2009591.

Saraçoğlu, Mehmet S. 2007. "Letters from Vidin: A Study of Ottoman Governmentality and Politics of Local Administration, 1864–1877." Ph.D., Ohio State University.

Sarigil, Zeki. 2014. "The Turkish Military: Principal or Agent?" *Armed Forces & Society* 40 (1):168–190. doi: 10.1177/0095327X12442309.

Shatzmiller, Maya. 1988. "Aspects of Women's Participation in the Economic Life of Later Medieval Islam: Occupations and Mentalities." *Arabica* 35 (1):36–58. doi: 10.1163/157005888X00422.

Sirman, Nükhet. 1988. *"Peasant Family Farms: the Position of Households in Cotton Production in a Village of Western Turkey."* University of London, SOAS.

Stirling, Paul. 1957. "Land, Marriage and the Law in Turkish Villages." *International Social Science Bulletin* 9 (1):21–33.

Stirling, Paul. 1965. *Turkish Village.* London: Weidenfeld and Nicolson.

Tekeli, Şirin. 1981. "Women in Turkish Politics." In *Women in Turkish Society*, edited by N. Abadan-Unat. Leiden: E. J. Brill.

Tekeli, Şirin. 1982. *Kadınlar ve Siyasal Toplumsal Hayat.* İstanbul: Birikim.

Tekeli, Şirin. 1990a. "The meaning and limits of feminist ideology in Turkey." In *Women, Family, and Social Change in Turkey*, edited by F. Özbay. Bangkok: UNESCO.

Tekeli, Şirin. 1990b. "Women in the changing patriarchal associations of the 1980s." In *Turkish State, Turkish Society*, edited by A. Finkel and N. Sirman. London, New York: Routledge.

Tekeli, Şirin. 1998. "Birinci ve ikinci dalga feminist hareketlerin karşılaştırmalı incelemesi." In *75 Yılda Kadınlar ve Erkekler*, edited by A. Berktay-Hacimirzaoglu. İstanbul: Tarih Vakfı.

The Ministry of Women and Family. 1997. Our Family. Edited by the Ministry responsible for Women and Family. Ankara.

The Republican State Archives. 1923–1960. Presidency of the State Archives of Turkey. edited by Presidency.

Timur, Hıfzı. 1957. "Civil Marriage in Turkey: Difficulties, Causes, and Remedies." *International Social Science Bulletin* 9 (1): 34–37.

Toktaş, Şule, and Mary Lou O'Neil. 2015. "Competing Frameworks of Islamic Law and Secular Civil Law in Turkey: A Case Study on Women's Property and Inheritance Practices." *Women's Studies International Forum* 48 (Supplement C):29–38. doi: 10.1016/j.wsif.2014.10.011.

Velidedeoğlu, Hıfzı V. 1944a. "Türk evlilik hukukunun bugünkü meseleleri." In *Medeni Kanunun XV. Yıl Dönümü için.* İstanbul: Istanbul Universitesi, Kenan matbaaası.

Velidedeoğlu, Hıfzı V. 1944b. "İsviçre medeni kanunu karşısında Türk medeni kanunu." In *Medeni Kanunun XV. Yıl Dönümü için.* Istanbul: Istanbul Universitesi.

Velidedeoğlu, Hıfzı V. 1970. *Türk Kanunu Medenisi ve Borçlar Kanunu.* Ankara: Ankara Universitesi Basım evi.

Yelbasi, Caner. 2019. *The Circassians of Turkey: War, Violence and Nationalism from the Ottomans to Atatürk.* London: I.B. Tauris.

Yerasimos, Stefanos. 2005. *Az Gelişmişlik Sürecinde Türkiye.* Vol. I, II and III. İstanbul: Belge Yayınları.

Yi, Eunjeong. 2004. *Guild Dynamics in Seventeenth-century İstanbul: Fluidity and Leverage.* Leiden, Boston: Brill.

Yıldız, Ahmet. 2001. *Ne Mutlu Türküm Diyebilene: Türk Ulusal Kimliginin Etno-Seküler Sinirlari (1919–1938).* İstanbul: İletişim.

Yılmaz, İhsan. 2003. "Non-Recognition of Post-Modern Turkish Socio-Legal Reality and the Predicament of Women." *British Journal of Middle Eastern Studies* 30 (1):25–41. doi: 10.1080/1353019032000059108.

Zarinebaf, Fariba. 2001. "The Role of Women In The Urban Economy Of Istanbul, 1700- 1850." *International Labour and Working Class History* 60 (Fall):141–152."

Zarinebaf, Fariba. 2010. "From Mahalle (neighbourhood) to the market and the courts: Women, credit, and property in eighteenth-century Istanbul." In *Across the Religious Divide: Women, Property, and Law in the Wider Mediterranean (ca. 1300-1800),* edited by J. G. Sperling and S. K. Wray. New York, London: Routledge.

Zihnioğlu, Yaprak. 2003. *Kadınsız Inkilap, Nezihe Muhiddin, Kadınlar Halk Fırkası, Kadın Birliği.* İstanbul: Metis.

5 EMERGENCE OF NEOLIBERAL PATRIARCHY

THE CONTEMPORARY PERIOD

Thus far, I have provided a historical account of the causes of the premodern and modern forms of domestic patriarchy as well as elaborating on the negotiation between the Turkish state and the patriarchal collective subject (1923–1940s). Focusing on the contemporary period, this chapter analyses, whether Turkey in the post-2000s has witnessed the emergence of the neoliberal form of public patriarchy and, if so, a shift away from the hegemony of premodern and modern domestic patriarchies.

According to my conceptual framework, under the dominance of premodern and modern domestic patriarchies, the gender-based exclusionary strategies confine women's labour to rural and urban household production. In contrast, in neoliberal or social-democratic public patriarchies, gender-based segregation and subordination are utilised to maintain women's double burden of paid and unpaid labour (see Chapter 3). Considering that the widespread experience of the double burden of paid and unpaid labour is a precondition for the transition away from domestic towards public patriarchies, this chapter investigates how far the case of double burden represents the majority of women's experience from the 2000s onwards. I further examine whether the Turkish state utilises commodification or decommodification based public provisioning to pull women out of household production or, on the contrary, that social policy confines the majority of women's labour to rural and urban household production. While the former signals the emergence of the public patriarchal state, the latter indicates the predominance of the domestic patriarchal state. In addition, I analyse changes within the civil society domain to consider if there has been a transition from gender-based exclusion towards segregation and subordination by measuring (i) gender gaps in education and (ii) public decision-making and political representation, (iii) women's control over their reproductive abilities and sexuality, as well as, (iv) investigating changes within cultural settings. Similarly, the forms and degrees of state intervention in the domain of violence shed light on the degree of hegemony in premodern and modern domestic patriarchies.

I use mixed methods of qualitative and quantitative analysis to investigate the contemporary variations of patriarchy in Turkey. Regarding the

DOI: 10.4324/9781003054511-8

qualitative research, I undertake documentary analysis of official texts (e.g. laws and regulations) derived from the archives of the Turkish state. In terms of the quantitative data, I draw upon the publicly available databases of the Turkish statistics office, the World Bank, the United Nations, the OECD, the ILO as well as drawing on the evidence gathered by the World Values Survey and Hacettepe University Institute of Population Studies.

5.1 Emergence of the neoliberal form of public patriarchy

Before investigating the emergence of neoliberal public patriarchy, the absence of the social-democratic form of public patriarchy within the historical context of Turkey requires attention. The relatively increased bargaining capacity of the working-class movement in Turkey – between the mid-1970s and the mid-1990s – did not give rise to a social democratic welfare regime. Existing research identifies various dynamics obstructing its development, including the nationalist and authoritarian characteristics of the leading Republican People's Party (*Cumhuriyet Halk Partisi*) and the lack of an organised labour movement (Emre 2019, 2015; Coşar and Özman 2008; Keyman and Öniş 2007; Ciddi 2009). Without a social democratic regime, state-led decommodification of domestic goods and services remained limited thereby preventing the transition from premodern and modern domestic patriarchies towards social-democratic public patriarchy. In addition, the initial weakness of the feminist movement (1950s–1980s), and later the lack of alignment between the feminist movement and working-class organisations (1980s–1990s) sustained the patriarchal character of the working-class movement, including trade unions, confederations, and political parties. These factors, in turn, meant that the domestic patriarchal character of the Turkish state was largely unchallenged. The relatively increased bargaining capacity of the working-class movement (1970s–1990s) did not therefore initiate a shift towards the social-democratic form of public patriarchy in Turkey.

Since the mid-2000s, the neoliberal form of public patriarchy appears to have developed a substantial foundation. Considering the comparatively high proportion of women in professional occupations and modest but stable proportion of female wageworkers in manufacturing (Ecevit, Gündüz-Hosgör, and Tokluoglu 2003; Smith and Dengiz 2010; Hacifazlioğlu 2010; Öncü 1979; Makal 2010, 2012), it can be argued that women in Turkey have always engaged with the circumstances specific to neoliberal public patriarchy. While a certain proportion of women have always experienced the double burden of paid and unpaid labour and gender-based segregation and subordination in the labour market, here my aim is to assess the predominance of neoliberal public patriarchy at the country level. Therefore, in my assessment, I examine (i) the extent to which women experience the double burden of paid and unpaid labour, and (ii) how far the public patriarchal character of the Turkish state is developed. I further investigate (iii) gender gaps in access to the key institutions of civil society as well as (iv) assessing state interventions in the domain of gendered violence.

5.1.1 Women's double burden of paid and unpaid labour

As Figure 5.1 illustrates, the female share (% of total) of paid employment has increased over time and, at the same time, the proportion of female labour in agriculture in comparison to other sectors has declined. This suggests that female unpaid family labour in agriculture has shifted towards paid labour (mostly in the services sector) and, as such, indicates women's increased access to paid employment.

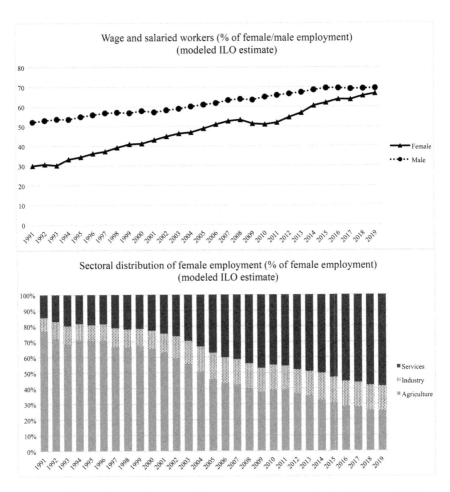

Figure 5.1 Women's access to paid employment in non-agricultural sectors, Turkey (1990–2019)

Source: World Development Bank (WDI 2020)

The time use survey for Turkey (2014– 2015) reveals a significant gender gap in time spent on housework. While men spend approximately *1 hour* per day, women spend *5 hours* per day on unpaid domestic work, including routine housework, shopping, care for household members, childcare, adult care, care for non-household members, volunteering, and travel related to household activities (OECD.Stat 2020e). Considering that average weekly working hours for female wage workers is 42 hours (in 2014), women's paid and unpaid working time totals approximately *80 hours* per week (ILOSTAT 2020b; TURKSTAT 2015). Women's increased access to paid employment in non-agricultural sectors, therefore, appears to give rise to a significant burden of paid and unpaid labour.

5.1.2 *The rise of the public patriarchal state*

Since the 2000s, the Turkish state appears to have transformed the polity in ways which, to a certain extent, remove the barriers to female paid employment and initiates public provisioning of childcare. With the elimination of the gender-based discriminatory articles within the constitution, Turkish criminal code, civil code and labour law, the state removed legal barriers to female paid employment in non-agricultural sectors. For example, the obligatory consent from husbands for married woman to work and some of the sectoral restrictions on women's employment as well as the night shift ban for female wage workers in industry have been repealed. In addition, gender-based discrimination and segregation at work have become increasingly outlawed, and sexual harassment within the workplace is forbidden by law. Furthermore, considering the positive correlation between women's access to education and female paid employment, the Turkish state has driven programmes to increase the schooling rate for girls, particularly in terms of the transition to secondary education (e.g. the Operation for Increasing the School Attendance Rate of Girls, KEP-1 and KEP-2). State-driven training programmes on literacy, preschool education, information technologies and the Internet have also increased women's access to various qualifications.

The state has further modified the labour law and regulations in a way which encourages female labour force participation following childbirth. The duration of paid parental leave for mothers has increased from 12 to 16 weeks (in 2003) and, for the first time, the 2016 Labour Law introduced one week paid parental leave for fathers. Working mothers are also allowed to work part-time in their previously full-time jobs after childbirth. Under the 2018 regulation, employers who employ more than 150 women workers have become responsible for providing nursery or day care services at the workplace. Tax exemptions are granted for the expenses of day care facilities in order to promote such provision by employers.

Where employers are not obligated to provide nursery or day care services, the state compensates the cost of childcare up to a certain limit

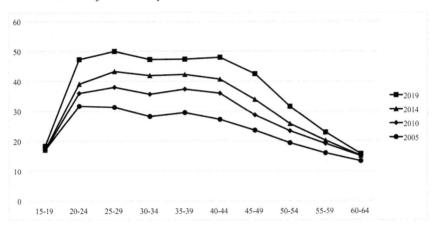

Figure 5.2 Female labour force participation, by age, Turkey (2005–2019)

Source: Calculated from the database provided by the Turkish Statistical Institute (TURKSTAT 2020c)

(per child, 50% of minimum monthly wage). In order to increase female labour force participation following childbirth, the Turkish state, temporarily and partially, has compensated the wages of care workers who look after working mothers' children in the three largest cities (İstanbul, Ankara, and İzmir). In addition, the project entitled "My Mum's Job is My Future" *(Annemin işi benim geleceğim)*, financed by both the state and employers, aims to establish nurseries in the industrial zones. Thus far, four zones have opened their nurseries (at the time of writing). The Turkish state has also provided loans and grants as well as various occupational courses in order to increase entrepreneurship and self-employment amongst women.

These state interventions seem effective in increasing mothers' access to paid employment. Evidence illustrated in Figure 5.2 suggests that since the mid-2000s, the M-shaped curve of female labour force participation by age has been increasingly flattened. This change suggests women can access childcare provision to allow them to re-join the labour force following childbirth.

Evidence on employment rates for all mothers (aged 15–64 years) with at least one child under 15 years supports the above findings; mothers' employment has increased from 21% to 30% between 2004 and 2013 (OECD.Stat 2020b). Public provisioning of childcare appears to play a significant role in supporting women to access paid employment. From the 1970s until the mid-1980s, pre-primary school enrolment (% gross) remained lower than 1%, and later rose up to 10% (in 2005). Since 2005, the same figure has increased to achieve its highest level; by 2017 the proportion (%) of children aged 3–5 years enrolled in pre-primary education had reached 40% (OECD. Stat 2020b; WDI 2020).

The evidence that I have investigated thus far provides support to the argument that Turkish social policy has shifted away from the enduring single male-breadwinner and full-time female homemaker model towards policy that encourages female paid employment (Kılıç 2010, 2008a, b). Since the mid-2000s, the state has increasingly utilised various degrees of commodification of childcare to uphold the sustainability of women's double burden of paid and unpaid labour. These commodification strategies draw on market-led provisioning of childcare (through private nurseries and day care centres) accompanied by state-compensations. The Turkish state, therefore, regulates childcare provision to maintain women's double burden of paid and unpaid labour suggesting the emergence of the public patriarchal state.

5.1.3 Changes within the gendered patterns of civil society

In assessing the domain of civil society, I analyse the forms of patriarchal domination in education, public decision-making and political representation, sexuality and cultural settings. In order to investigate women's access to education, I focus on gender gaps in educational attainment by calculating the Gender Parity Index (GPI) for gross enrolment ratio in primary, secondary, and tertiary education. GPI represents the ratio of women to men whose age corresponds to the selected level of education. While the gender gaps in literacy rate (aged 15–24 years) and primary and secondary school enrolment were eliminated between 2004 and 2013, tertiary school enrolment GPI figure indicates that the gap has become narrower over time (WDI 2020; UIS.Stat 2020).

Recent decades have also witnessed a modest but considerable change in women's access to public decision-making and political representation. From the mid-1990s until 2005, the proportion of seats held by women in the national parliament (% of total) remained lower than 4%, but the same figure achieved 17% in 2020 (WDI 2020). Although Turkey does not have a gender quota system for the parliament, the voluntary party quota system plays an important role in increasing women's access to parliament. The gender gaps in access to trade unions' decision-making mechanisms have, however, remained somewhat unchanged during this time period (Urhan 2014; Toksöz and Erdoğdu 1998). Nevertheless, given the decline in trade union density and collective bargaining coverage (OECD.Stat 2020d), women's limited access to trade union leadership is unlikely to significantly contribute to an increase in the gender gap in public decision-making and political representation. While trade unions may have lost their significance, the civil society domain is increasingly shaped by social movements concerned with women's rights, rights of the LGBTQ+ and Kurdish people and environmental concerns. Women's greater access to the decision-making mechanisms of these social movements has led the main opposition parties (*Halkların Demokratik Partisi* and *Cumhuriyet Halk Partisi*) to introduce the voluntary party quota system and thereby increase the proportion of women in the national parliament.

Women's control over their reproductive abilities also appears to have improved (see items A, C, D, E in Table 5.1). However, this change is

Table 5.1 Women's control over their reproductive abilities, Turkey (1992–2018)

	1993	*1998*	*2003*	*2008*	*2013*	*2018*
(A) Demand for family planning satisfied by modern methods (% of married women with demand for family planning)	45	49	56	57	56	62
(B) Unmet need for contraception (% of married women ages 15-49)	15	14	10	9	6	12
(C) Teenage mothers (% of women ages 15-19 who have had children or are currently pregnant)	9	10	8	6	4	..
(D) Adolescent fertility rate (% of women ages 15-19)	..	..	40	39	29	19
(E) Contraceptive prevalence rate - modern methods (% of women ages 15-49)	30	34	38	42	42	43

Sources: Calculated from the databases provided by the World Bank (WDI 2020) and the Turkish Statistical Institute (TURKSTAT 2020b)

associated with a counter trend: the percentage of fertile, married women (aged 15–49 years) who do not want to become pregnant but are not using contraception has recently increased from 6% to 12% (see item B in Table 5.1).

Women's control over their sexuality is not limited to their reproductive rights; it extends to their capacity for self-determination with respect to sexual orientation. The Turkish penal code (2004– current) has no mention of consensual same-sex sexual acts between adults meaning that neither criminalisation nor protection is in place. While same-sex marriage is not recognised, the right to change legal gender is acknowledged under particular conditions, including gender reassignment surgery, sterilisation and providing a mental health report. While the legal framework reinforces certain constraints regarding same-sex relationships, the state-led attacks towards the LGBTQ+ movement constitute a significant barrier to women's control over their sexuality.

In order to assess the extent to which changes within cultural settings signify the emergence of neoliberal public patriarchy, I address how far public perceptions and attitudes support women's greater access to education, employment, and political representation as opposed to their confinement within the domestic sphere. Table 5.2 shows that public support for women's access to education, paid employment, and high-ranking positions in the labour market and politics has increased over time. Despite the resurgence of patriarchal perceptions (in the period of 2010–2014), the hegemony of gender-based exclusionary attitudes appears to have been challenged over time. Those changes within the patriarchal character of

Table 5.2 Changes within patriarchal perceptions and attitudes, Turkey (1995–2020)

Do you strongly agree/ agree (A) or strongly disagree/ disagree (D) with the following statements?	1995–1999		2000–2004		2005–2009		2010–2014		2017–2020	
	A	*D*	*A*	*D*	*A*	*D*	*A*	*D*	*A*	*D*
Q1. If jobs are scarce, men should have more right to a job than women	66	27	59	28	52	29	*59*	*23*	51	26
Q2. Being a housewife just as fulfilling	78	20	77	21	74	22	*70*	*27*	62	34
Q3. Pre-school child suffers with working mother	..	32	..	36	..	37	*66*	*31*	52	46
Q4. Men make better political leaders than women do	61	64	60	70	59	79	*68*	*29*	52	45
Q5. University is more important for a boy than for a girl	34	..	29	..	19	44	*32*	*66*	32	66
Q6. Men make better business executives than women do	..	..	..	..	51		*64*	*32*	46	49
Q7. Percentage of women aged 15–49 years who consider a husband to be justified in hitting or beating his wife for at least one of the specified reasons, i.e., if his wife burns the food, argues with him, goes out without telling him, neglects the children or refuses sexual relations				39		20		*23*		13

Sources: Question from 1 to 6 are calculated from the database provided by the World Values Survey (WVS 2020), but Q7 is calculated from the databases provided by the OECD and the World Bank (WDI 2020; OECD.Stat 2020c)

perceptions and attitudes, furthermore, correlate with those regarding violence against women.

In light of the evidence investigated thus far, I suggest that changes within the domain of civil society indicate the emergence of neoliberal public patriarchy. Gender gaps in education have narrowed since the mid-2000s, and women's access to public decision-making and political representation as well as control over their reproductive abilities has also increased during this time period. Evidence also suggests a recent transformation in cultural values and attitudes towards supporting women's greater access to the key institutions of civil society (e.g. paid employment, education, and politics). The patriarchal characteristics of cultural conditions are, therefore, being adjusted in ways which support women's double burden of paid and unpaid labour and, as such, indicate erosion of the gender-based exclusionary strategies.

5.1.4 State interventions in violence against women

According to Walby (2009), the violence domain includes gendered violence, armies and militias, but my assessment here is limited to gendered violence which, in Turkey, is very prevalent. According to the evidence gathered by *Bianet* (the Independent Communication Network), 5–6 women are killed every week by a current or former intimate male partner (2016–2019) (Bianet 2020). In the context of such high levels of gendered violence and femicide, state interventions have increased since the 2000s (Güneş 2019; İlkkaracan and Amado 2011; Siska 2019). As a signatory to international agreements, including CEDAW, the Turkish state has taken measures to prevent custom and honour killings and violence against women and children (in 2006) and modified the legal framework, including Municipality Law (in 2000), Labour Act (in 2003), Turkish Penal Code (in 2005), the Constitution (in 2011) and the Law to Protect Family and Prevent Violence against Women (in 2007, 2012 and 2014). The social policy framework, furthermore, has addressed services and shelters to protect survivors of domestic violence (in 2008). Women Guesthouses for Combating Domestic Violence were established between 2014 and 2016. Currently, the number of shelters is 114 with a capacity for 3,454 people (at the time of writing). Violence Prevention and Monitoring Centres (ŞÖNİM) were also established in order to compensate the lack of shelters (there were 80 such centres in 2019).

Police officers, health-care professionals, and lawyers are trained in dealing with gendered violence and a number of programmes have been implemented in collaboration with media, faith-based organisations, and the military (2006–2017). Nation-wide awareness campaigns, such as *Stop Domestic Violence* (in 2004) and *Stop Violence Against Women* (in 2008) were also introduced. The Turkish state, furthermore, funded various research initiatives and conducted two nation-wide surveys to track domestic violence (in 2008 and 2014), as well as producing National Action Plans on combating violence against women, domestic violence, and intimate partner violence (2007–2010, 2012–2015 and 2016–2020) (UN.Women 2020). Since the 2000s, the Turkish state has therefore increasingly intervened to criminalize violence against women and introduce some preventative measures. This action by the state signals emergence of the neoliberal form of public patriarchy within the domain of violence.

To summarise, women's increased access to paid employment in non-agricultural sectors gives rise to the double burden of paid and unpaid labour which is sustained by the Turkish state's policies, such as the market-led provisioning of childcare. Moreover, women have greater access to the key institutions of civil society, including education, public decision-making and political representation, as well as increasing control over their reproductive capacity. Furthermore, evidence suggests that cultural values, perceptions and attitudes have changed in ways which support women's access to education, paid employment, and high-ranking positions within the labour market and politics, and to increasingly disapprove of violence against women. The state, further, has increasingly intervened in gendered violence by criminalising domestic violence and introducing some preventative measures. All of these changes suggest that since the mid-2000s neoliberal public patriarchy has achieved a substantial foundation in Turkey. Nevertheless, a detailed investigation is required to assess how far its emergence has challenged the predominance of premodern and modern domestic patriarchies.

5.2 Hegemony of premodern and modern domestic patriarchies

In this section, I investigate whether the predominance of premodern and modern domestic patriarchies has been maintained despite the emergence of neoliberal public patriarchy. This investigation thus enables an assessment of how far a shift away from the domestic towards the public forms of patriarchy has been initiated since the mid-2000s.

5.2.1 Limited coverage of the double burden experience

Under the conditions of increasing wage dependency, the gender-based division of labour in household production means female wageworkers experience a double burden of paid and unpaid labour. However, there are two major dynamics in Turkey which need to be considered to adequately assess how far the double burden represents the experience of the majority of women in the country. These are:

First, the pattern of small landownership has remained largely unchanged since the 1950s. While 8% of agricultural holdings constitute large-scale farms (20 hectares or larger), 80% of holdings are smaller than 10 hectares (TURKSTAT 2016a). This pattern of small landownership, furthermore, occurs together with a strong gender-based division of labour and persistent gender gaps in unpaid family work. Women constituted 76% of unpaid

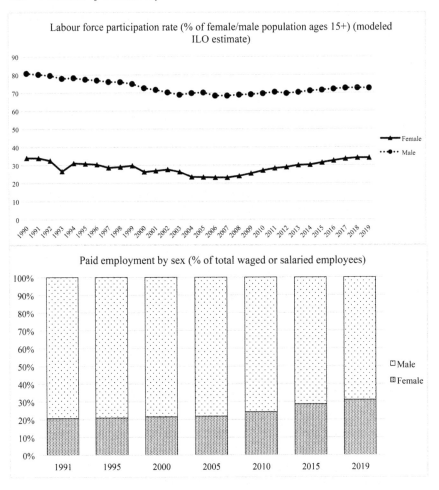

Figure 5.3 Gender gaps in paid employment, Turkey (1990–2019)

Source: Calculated from the database provided by the World Bank and the International Labour Organisation (ILOSTAT 2022; WDI 2020)

family workers in agriculture between 2010 and 2019 (ILOSTAT 2022). Considering that a quarter of female employment is still in agriculture (in 2019), then it is important to note that the double burden of paid and unpaid labour does not represent rural women's experience.

Second, persistent and large gender gaps in labour force participation indicate that a significant proportion of women do not engage with paid employment in non-agricultural sectors (see Figure 5.3); 66% of women in the working age population (aged 15–64 years) do not have any kind of paid employment (in agriculture or non-agricultural sectors) nor are they seeking a job. In contrast, the equivalent figure for men is 27% (in 2019)

(WDI 2020). Therefore, male dominance in paid employment needs to be taken into account when assessing the extent women experience the double burden.

Furthermore, evidence illustrated in Figure 5.3 shows that women's share of paid employment (% of total paid employment) remains low and, as such, correlates with the low levels of female labour force participation. I calculate that around 31% of women in the working age population (aged 15–64 years) have access to paid employment in formal or informal sectors thereby experiencing the double burden (in 2021), whereas the majority of women's labour is confined to rural or urban household production (ILOSTAT 2022).[1]

To a certain extent then, the emergence of neoliberal public patriarchy does impact on the lives of some women. Nonetheless, the majority of women are excluded from paid employment opportunities, and thereby continue to experience the conditions of premodern and modern forms of domestic patriarchy. Evidence on female labour force participation by level of education provides a detailed account of this division. In 2019, 71% of women with advanced education (in the working age population) were part of the labour force, whereas the same figure dropped to 29% for women with basic education. However, a lower level of education does not seem to prevent male employment: the labour force participation rate of men with basic level education was 69% (in 2019) (WDI 2020).

Furthermore, the ratio of female to male labour force participation rate signifies gender inequality across all levels of education, but the gender gap increases substantially when considering intermediate and basic education levels (see Figure 5.4). This suggests that women with a lower level

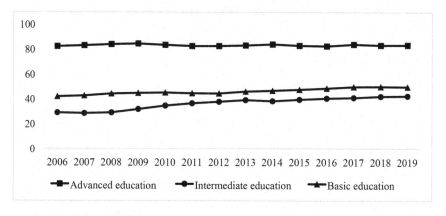

Figure 5.4 Ratio of female to male labour force participation, by education, Turkey (2006–2019)

Source: Ratio of female to male labour force participation rate is calculated by dividing female labour force participation rate by male labour force participation rate and multiplying by 100. A value closer to 100 represents a higher level of equality (WDI 2020)

of education are excluded from paid employment in non-agricultural sectors, whereas women with advanced education are more likely to have paid employment and experience conditions of the double burden.

In sum, the emergence of neoliberal public patriarchy is limited to women with advanced education; women with lower levels of education represent the majority of women of working age and are engaged in unpaid labour in rural or urban household production. This division raises the question of how the Turkish state responds.

5.2.2 Persistence of domestic patriarchal state

Thus far, I have demonstrated that since the mid-2000s, the Turkish state has increasingly regulated public provisioning of childcare and, in this way, has supported mothers' access to paid employment. However, given that the majority of women are excluded from paid employment, here I investigate whether the state's public policy interventions aim to increase all women's access to paid employment or to confine women with a lower educational level to rural and urban household production. While the former signifies a clear shift towards the public patriarchal state, the latter points to persistence in its domestic patriarchal character.

The net childcare costs for parents using childcare in Turkey appear to be lower than the OECD and European Union average (OECD.Stat 2020a).[2] Nevertheless, evidence on changes within female labour force participation by age, illustrated in Figure 5.5, shows that women with advanced education are the main beneficiaries of the recent policy interventions in childcare provision. The labour force participation of women with advanced education has sharply increased following childbirth (2006–2019), but women with basic or intermediate education have continued to leave the labour force and failed to return.

For women with less than basic education who predominantly work as unpaid family workers in agriculture, labour force participation increases following marriage and childbirth and does not decline until daughters in law join their extended family (see Figure 5.5). This supports the qualitative findings that pregnancy, childbirth, or lactation do not shape the gender-based division of labour in agrarian production, and at the same time, shows that policies on childcare provision are not relevant to the lives of rural women.

Mothers, mothers-in-laws, and other women within the extended family are involved in providing childcare (Özbay 1991). However, in 2016 only 11% of pre-school age children were looked after by their paternal or maternal grandmothers while their mothers were at work (TURKSTAT 2016b). More importantly, the proportion of women who rely on the unpaid labour of other women remained at the same level between 2008 and 2013 (HUIPS 2013, 2008). This indicates that the reserve army of unpaid care workers within the extended family has reached its capacity for various reasons,

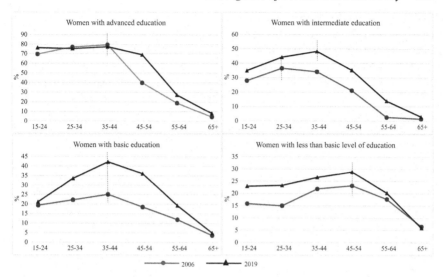

Figure 5.5 Female labour force participation, by age and education, Turkey (2006 and 2019)

Source: Calculated from the database provided by the International Labour Organisation (ILOSTAT 2022)

including aging, poverty, and an extended retirement age. The public provisioning of childcare, therefore, remains important for women's access to paid employment following childbirth.

Nonetheless, state interventions in childcare provision are not designed in ways which support the labour force participation of women with a lower level of education. As argued previously, the Turkish state draws heavily on commodification strategies together with a certain level of state compensation in childcare provision. Subsequently, the private childcare institutions and domestic workers constitute the backbone of childcare provision in the country. This market-led public provisioning system does not support women with basic and intermediate education who are more likely to receive lower wages. Affordable state-led institutions are extremely restricted, providing only for a special group of children under certain circumstances, thereby failing to constitute an alternative to profit-driven childcare institutions. As a result, the market-led provisioning of childcare limits the majority of women's access to nurseries and day care services and thus limits their access to paid employment.

The state, furthermore, confines women's labour to household production by establishing a family-based unpaid care system for elderly and disabled members of society. Unlike its strategy in the public provisioning of childcare, the Turkish state has not utilised a market-led provisioning of elderly and disabled care. For example, in 2016, the total capacity of state-owned and private care homes covered only 0.5% of the elderly population (aged 65+ years). The total capacity of care homes for disabled people constitutes only 0.2% of the population (ages 15+) who have considerable difficulties in living-independently (calculated from Karakuş 2018; TURKSTAT 2020a, 2016c). Home-based care services have also remained very limited in the country. This absence of elderly and disabled care provision is associated with state-driven incentives. Since 2005, the Turkish state has introduced conditional cash transfers to women who provide care for elderly and disabled members of the family. These benefits are described as necessary payments for the sustainability of a family-based unpaid care system (Karakuş 2018).

In addition, the Turkish state confines female peasants' labour to unpaid agricultural work. While the 1990s' policy strategy focused on rural poverty alleviation through women's access to non-traditional and non-agricultural skills (e.g. silk production and carpet making), the contemporary policy framework aims at "empower[ing] rural women in terms of their social and economic status and ensure that they are no longer unpaid family workers" (The Government of Turkey 2019: 70). Subsequently, the Turkish state removed the legal discrimination against women in inheritance of small-scale agricultural land (see Chapter 4) as well as providing a significant level of support to women's cooperatives in agriculture (e.g. loans with minimum or no interest rates, training programmes). Female peasants' increased access to rural assets and the market is expected to initiate a shift in their position from unpaid family workers to own-account workers. The evidence, however, demonstrates that between 2010 and 2019, the proportion of women own-account workers in agriculture (% of total) declined from 16% to 11%, whereas the proportion of unpaid family workers in agriculture who are women (% of total) has remained stable at 76% (ILOSTAT 2022). The state, therefore, confines women's labour to rural household production rather than implementing policy strategies which would increase rural women's mobility and access to advanced education, and paid employment in non-agricultural sectors.

In light of the evidence investigated thus far, I argue that the emergence of the public patriarchal character of the Turkish state has remained limited and has not supplanted its domestic patriarchal character. The state has increasingly utilised commodification strategies for childcare provision to regulate the double burden of paid and unpaid labour. Yet, those interventions are limited to women with advanced education. The policy framework is predominantly designed in ways which confine the majority of women to unpaid work in rural and urban household production. While urban women with basic or intermediate education are encouraged to stay at home and provide unpaid care for children, and elderly and disabled members of society, rural women are kept as unpaid family workers in small-medium scale farms. Rather than increasing all women's access to paid employment, policy interventions confine the majority of women's labour to rural and urban household production. The evidence therefore indicates the persistence of the domestic patriarchal character of the Turkish state.

5.2.3 *Male dominance over the civil society domain*

As argued previously, recent changes within the civil society domain signal the emergence of neoliberal public patriarchy. This section assesses how far the hegemony of domestic patriarchy within the domain of civil society has been challenged. As discussed previously, gender gaps in school enrolment in corresponding age have narrowed, but evidence on the ratio of female to male educational attainment (% of total population aged 25+ years) shows that gender inequality in intermediate and advanced education is higher than basic education (WDI 2020). This indicates that the state neglects gender gaps in adult education. Given that women with a low level of education are strongly disadvantaged against their male counterparts in the labour market (see Figure 5.4), gender gaps in education remain significant.

Moreover, with the emergence of an anti-democratic regime (since 2014–2015), women's improved access to the national parliament and social movements does not translate into greater access to public decision-making. The national parliament has lost its importance for public decision-making, and the anti-democratic regime has suppressed the feminist, LGBTQ+ and Kurdish rights-based movements and environmental activism. These developments, therefore, run counter to the increase in proportion of seats held by women in the national parliament as well as neutralising women's increased access to the decision-making mechanisms of the earlier mentioned social movements.

In addition, women's increased control over their reproductive abilities appears to be offset by a resurgence in pronatalist policies (since the 2010s). The pronatalist approach is strengthened with the public propaganda of the Justice and Development Party regime (since 2002), which encourages women to give birth to as many children as possible and condemns abortion. The former is achieved through using incentives for an increased number of births (The Ministry of Family 2020) and the latter by anti-abortion regulations. Women in Turkey are eligible to have access to abortion on request for economic or social reasons, in cases of rape or incest, or to save their life or preserve their mental health. However, in recent years, the government has utilised various regulations to limit access to the abortion services provided by the state-owned public hospitals. Abortion is still provided in private hospitals but is accessible only to women with high levels of income. The number of public hospitals which provide accessible abortion services in İstanbul has been reduced to one at the time of writing in 2021. Furthermore, the law seeking husbands' permission is kept despite legal conflict with the international agreements to which Turkey is signatory. Although the resistance of the feminist movement has prevented further restrictions (e.g. reduction to the time limit within which abortions can be performed) (Letsch 2012; Çatlak Zemin 2020), anti-abortion regulations have limited women's control over their reproductive abilities. These restrictions on women's reproductive rights, further, correlate with the limitations on women's sexuality. Since 2017, LGBTQ+ events, including Pride and

Table 5.3 Patriarchal perceptions and attitudes, Turkey (2005–2020)

	2005–2009		2017–2020	
On this list are various groups of people. Could you please mention any that you would not like to have as neighbors?				
Mentioned: Homosexuals	88		76	
Mentioned: Unmarried couples living together	65		55	
Please tell me for each of the following statements whether you think it cannot be justified (A), or always justified (B)				
	A	**B**	**A**	**B**
Justifiable: Divorce	94	5	94	4
Justifiable: Abortion	96	2	97	1
Justifiable: Casual sex	..	..	97	1

Sources: Calculated from the database provided by the World Values Survey (WVS 2020)

festivals, have been banned and activists are charged with prison sentences. These attacks on the LGBTQ+ community are sustained with police interventions and detentions (ILGA World 2019). Thus, although gender-based exclusionary perceptions and attitudes towards women's access to paid employment and political representation have gradually been eroded, women's control over their sexuality and reproductive rights has been strongly repudiated (see Table 5.3).

The evidence presented thus far, suggests that the emergence of the neoliberal form of public patriarchy has, to a certain degree, challenged the predominance of gender-based exclusionary strategies within the domain of civil society. Nevertheless, anti-democratic ruling (2014– current) has excluded women from public decision-making and political representation. Furthermore, gender gaps in intermediate and advanced education persist, and women's control over their sexuality, including their reproductive abilities, is restricted by the state-driven homophobic and pronatalist regulations. The predominance of gender-based exclusionary strategies within the institutions of politics and sexuality, furthermore, correlates with the transformation of values, meanings and perceptions. While there may be increased acceptance of improving women's access to paid employment, advanced education and political presentation, people are opposed to women having control over their own bodies and sexuality. Therefore, it appears that despite the emergence of neoliberal public patriarchy, the domain of civil society remains under the hegemony of domestic patriarchy.

5.2.4 Being trapped in a violent heterosexual family

Since the mid-2000s the Turkish state has increasingly intervened in gendered violence, but the key characteristics of this intervention represent a contradiction. The state-driven actions in the domain of gendered violence aim at preventing domestic violence, but at the same time, the cis-gender heterosexual family is shielded to such an extent that there continues to be a very high-level of femicides. Recently, the title of the relevant law has changed from 'the Protection of Women' to 'the Protection of Family' and this renaming represents more than just a shift in terminology. The parliamentary members of the ruling Justice and Development Party highlight that "they do not wish to increase the rate of divorce as an indirect and unintended result of trying to protect women against the violence of their husbands" (Akdoğan, Yildiz, and Çiner 2017: 404). Reviewing the evidence suggests that state-led interventions in gendered violence are shaped in various ways to confine survivors within violent households.

First, the capacity of shelters is limited and insufficient which means that the state avoids providing viable alternatives to the heterosexual family (Diner and Toktaş 2013). Over the last two decades, the total capacity of shelters and the maximum duration of stay in those shelters have been kept to a minimum level. Second, state practitioners believe that they should protect the family which leads to the perception of domestic violence as being a private and familial matter (Yücel 2017). This perception, in turn, prevents the execution of laws and regulations. Third, adopting a heterosexual family-focused approach means that little attention is paid to the preventative and protective measures to address femicides of single, separated, or divorced women, and violence against LGBTQ+ people is ignored. Although international institutions have highlighted the significance of femicides, the Turkish state has, thus far, not initiated any surveys, research, campaigning, or training to address the level of femicides in the country (e.g. at the time of writing in 2021, there are no official statistics on femicides). Far from acting to prevent femicides, prison sentences of perpetrators have actually been shortened – if not abandoned- through application of the law on "unjust provocation". The state's lack of intervention in femicides of single, separated or divorced women and violence against LGBTQ+ people thereby effectively discourages forms of relationships alternative to the cis-gender heterosexual family.

5.3 Conclusion

On the basis of the evidence discussed in this chapter, I argue that the emergence of the neoliberal form of public patriarchy (since the mid-2000s) is limited and its scale insufficient to challenge the hegemony of premodern and modern domestic patriarchies. While women with advanced education are increasingly subjected to the double burden of paid and unpaid labour, the majority of women are excluded from paid employment in non-agricultural sectors – around 70% of women in the working age population (15-64) do not have access to any form of paid employment (in 2021). Thus, the absence of a shift from women's unpaid labour towards the double burden of paid and unpaid labour indicates the continued predominance of domestic patriarchy.

In addition, the state's role in confining women's labour to rural and urban household production remains significant which points to the Turkish state's continuing domestic patriarchal character. Market-led strategies limit the accessibility of childcare meaning that the majority of women are excluded from paid employment following childbirth. The state also confines those women's labour to household production by maintaining its family-based unpaid care system for elderly and disabled members of society. At the same time, as these policies confine women to urban household production, agrarian policies and regulations serve to uphold the role of women as unpaid family workers in rural household production.

Furthermore, while the emergence of neoliberal public patriarchy does impact the domain of civil society, the dominance of gender-based exclusionary strategies appears to be preserved. Gender gaps in school enrolment have narrowed, but less attention is paid to gender gaps in adult education, thus women's overall access to intermediate and advance education (aged 25+ years) continues to be more restricted than that of men. Neoliberal patriarchy also appears to initiate a shift in cultural attitudes in terms of increasing support for women's education, paid employment and political representation. However, the notion of women gaining greater control over their sexuality, including their reproductive abilities, is strongly rejected. The recently established anti-democratic regime, further, transforms the dynamics of public decision-making in a way which undermines the significance of women's political representation in the national parliament and social movements. The resurgence of pronatalist policies and homophobic regulations also sustain women's limited control over their sexuality. The key institutions of the civil society domain, therefore, are marked by the continuing predominance of gender-based exclusionary strategies and domestic forms of patriarchy rather than neoliberal public patriarchy.

Finally, state interventions in the domain of gendered violence are increased; yet a closer look at those interventions shows that the Turkish state traps women in the confines of the violent heterosexual family setting by limiting women's access to viable alternatives and tolerating male violence against single, separated or divorced women and violence against LGBTQ+ people. Such policies and regulations in the domain of gendered violence also serve to signify the predominance of domestic patriarchy.

To conclude, despite the emergence of neoliberal public patriarchy, Turkey remains under the hegemony of premodern and modern domestic patriarchies, sustaining the dominance of gender-based exclusionary strategies in paid employment, public decision-making and political representation, cultural settings, sexuality as well as tolerating gendered violence. As discussed in Chapter 4, the patriarchal gender contract during the early Republican period was established on the grounds of gender-based exclusionary strategies. In light of the evidence investigated in this chapter, I argue that the contemporary patriarchal gender contract continues to predominantly draw on such exclusionary strategies rather than gender-based segregation and subordination. Rural and urban household production remain the primary place for the majority of women's labour and, at the same time, the domestic patriarchal character of the state and the dominance of gender-based exclusionary strategies within the domains of civil society and gendered violence are preserved.

Next, I elaborate on the uneven and combined development of premodern and modern domestic as well as neoliberal public patriarchies by investigating the geopolitics of patriarchal transformation in Turkey.

Notes

1 In my calculations, I deduct total number of female contributing family workers from total number of female labour force as well as calculating working age female population (aged between 15 and 64).
2 This indicator measures the net childcare costs for two-parent households assuming full-time centre-based childcare after any benefits designed to reduce the gross childcare fees (e.g. childcare allowances, tax concessions, fee rebates and increases in other benefit entitlements). The calculation also assumes that the couple has two children ages 2 and 3, one parent earns 100% of the average wage, and the other earns 67% of the average wage (see OECD indicators)

References

Akdoğan, Argün A., Mete Yildiz, and Can U. Çiner. 2017. "An analysis of policy transfer the policy on protecting women against domestic violence in Turkey." In *Public Policy Making in a Globalized World*, edited by R. J. Lewis. London, New York: Routledge.

Bianet. 2020. Bianet femicide map (2016–2019). Edited by Independent Communication Network.

Çatlak Zemin. 2020. "8 Haziran 2012: 22 ilde eşzamanlı eylem: Kürtaj Haktır Karar Kadınların!", 12.08.2020. https://www.catlakzemin.com/8-haziran-2012-22-ilde-eszamanli-eylem-kurtaj-haktir-karar-kadinlarin/.

Ciddi, Sinan. 2009. *Kemalism in Turkish Politics: The Republican People's Party, Secularism and Nationalism*. London, New York: Routledge.

Coşar, Simten, and Aylin Özman. 2008. "Representation Problems of Social Democracy in Turkey." *Journal of Third World Studies* 25 (1):233–252.

Diner, Çağla, and Şule Toktaş. 2013. "Women's Shelters in Turkey: A Qualitative Study on Shortcomings of Policy Making and Implementation." *Violence Against Women* 19 (3):338–355. doi: 10.1177/1077801213486258.

Ecevit, Yıldız, Ayşe Gündüz-Hosgör, and Ceylan Tokluoğlu. 2003. "Professional Women in Computer Programming Occupations: The Case of Turkey." *Career Development International* 8 (2):78–87. doi: 10.1108/13620430310465480.

Emre, Yunus. 2015. "Why Has Social Democracy Not Developed in Turkey? Analysis of an Atypical Case." *Journal of Balkan and Near Eastern Studies* 17 (4):392–407. doi: 10.1080/19448953.2015.1063298.

Emre, Yunus. 2019. "The Legalization of the Right to Strike in Turkey in the 1960s." *Journal of Balkan and Near Eastern Studies* 21 (4):427–442. doi: 10.1080/19448953.2018.1506281.

Güneş, Ayşe. 2019. "Legal Implications of Turkey's Accessions to the Istanbul Convention by Enacting and Refining its Laws on Violence Against Women." *Women & Criminal Justice*:1–15. doi: 10.1080/08974454.2019.1697792.

Hacifazlioğlu, Özge. 2010. "Balance in Academic Leadership: Voices of Women from Turkey and the United States of America (US)." *Perspectives in Education* 28 (2):51–62.

HUIPS. 2008. *Population and Health Survey*. Edited by Hacettepe University Institute of Population Studies. Ankara: Hacettepe University Institute of Population Studies.

HUIPS. 2013. Population and Health Survey. Edited by Hacettepe University Institute of Population Studies. Ankara.

ILGA World. 2019. State-Sponsored Homofobia: Global Legislation Overview Update.

ILOSTAT. 2022. Statistics on the Working-age Population and Labour Force– ILO modelled estimates. In *The ILOSTAT database*, Geneva: The International Labour Organisation.

ILOSTAT. 2020b. Statistics on Working Time. Edited by The International Labour Organisation.

İlkkaracan, Pınar, and Liz Erçevik Amado. 2011. "Legal reforms on violence against women in Turkey: Best practices." In *Gender and Violence in the Middle East*, edited by D. Ghanim. London, New York: Routledge

Karakuş, Bülent. 2018. *Türkiye'de Yaşlılara Yönelik Hizmetler, Kurumsal Yaşlı Bakımı ve Kurumsal Yaşlı Bakımında İllerin Durumu*. Ankara: Aile ve Sosyal Politikalar Bakanlığı.

Keyman, Fuat E., and Ziya Öniş. 2007. "Globalization and Social Democracy in the European Periphery: Paradoxes of the Turkish Experience." *Globalizations* 4 (2):211–228. doi: 10.1080/14747730701345226.

Kılıç, Azer. 2008a. "Continuity and Change in Social Policy Approaches Toward Women." *New Perspectives on Turkey* 38:135–158.

Kılıç, Azer. 2008b. "The Gender Dimension of Social Policy Reform in Turkey: Towards Equal Citizenship?" *Social Policy & Administration* 42 (5):487–503. doi: 10.1111/j.1467-9515.2008.00620.x.

Kılıç, Azer. 2010. "Gender, family and children at the crossroads of social policy reform in Turkey: Alternating between familialism and individualism." In *Children, Gender and Families in Mediterranean Welfare States*, edited by M. Ajzenstadt and J. Gal. London, New York: Springer.

Letsch, Constanze. 2012. "Turkish Women Join Pro-Choice Rally as Fears Grow of Abortion Ban." The Guardian, accessed 6 June. http://www.guardian.co.uk/world/2012/jun/03/turkish-women-rally-abortion-ban.

Makal, Ahmet. 2010. "Türkiye'de erken Cumhuriyet Döneminde Kadın Emeği." *Çalışma ve Toplum* 2:12–39.

Makal, Ahmet. 2012. "Türkiye'de kadın emeğinin tarihsel kökenleri 1920–1960." In *Geçmişten Günümüze Türkiye'de Kadın Emeği*, edited by A. Makal and G. Toksöz. Ankara: Ankara Universitesi Yayinevi.

OECD.Stat. 2020a. Benefits, Taxes and Wages. Edited by OECD.

OECD.Stat. 2020b. Family database. Edited by OECD.

OECD.Stat. 2020c. Gender database. Edited by OECD.

OECD.Stat. 2020d. Labour database. Edited by OECD.

OECD.Stat. 2020e. Time use survey. Edited by OECD.

Öncü, A. 1979. "Uzman mesleklerde Türk kadını." In *Türk Toplumunda Kadın*, edited by N. Abadan-Unat. Ankara: Türk Sosyal Bilimler Derneği

Özbay, Ferhunde. 1991. "Türkiye'de Kadın ve çocuk emeği." *Toplum ve Bilim* 53 (Bahar):41–54.

Siska, Katalin. 2019. ""You Cannot Put Women and Men on an Equal Footing, It Is Against Nature." A Review of the Evolution of Women's Rights Since the Establishment of the Republic of Turkey." *Journal on European History of Law* 10 (1):149–156.

Smith, Alice, and Berna Dengiz. 2010. "Women in Engineering in Turkey – A Large Scale Quantitative and Qualitative Examination." *European Journal of Engineering Education* 35 (1):45–57. doi: 10.1080/03043790903406345

The Government of Turkey 2019. Turkey's 2nd Voluntary National Review (VNR) Sustainable Development Goals. New York.

The Ministry of Family. 2020. Doğum yardımı. The Ministry of Family Labour and Social Services.

Toksöz, Gülay, and Seyhan Erdoğdu. 1998. *Sendikacı Kadın Kimliği*. İstanbul, Ankara: İmge Yayınevi.

TURKSTAT. 2015. Time use survey. Edited by Turkish Statistical Institute.

TURKSTAT. 2016a. Agricultural Farm Structure Survey.

TURKSTAT. 2016b. Aile yapısı araştırması. Edited by Turkish Statistical Institute.

TURKSTAT. 2016c. Türkiye sağlık araştırması. Edited by Turkish Statistical Institute.

TURKSTAT. 2020a. Address Based Population Registration System (ABPRS). Edited by Turkish Statistical Institute.

TURKSTAT. 2020b. HUIPS, Turkey Demographic and Health Survey, 1993–2018. Edited by The Turkish Statistical Institute.

TURKSTAT. 2020c. Labour Force Database. Edited by Turkish Statistical Institute. Ankara.

UIS.Stat. 2020. The UNESCO Institute for Statistics.Edited by The UNESCO.

UN.Women. 2020. UN Women – Global Database on Violence Against Women. The United Nations.

Urhan, Betül. 2014. *Sendikasız kadınlar, kadınsız sendikalar: Sendika- kadın ilişkisinde görülen sorun alanlarını belirlemeye yönelik bir araştırma*. İstanbul: KADAV.

Walby, Sylvia. 2009. *Globalisation and Inequalities: Complexity and Contested Modernities*. London: Sage Publications Ltd.

WDI. 2020. World Development Indicators. Edited by The World Bank.

WVS. 2020. World Values Survey. Edited by The WVS Association. Vienna, Austria.

Yücel, Özge. 2017. "Efficiency and Expediency of Preventive and Protective Measures Against Domestic Violence Taken by the Family Courts in Ankara." *International Journal of Law, Policy, and the Family* 31 (3):311–327. doi: 10.1093/lawfam/ebx012

6 UNEVEN AND COMBINED DEVELOPMENT OF PATRIARCHY

Thus far, I have proposed that Turkey remains under the hegemony of pre-modern and modern domestic patriarchies despite the emergence of neoliberal public patriarchy (since the mid-2000s). In this chapter, I differentiate the regions dominated by forms of domestic patriarchies from those where neoliberal public patriarchy has emerged alongside modern domestic patriarchy. In this way, I provide a detailed account of the geopolitics of patriarchal transformation which, in turn, is significant in terms of diversifying the experiences of women (Sections 6.1 and 6.2). I further examine how far the religion and ethnicity based oppression diversifies Alevi and Kurdish women's experiences (Sections 6.3 and 6.4) as well as, focusing on class differences amongst women (Section 6.5).

6.1 The geopolitics of patriarchal transformation in Turkey

Conventional ways of differentiating rural from urban populations tend to conceal the significance of gendered relations of labour for social transformation. The Turkish Statistical Institute, for example, used to classify areas with a population greater than 20,000 as urban and the remainder as rural. Since 2014, areas with city councils have been classified as urban areas. Populist policies have permitted areas with a population over 5,000 to have a city council (The Official Paper 2005) which meant areas once classified as rural became urban. Changes in this classification system complicate attempts to assess rural and urban populations. As the World Bank highlights, "[t]here is no consistent and universally accepted standard for distinguishing urban from rural areas, in part because of the wide variety of situations across countries" (WDI 2020).

Furthermore, the rural/urban or village/town divisions as well as the decline within the overall share of agriculture in GDP (%) obscure the continuum between the gendered patterns in agriculture and non-agricultural sectors. The dominance of small-landownership gives rise to agrarian and semi-agrarian cities, where the main economic activity is agrarian commerce (e.g. merchandise, trade, transportation and warehousing). Patriarchal relations of agrarian production tend to expand into these commercial activities

DOI: 10.4324/9781003054511-9

and lead to women's exclusion from the public sphere (Hoşgör-Gündüz and Smits 2007). In order to distinguish the geographies of women's paid labour from others where women's labour is confined to rural and urban household production, I differentiate agrarian, semi-agrarian and non-agrarian cities. I use various indicators to classify areas, including women's access to education, gender gaps in paid employment and share of agriculture in GDP (%) across all 26 regions of Turkey.

Table 6.1 demonstrates that, while the majority of male employment is in non-agricultural sectors in all 26 regions, female employment is mostly in agriculture, in half of those regions. While there are some regions where a shift towards female paid employment in non-agricultural sectors has been initiated (İstanbul-TR10, Ankara-TR51, İzmir-TR31, Bursa, Eskişehir, Bilecik-TR41, Tekirdağ, Edirne, Kırklareli-TR21), and women's access to education and paid employment in these regions is higher than others, these regions account for only 38% of the total population (in 2018) (TURKSTAT 2020a). This means that roughly 60% of the total population lives in agrarian and semi-agrarian cities where women's mobility and access to education and paid employment is more restricted than in non-agrarian cities.

While agrarian and semi-agrarian cities are shaped by the predominance of premodern and modern domestic patriarchies, non-agrarian cities comprise modern domestic and neoliberal public patriarchies. In those agrarian and semi-agrarian cities, gender-based exclusionary strategies confine women's labour to rural and urban household production. Alongside the domestic patriarchal form, neoliberal public patriarchy is emerging in non-agrarian cities with its gendered segregation and subordination sustaining women's double burden of paid and unpaid labour. This structure of patriarchal transformation indicates a combined 'development of premodern and modern domestic' and 'development of neoliberal public' patriarchies in Turkey (See Figure 6.1).

6.2 Diversified experiences of women

The uneven and combined development of premodern and modern domestic and neoliberal public patriarchies diversify women's experiences, thereby dividing women on the grounds of patriarchal domination. For example, under conditions of premodern domestic patriarchy, rural women work as unpaid family workers on the farm as well as doing housework and care work within the home. As women's unpaid family labour is crucial for those small-medium scale farms, women are kept in the village as mothers, wives, daughters, sisters and sisters-in-law. In contrast, young men who are disadvantaged in land inheritance are encouraged to migrate for education and paid employment. Rural women's mobility and access to education and paid employment are therefore more restricted than their male counterparts. Furthermore, women's exclusion from agrarian commerce and the ownership of land and other forms of agricultural property is associated with a

Table 6.1 Agrarian, semi-agrarian and non-agrarian cities, Turkey (in 2018)

	Share of Agriculture in			Female Labour Force		
	female employment (% of total employed, 15+)	*male employment (% of total employed, 15+)*	*Share of agriculture in GDP (%)*	*illiterate (% of total, 15+)*	*with secondary education (% of total, 15+)*	*tertiary education (% of total, 15+)*
Ağrı, Kars, Iğdır, Ardahan-TRA2	76	44	27	33	7	11
Van, Muş, Bitlis, Hakkari-TRB2	60	28	17	28	12	16
Trabzon, Ordu, Giresun, Rize, Artvin, Gümüşhane-TR90	59	30	10	12	15	20
Samsun, Tokat, Çorum, Amasya-TR83	56	34	14	14	12	18
Kastamonu, Çankırı, Sinop-TR82	56	39	17	12	10	18
Şanlıurfa, Diyarbakır-TRC2	54	29	18	30	12	20
Erzurum, Erzincan, Bayburt-TRA1	54	28	16	14	10	25
Malatya, Elazığ, Bingöl, Tunceli-TRB1	52	26	10	19	12	23
Zonguldak, Karabük, Bartın-TR81	48	24	4	11	12	23
Manisa, Afyonkarahisar, Kütahya, Uşak-TR33	43	25	15	7	15	22
Kırıkkale, Aksaray, Niğde, Nevşehir, Kırşehir-TR71	42	23	19	7	14	24
Konya, Karaman-TR52	40	20	18	7	12	22
Balıkesir, Çanakkale-TR22	36	25	13	4	17	25
Kayseri, Sivas, Yozgat-TR72	36	18	10	9	15	28
Hatay, Kahramanmaraş, Osmaniye-TR63	34	20	8	13	16	20
Aydın, Denizli, Muğla-TR32	34	22	12	4	17	26
Antalya, Isparta, Burdur-TR61	27	15	9	3	18	30
Adana, Mersin-TR62	26	16	10	6	22	28
Gaziantep, Adıyaman, Kilis-TRC1	23	13	8	11	16	31
Kocaeli, Sakarya, Düzce, Bolu, Yalova-TR42	22	12	3	4	19	29
Mardin, Batman, Şırnak, Siirt-TRC3	19	13	11	19	17	25
Tekirdağ, Edirne, Kırklareli-TR21	17	16	7	3	20	26
Bursa, Eskişehir, Bilecik-TR41	14	10	5	3	21	31
İzmir-TR31	11	7	4	3	19	39
Ankara-TR51	4	4	2	1	20	47
İstanbul-TR10	1	1	0	2	21	40

(Left margin labels, top to bottom: Agrarian cities; Semi-agrarian cities; Non-agrarian cities)

Source: Calculated from the database provided by the Turkish Statistical Institute (TURKSTAT 2020c)

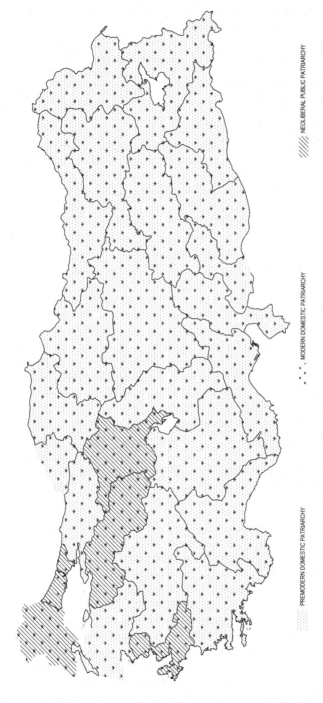

PREMODERN DOMESTIC PATRIARCHY

MODERN DOMESTIC PATRIARCHY

NEOLIBERAL PUBLIC PATRIARCHY

Figure 6.1 Uneven and combined development of patriarchy in Turkey (2018)

Graphic design: Evren Kocabıçak

clear gender-based division of labour which supports male peasants in establishing strong control over women's unpaid family labour (Karkiner 2009;
Hoşgör-Gündüz and Smits 2007; Onaran-İncirlioğlu 1999; Morvaridi 1992;
GDSW 2000; Ecevit 1993). By excluding women from technical skills and
possession of mechanical technologies, male peasants utilise the mechanisation of agriculture to sustain the gendered division of labour (Karkiner 2009;
Hoşgör-Gündüz and Smits 2007; Morvaridi 1992), as well as drawing on the
cultural and religious conditions, landowning male peasants utilise violence
to force women to work for longer hours under arduous conditions. Rural
women also have more pregnancies, miscarriages and stillbirths in comparison to urban women (Özdemir, Çevik, and Çiçeklioğlu 2019). Living under
such conditions of patriarchal labour exploitation, getting married to a male
wageworker or income earner appears to be the only way for rural women
to migrate to semi-agrarian or non-agrarian cities and leave the heavy workload behind. Therefore, it is unsurprising that rural women usually perceive
modern domestic patriarchy as an elite form of womanhood which does not
require long hours of work on the land. The deeply exploitative conditions of
premodern domestic patriarchy sustain the perception of 'lady of her household' amongst female peasants.

Meanwhile, those 'ladies', the full-time homemakers, whose labour
is entirely confined to household production, experience gender-based
exclusionary strategies under modern domestic patriarchy. In agrarian,
semi-agrarian and also non-agrarian cities, those women represent the
largest group within female population. As argued previously, the majority of urban women cannot access market-led childcare provision. The
absence of care provision for elderly and disabled members of society also
confines those women's labour to the home. In fact, Turkey's family-based
care system for elderly and disabled members of society could not survive
without these women undertaking unpaid family labour. As well as being
at risk of poverty, the exploitative nature of their unpaid work damages
both psychological and physical health (Şafak et al. 2016; Topuzoğlu et al.
2015). Nevertheless, full-time homemakers insist on an alternative future for
themselves as well as fighting for their daughters' access to advanced education and paid employment. For them, the double burden of paid and unpaid
labour is a price that needs to be paid for women's empowerment and relative independence. Their exclusion from paid employment allows these
women to become involved in caring for their grandchildren which leads to
a solidarity with younger women in the family (Can 2019). Grandmothers'
role in childcare implies that, in part, modern domestic patriarchy supplies
care labour required for childcare and thus supports mothers' labour force
participation in non-agrarian cities.

Simultaneously, female wageworkers living under the conditions of
neoliberal public patriarchy in non-agrarian cities deal relentlessly with
gender-based segregation and subordination within the labour market. As
discussed earlier, the experience of female wageworkers with basic and intermediate education is different to others with advanced education. The latter

group has relatively greater access to childcare provision and more bargaining capacity within the family. In contrast, the former group of female wageworkers is ghettoised in precarious and low paying jobs, which in turn, weakens their bargaining power within the heterosexual family. Moreover, state policies discriminate against female wageworkers with basic or intermediate education in terms of their access to the market-led provisioning of childcare, thereby leading to a weaker attachment to the labour market. Despite those differences, both groups of women work for nearly 80 hours per week (see Chapter 5), including paid and unpaid work, thus facing the deeply exploitative conditions of the double burden.

Drawing on my assessment, it appears that women's mobility and access to education and paid employment in agrarian and semi-agrarian cities is more limited than for women in non-agrarian cities; but, at the same time, women in non-agrarian cities who have a basic or intermediate education do not benefit from childcare provision and paid employment to the same extent as women with advanced education. Hence, although all women are involved in household production without any kind of payment, varieties of patriarchy differentiate the experiences of female peasants, fulltime homemakers and female wageworkers.

	Female peasants	*Full-time homemakers*	*Female wageworkers*
Primary location	Agrarian and semi-agrarian cities	Agrarian, semi-agrarian, and non-agrarian cities	Non-agrarian cities
Labour	Unpaid labour in rural household production, particularly farm work	Unpaid labour in urban household production, particularly care work	The double burden of paid and unpaid labour, including care work
Education	Basic level	Basic and intermediate levels	Intermediate and advanced levels
Public provisioning of care	No access	Very limited access	Relatively higher level of access
Mobility	Very limited	Very limited	Relatively higher
Control over sexuality including reproductive abilities	Very limited	Very limited	Limited
Gendered violence	No protection	Low level of protection	Low level of protection

Thus far, I have demonstrated that the uneven and combined development of the premodern and modern domestic and neoliberal public patriarchies diversifies women's experiences in agrarian, semi-agrarian and non-agrarian cities. While women living in different spaces are divided on the grounds of patriarchal domination and exploitation, it is important to note that women can travel between varieties of patriarchy and experience different forms in their lifetime. For example, upon marrying a male breadwinner, a female peasant may leave agriculture and migrate to work as a full-time home-maker. If her husband's limited income pushes her to join the labour market, then this rural migrant woman becomes a female wageworker. Again, depending on her working conditions and husband's income, a female wage-worker might choose to work as a fulltime homemaker. Therefore, there are not only divisions across space, but also changes over time, which mean variations in the experiences of different groups of women. Religious, ethnicity and class based differences amongst women also play an important role in dividing as well as uniting women in this context of patriarchy.

6.3 Alevi women and religion-based oppression

While Kurdish people are the largest ethnic minority in Turkey, the biggest religious minority consists of Alevi people. Alevis are comprised of Turkish and Kurdish people and constitute approximately 15% of total population (Shankland and Çetin 2005). Alevi people follow a fundamentally differ-ent practice (called Alevism) than the Sunni Muslim majority. While some describe Alevism as a religion in its own right, others suggest that it draws on a different interpretation of Islam.

Alevi female peasants' experience of landownership does not seem to be different to that of other women in Turkey. Legal discrimination against women in land inheritance (1926- 2015) sustained male dominance in land-ownership thereby upholding the premodern form of domestic patriarchy in rural areas where Alevi villages are based (e.g. Sivas, Dersim, Tokat, Çorum, Maraş, Bingöl, Erzincan, Amasya, Erzurum, and Malatya). Alevi men also utilise culture and religion to exclude women from inheriting agrarian land (Okan 2018). Nonetheless, Alevi villages have had a much higher rate of outward migration in comparison to Sunni Turkish villages (Shankland 1993; Salman 2019). Salman (2019) identifies two significant waves of rural to urban migration amongst rural Alevi population: (i) the post-1980s' migration wave which followed the 1978–1980 massacres (in Sivas, Maraş and Çorum) whereby hundreds of Alevi men and women were killed, and (ii) the post-2000s' migration following the 1993 Sivas (Madımak) massacre in which Alevis, artists and writers were killed in an Alevi festival. This latter massacre, Salman suggests, revealed the Sunni-Muslim character of the Turkish state and thereby broke Alevis' trust. These waves of forced migration have reduced the population of Alevi villages to a greater degree than Sunni villages, e.g. the total population of villages in the Sivas Yıldızeli province has declined by 72% (1965– 2010) (Salman 2019).

These migrations have, on the one hand, pulled Alevi women out of pre-modern domestic patriarchy and, on the other, reinforced the conditions of neoliberal public patriarchy. Alevi women who remain in the villages continue to be subject to the patriarchal property and labour relations in agriculture. However, considering that non-agrarian cities (İstanbul and Ankara in particular) are the major receivers of Alevi immigrants, Alevi women are increasingly subjected to the neoliberal form of public patriarchy.

Furthermore, Alevi women appear to successfully utilise religious discourses and practices in fighting against gendered seclusion in their communities (Akdemir 2020). In comparison to the Sunni Islam, the Alevi cultural and religious settings allow for women's greater access to the public sphere, including religious ceremonies, higher ranks in Alevi organisations, as well as education and paid employment (Güneş-Ayata 1992). As a result, despite gendered subordination in the public sphere, Alevi women are less likely to be confined to the domestic sphere. In addition, education has a particular importance for Alevi communities (Massicard 2007) and these families encourage their children, both boys and girls, to have an advanced education. Women's relatively high level of access to the public sphere, particularly education, leads to the predominance of neoliberal domestic patriarchy in this religious minority. Nevertheless, it should be noted that discrimination against Alevi wageworkers in the labour market counters this shift for Alevi women.

Forced migrations and the weakness of the gender-based exclusionary strategies in Alevi community have, therefore, initiated a shift from premodern and modern domestic towards neoliberal public patriarchy. Alevi women with advanced education are more likely to experience gender-based segregation and subordination under neoliberal public patriarchy but, at the same time, discrimination against Alevi wageworkers in hiring practices reinforces the modern form of domestic patriarchy especially for Alevi women with basic and intermediate education.

6.4 Kurdish women and ethnicity-based oppression

As Table 6.1 shows, the majority of Kurdish provinces are comprised of agrarian and semi-agrarian cities (e.g. Ağrı, Kars, Iğdır, Van, Erzurum, Erzincan, Elazığ, Muş, Bitlis, Hakkari, Urfa, Diyarbakır, Malatya, Bingöl, Dersim and Adıyaman). Premodern domestic patriarchy appears to be dominant in these provinces, indicated by large gender gaps in property ownership and access to education and paid employment, a lower age of marriage, higher fertility rates and cousin marriage. However, rejecting the perception that Kurdish culture is more patriarchal than others, I suggest that premodern domestic patriarchy needs to be examined to explain the dynamics of uneven gender relations in those regions.

Veli Yadırgı (2017) has investigated the ways in which state-led policies have maintained the socio-economic underdeveloped condition of the Kurdish-populated provinces. He claims that the Turkish state distributed land to recruit Kurdish elites to the regime, meaning that land is concentrated in the hands of a few Kurdish landlords. However, the evidence shows that the Kurdish-populated provinces share a similar pattern of small landownership and gendered unpaid family work in agriculture to the other regions of Turkey (TURKSTAT 2011). Thus, Kurdish women's role in agriculture does not seem to be different to that of other women.

Nevertheless, ethnicity-based oppression and discrimination plays a considerable role in differentiating Kurdish women's experience of uneven and combined development of patriarchy. State-led policies and strategies do appear to have prevented economic development of the Kurdish-populated provinces (Yadırgı 2017; Yoltar 2020). At the same time, the four decade of low intensity warfare that the Turkish Army waged against Kurdish dissidents and the Kurdistan Workers' Party (*Partîya Karkerên Kurdistanê*) also constitutes a barrier to the development of non-agricultural sectors and thus upholds the predominance of premodern domestic patriarchy.

The low-intensity conflict has also produced complexity in terms of Kurdish women's experiences of patriarchy. Forced migrations have introduced an unintentional shift towards modern domestic patriarchy by pulling many Kurdish women out of the conditions of premodern domestic patriarchy. Migration to non-agrarian cities in Turkey or abroad has increased Kurdish women's access to higher education and paid employment thereby, reinforcing the conditions of neoliberal (or social-democratic) public patriarchy. Furthermore, despite the high risk of death and imprisonment, engagement within the Kurdish movement either legally through the pro-Kurdish parties and civil society organisations or by joining the outlawed Kurdish guerrilla forces have provided an opportunity for women to leave the patriarchal family structure and engage with an active struggle against gendered oppression and inequality within their society and organisations. As a result, women's struggle within the Kurdish movement has given rise to a strong gender-equality consciousness within the movement and to Kurdish feminism (Kurdish Women Conference 2014; Kışanak 2018; Açık 2013; Çaha 2011; Düzgün 2016; Tank 2017).

A lack of education in the mother tongue also tends to limit Kurdish women's access to education and to public services to a greater extent than for Kurdish men, thereby maintaining the predominance of gender-based exclusionary strategies. The importance of the educational system for the assimilation of the Kurdish population into the dominant nation is widely discussed (Mojab 2001; 2000). However, evidence points to considerable gender gaps in the use of Turkish language. According to the 1998 survey, roughly 23% of Kurdish women (aged 15–49) do not speak Turkish, but only 2% of Kurdish men within the same age group cannot speak Turkish (Smits and Gündüz-Hoşgör 2003). In 2018, the Kurdish-populated provinces continue to have higher gender gaps in Turkish literacy in comparison to other provinces (TURKSTAT 2020c, b). In explaining such gender gaps, Shahrzad Mojab points to the nationalist perception of Kurdish women as "the guardians of Kurdish culture, heritage, and language" (2000: 89). However, as Jeroen Smits and Ayşe Gündüz-Hoşgör (2003) highlight, the ethnicity-based discrimination in language increases the dependency of

Kurdish women on their male family members with respect to legal rights and other issues. In the context of the gendered patterns of rural to urban migration, the lack of education in mother tongue further presents a barrier to Kurdish migrant women's access to paid employment, thereby sustaining modern domestic patriarchy.

In light of the evidence investigated thus far, I suggest that the ethnicity-based oppression diversifies Kurdish women's experience in complicated ways. The armed conflict alongside rural to urban migration pulls women out of premodern domestic patriarchy and provides a suitable context for women's empowerment thereby giving rise to Kurdish feminism. However, armed conflict and the state-led policies and regulations prevent industriali-sation leading to the predominance of patriarchal agriculture thereby block-ing the shift towards neoliberal public patriarchy in the Kurdish-populated provinces. In addition, the lack of education in mother tongue maintains the gender-based exclusionary strategies in education, paid employment and access to legal services, thereby strengthening the premodern and mod-ern forms of domestic patriarchy.

6.5 Class based oppression and exploitation

My assessment of the emergence of neoliberal public patriarchy and the hegemony of premodern and modern domestic patriarchies demonstrates that women's experiences are differentiated according to class. In other words, women with basic and intermediate education experience gendered oppression and inequality differently to women with advanced education. While the latter group of women has greater access to childcare provision and paid employment thereby experiencing the double burden of paid and unpaid labour, market-led childcare provision disadvantages the former group against their male counterparts in the labour market. Women with basic and intermediate education, therefore, fail to re-join the labour force following childbirth. Moreover, the Turkish state reliance upon the family-based (informal) care system for disabled and elderly members of society constitutes a significant barrier to women's access to paid employment in non-agricultural sectors. These gender-based exclusionary strategies, therefore, effectively confine relatively less educated women's labour to household production leading to the predominance of modern domestic patriarchy.

Furthermore, poorer women are less likely to benefit from the limited shift away from the gender-based exclusionary strategies in the civil soci-ety domain. Research shows that the lack of accessible childcare provi-sion prevents mothers with low levels of education from voting, registering to vote or taking part in social movements (Güvercin 2019). Considering that pronatalist policies have abolished accessible abortion services in the state-owned hospitals, working class women's control over their reproductive abilities is more restricted than that of other women who can afford private hospitals. Moreover, women with lower levels of education are exposed to domestic violence to a greater extent than other women (Dildar 2020).

To summarise, ethnicity and religion based oppression diversifies the experiences of Kurdish and Alevi women but, at the same time, converges their experience with women from the dominant ethnicity and religion. This means that the division of women on the grounds of patriarchal powers of labour exploitation crosscuts ethnicity and religious differences thereby dividing Alevi and Kurdish women. Meanwhile, class-based oppression and exploitation change women's experiences of patriarchy, including Alevi and Kurdish women. Sunni or Alevi, as well as Turkish or Kurdish women who can access advanced education are more likely to experience neoliberal public patriarchy, whereas, others live under conditions of premodern and modern domestic patriarchy.

6.6 Conclusion

The transition from domestic forms of patriarchy towards the public forms does not follow a linear path. Geopolitical analysis of a patriarchal transformation suggests that women in agrarian and semi-agrarian cities live under the predominance of premodern and modern domestic patriarchies, whereas, neoliberal public patriarchy occurs along with modern domestic patriarchy in non-agrarian cities. Patriarchal transformation in Turkey thus consists of the uneven and combined development of premodern and modern domestic as well as neoliberal public patriarchies.

While those spatial dimensions impact women's experiences, religion and ethnicity based oppression and discrimination also play a significant role in *dividing* as well as *uniting* women on the grounds of patriarchal domination. For example, premodern domestic patriarchy has remained significant not only for women from the dominant religion and ethnicity, but also for Alevi and Kurdish women. At the same time, the dispossession and forced migrations of Alevi and Kurdish rural populations have pulled these women out of premodern domestic patriarchy. Despite discrimination against this religious minority in hiring processes, Alevi women's relatively higher level of access to the public sphere, particularly education, has supported their engagement with paid employment, thereby initiating a shift towards neoliberal public patriarchy. The lack of education in mother tongue has, however, prevented Kurdish migrant women from joining the labour force and, as such, reinforced modern domestic patriarchy following their detachment from premodern domestic patriarchy. The racist agenda of the Turkish state and the low-intensity conflict have exacerbated underdevelopment in the Kurdish-populated provinces and thereby strengthened premodern domestic patriarchy. However, at the same time, such conflict has had complex implications for Kurdish women's experience of patriarchy. As well as initiating forced migrations out of villages thereby weakening premodern patriarchy, the unjust character of this conflict has reinforced women's choice to leave behind the patriarchal family structure and establish independent organisations leading to increased questioning of gender inequality and to Kurdish feminism. In summary, religion and ethnicity based regimes of oppression diversify women's experiences but, at the same time, patriarchal labour exploitation divides Alevi and Kurdish women thereby meaning their experiences converge towards those of Turkish and Muslim majority women.

Class-based oppression and exploitation, however, appear to drastically transform women's experiences of patriarchal transformation. Women with advanced education are more likely to live under the conditions of neoliberal public patriarchy and benefit from better access to childcare provision, paid employment, education, political representation, and changes within the cultural settings. In contrast, the Turkish state keeps women with basic and intermediate education under the hegemony of premodern and modern domestic patriarchies. The commodification-based childcare provision constitutes a barrier to their access to paid employment following childbirth, and this situation is compounded by the state's use of working-class women's unpaid labour to uphold a family-based care system for elderly and disabled members of society. For these women, limited access to education and paid employment is further associated with restricted access to political representation and abortion. Meanwhile, the family centred approach embedded in state intervention regarding gendered violence significantly risks those women's lives. Class, therefore, influences women's experiences of patriarchy and, as such, crosscuts religious and ethnicity based differences.

Next I investigate the extent to which the uneven and combined development of patriarchy in Turkey has shaped capital accumulation, proletarianisation, and cultural settings as well as creating an enduring bond between the Turkish bourgeoisie and authoritarian state regimes.

Reference

Akdemir, Ayşegül. 2020. "The Construction of Gender Identity in Alevi Organisations: Discourses, Practices, and Gaps." *Ethnography* May doi: 10.1177/1466138120924435

Açık, Necla. 2013. "Re-defining the role of women within the kurdish national movement in Turkey in the 1990s." In *The Kurdish Question in Turkey: New Perspectives on Conflict, Representation and Reconciliation*, edited by W. Zeydanlıoglu and C. Güneş. London: Routledge.

Can, Başak. 2019. "Caring for Solidarity? The Intimate Politics of Grandmother Childcare and Neoliberal Conservatism in Urban Turkey." *New Perspectives on Turkey* 60 (1):85–107. doi: 10.1017/npt.2019.4.

Çaha, Ömer. 2011. "The Kurdish Women's Movement: A Third-Wave Feminism Within the Turkish Context." *Turkish Studies* 12 (3):435–449. doi: 10.1080/14683849.2011.604211.

Dildar, Yasemin. 2020. "Is Economic Empowerment a Protective Factor Against Intimate Partner Violence? Evidence from Turkey." *The European Journal of Development Research* 33: 1695–1728. doi: 10.1057/s41287-020-00311-x.

Düzgün, Meral. 2016. "Jineology: The Kurdish Women's Movement." *Journal of Middle East Women's Studies* 12 (2):284–287.

Ecevit, Mehmet. 1993. "Rural Women and the Small Peasant Economy." *Turkish Public Administration Annual* 17–19:87–99.

GDSW. 2000. Kırsal Alan Kadınının İstihdama Katkısı. Ankara: Head Quarter of Women's Problems and Status, Turkish Republic Prime Ministry.

Güneş-Ayata, Ayşe. 1992. "The Turkish Alevis." *Innovation: The European Journal of Social Science Research* 5 (3):109–114. doi: 10.1080/13511610.1992.9968312.

Güvercin, Deniz. 2019. "Going to the Polls or Feeding Children? An Empirical Investigation of Voter Turnout Among Turkish Women With Children at Home." *Boğaziçi Journal* 33 (1):1–16.

Hoşgör-Gündüz, Ayşe, and Jeroen Smits. 2007. "The status of rural women in Turkey: What is the role of regional differences?" In *From patriarchy to empowerment women's participation, movements, and rights in the Middle East, North Africa, and South Asia*, edited by V. M. Moghadam. Syracuse, New York: Syracuse University Press.

Karkiner, Nadide. 2009. *Feminist Analysis of Rural Woman in a Village of Turkey: Feminist Theory, Method, Research, London, New York*: LAP Lambert Academic Publishing.

Kışanak, Gültan. 2018. *Kürt Siyasetinin Mor Rengi*. Ankara: Dipnot Yayınları.

Kurdish Women Conference. 2014. "The Jineoloji Conference." accessed 6 July.

Massicard, Elise. 2007. *Türkiye'den Avrupa'ya Alevi Hareketinin Siyasallaşması*. İstanbul: İletişim yayınları.

Mojab, Shahrzad. 2000. "Vengeance and Violence: Kurdish Women Recount the War." *Canadian Woman Studies* 19 (4).

Mojab, Shahrzad. 2001. *Women of a Non-state Nation: the Kurds*. Costa Mesa, California: Mazda Publishers.

Morvaridi, Behrooz. 1992. "Gender Relations in Agriculture: Women in Turkey." *Economic Development and Cultural Change* 40 (3):567–586.

Okan, Nimet. 2018. "Thoughts on the Rhetoric That Women and Men are Equal in Alevi Belief and Practice." *National Identities* 20 (1):69–89. doi: 10.1080/14608944.2016.1244936.

Onaran-İncirlioğlu, Emine. 1999. "Images of village women in Turkey: Models and anomalies." In *Deconstructing Images of 'the Turkish Women'*, edited by Z. Arat. New York: Palgrave Macmillan US.

Özdemir, Raziye, Celalettin Çevik, and Meltem Çiçeklioğlu. 2019. "Unmet Needs for Family Planning Among Married Women Aged 15–49 Years Living in Two Settlements With Different Socioeconomic and Cultural Characteristics: A Cross-Sectional Study From Karabuk Province in Turkey." *Rural and Remote Health* 19 (3). doi: 10.22605/RRH5125.

Şafak, Elif Deniz, Şemsinur Göçer, Salime Mucuk, Ahmet Öztürk, Sibel Akın, Sibel Arguvanlı, and Mümtaz M. Mazıcığlu. 2016. "The Prevalence and Related Factors of Restless Leg Syndrome in the Community Dwelling Elderly in Kayseri, Turkey: A Cross-Sectional Study." *Archives of Gerontology and Geriatrics* 65: 29–35. doi: 10.1016/j.archger.2016.02.012.

Salman, Cemal. 2019. *Lamekandan Cihana Göç Kimlik Alevilik*. Ankara: Dipnot Yayınları.

Shankland, David, and Atilla Çetin. 2005. "Culturalism and social mobility, or an Alevi village in Germany: Initial considerations." In *Alevis and Alevism: Transformed Identities*, edited by H. I. Markussen. New York: Isis Press

Shankland, David. 1993. "Alevi and sunni in rural Anatolia: Diverse paths of change." In *Culture and Economy: Changes in Turkish Villages*, edited by P. Stirling. London: Eothen Press.

Smits, Jeroen, and Ayşe Gündüz-Hoşgör. 2003. "Linguistic Capital: Language as a Socio-Economic Resource Among Kurdish and Arabic Women in Turkey." *Ethnic and Racial Studies* 26 (5):829–853. doi: 10.1080/0141987032000109050.

Tank, Pınar. 2017. "Kurdish Women in Rojava: From Resistance to Reconstruction." *Die Welt des Islams* 57 (3–4):404–428. doi: 10.1163/15700607-05734p07

The Official Paper. 2005. The Law of City Council 5393. In *25874*. Ankara.

Topuzoğlu, Ahmet, Tolga Binbay, Halis Ulaş, Hayriye Elbi, Feride Aksu Tanık, Nesli Zağlı, and Köksal Alptekin. 2015. "The Epidemiology of Major Depressive Disorder and Subthreshold Depression in Izmir, Turkey: Prevalence, Socioeconomic Differences, Impairment and Help-Seeking." *Journal of Affective Disorders* 181:78–86. doi: 10.1016/j.jad.2015.04.017.

TURKSTAT. 2011. Summary of Agricultural Statistics. Turkish Statistical Institute.

TURKSTAT. 2020a. Address Based Population Registration System (ABPRS). edited by Turkish Statistical Institute.

TURKSTAT. 2020b. National Education Survey. Edited by The Turkish Statistical Institute.

TURKSTAT. 2020c. Regional Dataset. Edited by Turkish Statistical Institute.

WDI. 2020. World Development Indicators. Edited by The World Bank.

Yadırgı, Veli. 2017. *The Political Economy of the Kurds of Turkey: From the Ottoman Empire to the Turkish Republic*. Cambridge, New York, Melbourne, Delhi: Cambridge University Press.

Yoltar, Çağrı. 2020. "Making the Indebted Citizen: An Inquiry into State Benevolence in Turkey." *Political and Legal Anthropology Review* 43 (1):153–171. doi: 10.1111/plar.12347.

7 THE TURKISH TRAJECTORY OF SOCIAL CHANGE
A COMPARATIVE PERSPECTIVE

This chapter presents an alternative framework to those theories previously discussed (in Chapter 1) which tend to reduce the dynamics of social change to the capitalist system or portray the Islamic cultural and religious settings as inherently hostile to gender equality. Instead, it is proposed that varieties of patriarchy are, in fact, instrumental in shaping socio-economic transformation. Under the conditions in which women's exclusion from landownership is associated with the predominance of small landownership, the dynamics of social change are strongly linked to rural forms of patriarchy. Drawing on the case of Turkey, and using comparative analysis, I examine the way in which the premodern form of domestic patriarchy has effectively shaped proletarianisation, urban wage levels, labour supply, capital accumulation strategies and state formation as well as giving rise to gendered patterns of culture and religion.

The chapter starts with a brief introduction concerning my comparative methodology (Section 7.1) and continues with an analysis of the ways in which premodern domestic patriarchy establishes significant gender gaps within the proletarianisation process by limiting women's mobility, access to education and paid employment, thereby preventing the movement of female labour from agricultural to non-agricultural sectors (Section 7.2). I then focus on the implications for capitalist transformation, including the impact upon urban wage levels, labour supply, and industrial capacity and quality. This discussion is followed by a detailed assessment of manufacturers' response to the conditions imposed by premodern domestic patriarchy (Section 7.3). In contrast to essentialist approaches that portray Islamic cultural and religious conditions as inherently hostile to gender equality, I also investigate how far the hegemony of premodern and modern domestic patriarchies in Turkey maintain the gender-based exclusionary character of cultural and religious settings (Section 7.4).

7.1 Brief note on the methodology

I use comparative analysis to investigate the ways in which premodern domestic patriarchy diversifies socio-economic transformation. The analysis considers two main variables: the level of economic development and

DOI: 10.4324/9781003054511-10

gender gaps in agricultural production. I identify the ways the Turkish trajectory of social change is different to that observed in countries which share a similar level of economic development but have differently gendered patterns of agriculture. I further compare Turkey with countries which have a similar gendered pattern of agriculture to examine the extent to which this pattern brings about convergence in the trajectories of less developed countries. In this way, the comparison of Turkey with the selected countries allows the implications of patriarchal property and labour relations in agriculture to be differentiated. Countries were selected on the basis of the following criteria:

i *The level of economic development:* I identify countries having a similar level of economic development to Turkey by calculating manufacturing, value added (% of Gross Domestic Product- GDP); energy use (kg of oil equivalent per capita); GDP per capita (constant 2010 US$) and Gross National Income (GNI) per capita (constant 2010 US$). Countries missing historical data (1960s-current) are removed from the analysis. Considering the significance of oil revenues in shaping trajectories of social change (Karshenas and Moghadam 2001) and thereby skewing the analysis, I also exclude oil rich countries from my selection.

ii *Gender gaps in agricultural production:* Cheryl Doss et al. (2015) make an important methodological contribution by arguing that the dominance of small landownership results in differently gendered outcomes to those associated with large-scale capitalist farms hiring wage labour. Engaging with their argument, I examine agricultural holdings by size (% of total) rather than using land distribution amongst landowners. The latter measures class-based inequalities, whereas the former sheds light on gender-based inequalities. Employment in agriculture and contributing family workers are examined to assess the labour supply of unpaid family workers in the households of landowning farmers.

Group A

Countries sharing a similar level of economic development to Turkey but characterised by large-scale capitalist farms and paid labour in agriculture	Argentina, Brazil, Chile, Malaysia and South Africa

Group B

Less developed countries characterised by the dominance of small landownership and women's unpaid family labour in agriculture	Bangladesh, Egypt, India, Morocco and Pakistan

---

The period considered (1960s- current) encompasses increased agrarian commercialisation and thus enables investigation of the interaction between the patriarchal and capitalist systems of exploitation. I draw on statistics from the publicly available databases of the World Bank, the IMF, the United Nations, the ILO, and the Turkish statistics office. I further draw on evidence provided by the FAO's World Census of Agriculture and datasets and reports provided by the Ministry of Agriculture.

7.2   Implications for the gendered patterns of proletarianisation

This section provides a detailed analysis of the ways in which premodern domestic patriarchy prevents the movement of female labour from agriculture to non-agricultural sectors thereby establishing significant gender gaps within the proletarianisation process. I use the concept of proletarianisation refer to labourers' dispossession of the means of production and the shift away from non-waged forms of labour towards waged/salaried labour under conditions of increasing wage dependency. My analysis begins by examining how far the gendered patterns of land dispossession give rise to patriarchal exploitation of labour in small-medium scale farms and continues by looking at the ways patriarchal exploitation in agriculture excludes rural women from paid employment in non-agricultural sectors.

7.2.1   Gendered dispossession and labour exploitation

In Chapter 4, I analysed the dynamics of a centuries-long gendered dispossession of land, demonstrating that the 1926 civil code discriminated against women in inheritance of agrarian land and establishing that this legal dispossession continued with the 2001 civil code until the recent (2015) regulation introducing a points based system. Research based on qualitative methods shows that women's exclusion from landownership leads to a strong gender-based division of labour in agriculture, thereby sustaining the patriarchal exploitation of women's labour. While men handle commercial and bureaucratic tasks, women are responsible for the heaviest and most labour-intensive and repetitive tasks (Karkiner 2009; Hoşgör-Gündüz and Smits 2007; Onaran-İncirlioğlu 1999; Morvaridi 1992, 1993; GDSW 2000; Ecevit 1993). At the same time, male peasants control the agrarian surplus as well as spending more time and money on leisure, eating more and having more nutritious food than women (Kandiyoti 1990). Agrarian technologies or changes in cultivated goods do not appear to challenge the landowning male peasants' position as appropriators nor the female peasants' position as direct producers (Karkiner 2009; Hoşgör-Gündüz and Smits 2007; Morvaridi 1992) but instead seem to intensify the gender-based division of labour in agriculture (Hoşgör-Gündüz 2014).

Evidence provided in Table 7.1 and 7.2 supports the qualitative findings that a pattern of small landownership along with women's exclusion from landownership leads to large gender gaps in unpaid family work. Table 7.1 shows that the percentage of large-scale farms (larger than 20 hectares) in total agricultural holdings in Turkey and Group B countries is much smaller than in Group A countries. Moreover, historical evidence demonstrates that the proportion of large-scale farms in Turkey, India and Pakistan has

Table 7.1 Agrarian structure, Group A and B countries and Turkey

Agricultural Holdings, by size (% of total, hectares)

		Year of survey	Very small scale farms (0,1–5)	Small and middle scale farms (5–20)	Large scale farms (larger than 20)	
Group A countries	Argentina	1988	15	20	66	100
	Brazil	1996	37	27	35	100
	Chile	1997	43	31	25	100
	Malaysia	2009	85% of total agrarian land is cultivated by large scale agricultural holdings (larger than 40 hectares).			
	South Africa	1988	2	5	93	100
	Turkey	2001	65	29	6	100
Group B countries	Bangladesh	2008	87% of agricultural holdings are smaller than 6 hectares			
	Egypt	1999–2000	99	1	0	100
	India	2001	95	4	0	100
	Morocco	1996	71	25	4	100
	Pakistan	2000	86	13	2	100

Agricultural Holdings, by size, over time (% of total, hectares)

	Year of survey	Very small scale farms (0,1–5)	Small and Middle scale farms (5–20)	Large scale farms (larger than 20)	
India	1971	89	11	1	100
	2001	95	4	0	100
Pakistan	1971–1973	68	29	3	100
	2000	86	13	2	100
Turkey	1980	62	32	6	100
	2001	65	29	6	100

Turkey, Agricultural Holdings, by size, over time (% of total, hectares)

	Year of survey	Very small scale farms (0.1–4.9)	Small and Middle scale farms (5–19.9)	Large scale farms (larger than 20)	
	1950	62	32	6	100
	1963	69	28	4	100
	2001	65	29	6	100
	2006	64	29	6	99

Note: In 2006, 1% of agricultural holdings do not own land in Turkey

Source: Calculated from the existing databases and reports provided by the Food and Agricultural Organisation and the Turkish Statistical Institute (FAO 2013, 2001; TURKSTAT 2011a, b)

remained stable over time. As Table 7.2 demonstrates, women's exclusion from landownership in conjunction with the predominance of small land-ownership leads to gender inequality in unpaid family work in Turkey and Group B countries, whereas the dominance of large-scale farms does not have the same gendered outcomes in Group A, countries.

Table 7.2 Gender gaps within unpaid family work, Group A and B countries and Turkey

| | | Group A countries | | | | | | Group B countries | | | |
		Argent.	Brazil	Chile	Malay.	S.Africa	Turkey	Bangla.	Egypt	India	Morocco	Pakistan
Contributing family workers, by sex (% of female and male employment) (modelled ILO estimate)												
1990-94	Female	2	13	5	13	2	60	59	33	35	33	62
	Male	1	6	3	3	1	20	11	9	14	18	18
1995-99	Female	2	8	4	13	1	57	58	27	34	54	61
	Male	1	4	2	3	1	16	10	9	14	18	16
2000-04	Female	2	9	4	10	1	45	62	24	41	54	49
	Male	1	5	1	2	1	8	9	8	14	24	17
2005-09	Female	1	8	3	8	1	36	59	33	37	53	61
	Male	1	4	1	3	0	5	8	9	12	18	18
2010-14	Female	1	5	5	8	1	33	45	32	31	48	60
	Male	1	2	3	2	0	5	6	6	10	13	15
2015-19	Female	1	4	4	8	1	26	34	27	48	48	55
	Male	0	1	3	2	0	4	4	5	8	13	15
Employment in agriculture, by sex (% of female and male employment) (modelled ILO estimate)												
1990-94	Female	0	24	6	20	18	72	89	46	76	35	69
	Male	1	30	23	24	17	33	63	32	58	42	45
1995-99	Female	0	20	5	15	18	68	82	33	75	48	68
	Male	1	27	20	21	17	31	61	31	56	41	43
2000-04	Female	1	16	5	12	10	58	69	37	73	57	69
	Male	1	24	18	17	13	25	53	28	53	40	41
2005-09	Female	0	14	6	10	6	42	68	46	69	61	72
	Male	2	22	16	17	8	17	42	28	48	36	37
2010-14	Female	0	8	5	8	4	37	60	42	62	59	74
	Male	1	17	13	16	6	17	42	25	44	32	34
2015-19	Female	0	4	5	7	4	29	61	39	58	59	73
	Male	0	14	13	14	7	15	33	22	41	32	33

Source: Calculated from the database provided by the World Bank (WDI 2020)

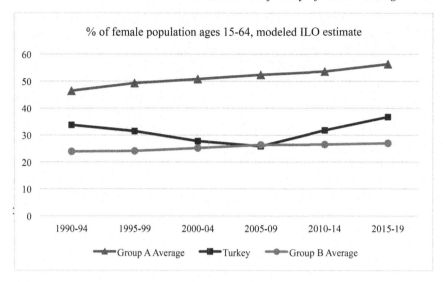

Figure 7.1 Female labour force participation rate, Group A and B countries and Turkey

Source: Calculated from the database provided by the World Bank (WDI 2020)

Moreover, evidence illustrated in Figure 7.1 suggests that the female labour force participation rate is much lower in Turkey than in Group A countries and instead tends to reflect that found in Group B countries (1995–2019). Thus, it is important to investigate whether the premodern form of domestic patriarchy prevents the movement of female labour from agriculture to non-agricultural sectors.

7.2.2 Rural women's exclusion from proletarianisation

Premodern domestic patriarchy appears to inhibit female paid employment in four major ways: First, women in their position as mothers, sisters, wives and daughters are kept in agriculture and continue to work as unpaid family workers. In contrast, younger men, who are disadvantaged in relation to their elder brother(s) concerning land inheritance, are encouraged to gain an education, migrate to urban areas, and join paid employment. However, the only way for women to migrate to urban areas is marriage (Öztürk et al. 2017; Kentel, Emre-Öğün, and Öztürk 2017; Erman 2001; Suzuki-Him and Hoşgör-Gündüz 2019). Husbands of immigrant brides are often single male breadwinners providing regular income either as wageworkers or through self-employment (Erman 1998). The patriarchal property and labour relations in agriculture, therefore, give rise to gendered patterns of rural to urban migration and, as such is a significant barrier to the movement of female labour from agriculture to non-agricultural sectors.

Second, girls' access to education in rural areas is more restricted than that of boys (Dayıoğlu 2005) meaning that immigrant brides who migrate to urban areas are disadvantaged in finding paid employment since they are less able to compete with their more educated male counterparts. Even when husbands' limited incomes push women to join the labour market, rural migrant women are unlikely to find employment other than domestic or home-based work (Erman 1998). Less educated migrant women can only access informal unskilled jobs which, in turn, destabilises any involvement in paid employment. Nadide Karkıner (2009) also suggests that rural women are aware that the likelihood of finding jobs in cities is very low so marriage is seen as the only way to migrate and leave behind the heavy workload. Immigrant brides' limited access to education is therefore a barrier to female paid employment in non-agricultural sectors.

Third, immigrant rural women continue to work as seasonal unpaid family workers on their fathers', brothers' or in-laws' farms (Erman 2001, 1998). They are not therefore completely free from patriarchal labour relations in agriculture which means any attachment to formal employment in non-agricultural sectors is precarious.

Last, considering that one third of rural migrants migrate within the same agrarian or semi-agrarian city (Kentel, Emre-Öğün, and Öztürk 2017), rural women's exclusion from the public sphere supports male merchants in excluding women from agrarian commerce (Hoşgör-Gündüz and Smits 2007). Such exclusion further contributes to the low level of female paid employment in those agrarian and semi-agrarian cities.

Drawing on patriarchal property and labour relations in agriculture, the premodern form of domestic patriarchy appears to play a considerable role in preventing female paid employment by limiting women's mobility and access to education and establishing gendered patterns of rural to urban migration. In order to assess this finding in greater depth, I draw on comparative analysis of gender gaps in education and paid employment. As Table 7.3 shows, Turkey has waited for several decades to catch up with Group A countries with respect to gender gaps in primary and secondary education, and continues to have large gender gaps in tertiary education. Gender gaps in education in Turkey thus appear to converge towards Group B countries despite these countries having a lower level of economic development.

Furthermore, Figure 7.2 points to a significant gap between Turkey and Group A countries regarding the proportion of women with lower and upper secondary levels of education; there is no such a gap with respect to men's educational attainment. This means that women's access to secondary education in Turkey is more limited than it is Group A countries. The evidence illustrated in Figure 7.2 supports the initial findings addressed in Chapter 5 that women with a relatively lower level of education are excluded from paid employment in non-agricultural sectors. As Mine Çınar (1994) suggests, the female labour force in Turkey is divided between two poles: women with tertiary level education and women with primary education. The former group occupies qualified jobs in non-agricultural sectors, whereas, the latter

Table 7.3 Gender gaps in education, Group A and B countries and Turkey

	Group A countries						Group B countries				
	Argentina	Brazil	Chile	Malaysia	S.Africa	Turkey	Bangladesh	Egypt	India	Morocco	Pakistan
School enrolment, primary (gross), gender parity index (GPI)											
1970-74	1.0	..	1.0	0.9	1.0	0.8	0.5	0.7	0.6	0.6	0.4
1975-79	1.0	..	1.0	1.0	..	0.8	0.6	0.7	0.7	0.6	0.5
1980-84	1.0	..	1.0	1.0	..	0.9	0.7	0.7	0.7	0.6	0.5
1985-89	1.0	..	1.0	1.0	1.0	0.9	0.7	0.8	0.7	0.6	0.5
1990-94	1.0	..	1.0	1.0	1.0	0.9	0.8	0.9	0.8	0.7	0.5
1995-99	1.0	1.0	1.0	1.0	1.0	0.9	..	0.9	0.8	0.8	..
2000-04	1.0	0.9	1.0	1.0	1.0	0.9	..	0.9	0.9	0.9	0.7
2005-09	1.0	0.9	1.0	1.0	1.0	1.0	1.1	1.0	1.0	0.9	0.8
2010-14	1.0	1.0	1.0	1.0	1.0	1.0	1.1	1.0	1.1	1.0	0.9
2015-19	1.0	1.0	1.0	1.0	1.0	1.0	1.1	1.0	1.1	1.0	0.9
School enrolment, secondary (gross), gender parity index (GPI)											
1970-74	1.1	..	1.1	0.7	..	0.4	0.3	0.5	0.4	0.4	0.3
1975-79	1.1	..	1.1	0.9	..	0.5	0.3	0.6	0.5	0.6	0.3
1980-84	1.1	..	1.1	1.0	..	0.5	0.3	0.6	0.5	0.7	0.4
1985-89	1.1	..	1.1	1.0	1.1	0.6	0.5	0.7	0.6	0.7	0.4
1990-94	..	..	1.0	1.1	1.2	0.6	0.5	0.8	0.6	0.7	0.5
1995-99	1.1	..	1.0	1.1	1.1	0.7	1.0	0.9	0.7	0.8	..
2000-04	1.1	1.1	1.0	..	1.1	0.7	1.1	0.9	0.8	0.8	..
2005-09	1.1	1.1	1.0	..	1.1	0.9	1.1	1.0	0.9	0.9	0.8
2010-14	1.1	1.1	1.0	1.1	1.1	0.9	1.1	1.0	1.0	0.9	0.8
2015-19	1.0	1.0	1.0	1.1	1.1	1.0	1.1	1.0	1.0	0.9	0.8

(Continued)

Table 7.3 Gender gaps in education, Group A and B countries and Turkey *(Continued)*

	Group A countries					Turkey	Group B countries				
	Argentina	*Brazil*	*Chile*	*Malaysia*	*S.Africa*	*Turkey*	*Bangladesh*	*Egypt*	*India*	*Morocco*	*Pakistan*
School enrolment, tertiary (gross), gender parity index (GPI)											
1970-74	0.8	..	0.6	..	..	0.2	0.1	0.4	0.3	0.2	0.3
1975-79	1.0	..	0.7	0.6	..	0.2	0.2	0.5	0.4	0.3	0.4
1980-84	1.1	..	0.8	0.8	..	0.4	0.2	0.5	0.4	..	0.4
1985-89	1.1	..	0.8	0.8	0.8	0.5	0.2	0.5	0.5	0.5	0.4
1990-94	..	..	0.9	..	0.8	0.5	0.2	0.6	0.5	0.6	0.3
1995-99	1.6	1.2	0.9	..	..	0.6	0.5	..	0.6	0.7	..
2000-04	1.5	1.3	0.9	..	..	0.7	0.5	0.8	0.7	0.8	0.8
2005-09	1.5	1.3	1.0	..	..	0.8	0.6	0.9	0.7	0.9	0.9
2010-14	1.6	1.3	1.1	1.4	1.4	0.8	0.7	0.9	0.9	0.9	1.0
2015-19	1.7	1.4	1.1	1.2	1.4	0.9	0.7	1.0	1.0	1.0	0.9

Notes: The Gender Parity Index (GPI) indicates the level of parity between girls and boys. A GPI of less than 1 suggests girls are more disadvantaged than boys in learning opportunities and a GPI of greater than 1 suggests the reverse.

Source: Calculated from the database provided by the World Bank (WDI 2020)

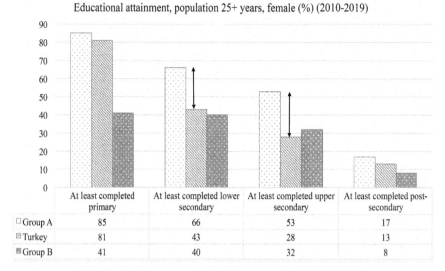

Educational attainment, population 25+ years, female (%) (2010-2019)

	At least completed primary	At least completed lower secondary	At least completed upper secondary	At least completed post-secondary
Group A	85	66	53	17
Turkey	81	43	28	13
Group B	41	40	32	8

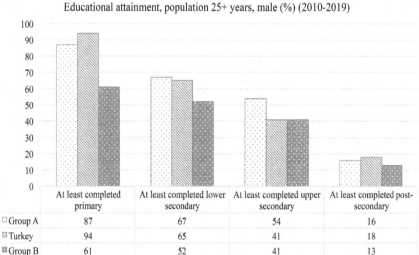

Educational attainment, population 25+ years, male (%) (2010-2019)

	At least completed primary	At least completed lower secondary	At least completed upper secondary	At least completed post-secondary
Group A	87	67	54	16
Turkey	94	65	41	18
Group B	61	52	41	13

Figure 7.2 Educational attainment, Group A and B countries and Turkey

Source: Calculated from the databases provided by the World Bank and the International Standard Classification of Education (WDI 2020; ISCED 2012)

group works as unpaid family workers in agriculture with restricted mobility and limited access to education and paid employment. Increases in the female labour force participation rate in Turkey are largely due to the former group of women gaining employment in non-agrarian cities.

Table 7.4 provides support to those findings that gendered property and labour relations in agriculture constitute a significant barrier to the

Table 7.4 Gender gaps in paid employment, Group A and B countries and Turkey

Share of women in waged employment in the non-agricultural sector (% of total non-agricultural employment)

	1980-84	1985-89	1990-94	1995-99	2000-04	2005-09	2010-14	2015-17
Argentina	..	..	..	..	..	..	41	42
Brazil	37	39	41	42	44	45	45	45
Chile	35	35	36	37	37	31	42	43
Malaysia	32	35	35	35	37	38	39	40
South Africa	..	..	..	..	43	44	44	44
Turkey	11	13	14	15	20	22	24	27
Bangladesh	19	25	18	23	21	15	22	20
Egypt	13	18	17	17	17	16	16	17
India	..	..	13	15	17	19	19	..
Morocco	..	..	21	..	23	21	21	..
Pakistan	..	6	8	8	8	10	10	11

Employment in agriculture, by sex (% of total female and male employment) (modelled ILO estimate)

		1957-65	1970-72	1980-82	1990-94	1995-99	2000-04	2005-09	2010-14	2015-17
Argentina	Fem.	5	4	3	0	0	1	0	0	0
	Male	22	19	15	1	1	1	2	1	1
Brazil	Fem.	30	20	14	24	20	16	14	8	5
	Male	57	51	36	30	27	24	22	17	14
Chile	Fem.	4	3	2	6	5	5	6	5	5
	Male	34	27	23	23	20	18	16	13	13
Malaysia	Fem.	76	55	39	20	15	12	10	8	7
	Male	52	44	31	24	21	17	17	16	14
S.Africa	Fem.	15	26	11	18	18	10	6	4	4
	Male	34	29	17	17	17	13	8	6	7
Turkey	Fem.	94	89	86	72	68	58	42	37	29
	Male	58	54	42	33	31	25	17	17	15
Bangla.	Fem.	92	70	59	89	82	69	68	60	62
	Male	85	77	59	63	61	53	42	42	33
Egypt	Fem.	44	..	..	46	33	37	46	42	39
	Male	58	..	..	32	31	28	28	25	22
India	Fem.	82	83	76	76	75	73	69	62	57
	Male	68	70	63	58	56	53	48	44	39
Morocco	Fem.	42	..	31	35	48	57	61	59	57
	Male	65	..	41	42	41	40	36	32	31
Pakistan	Fem.	71	..	..	69	68	69	72	74	73
	Male	59	53	52	45	43	41	37	34	33

Sources: Data is calculated from the existing databases and reports (WDI 2020; ILOSTAT 2020a). Data between the 1960s and the 1980s are calculated from the dataset provided by the ILO (1990).

movement of female labour from agriculture to non-agricultural sectors. As the table shows, historically, Group A countries have had a higher share of women in waged employment in the non-agricultural sectors than Turkey. Although, the majority of women's employment in Group A has shifted towards non-agricultural sectors *before or around the same time* as that of men's, in Turkey women's employment has remained concentrated in agriculture for *longer* than is the case for their male counterparts, i.e. men's employment in Turkey shifted almost 35 years before that of women. The table also shows that gender gaps in paid employment in Turkey tend to converge with the less developed Group B countries where there are large gender gaps in the shift from agricultural to non-agricultural employment.

In light of the evidence investigated thus far, I suggest that patriarchal control over women in agriculture leads to a reduction of female paid employment in the non-agricultural sectors. Women are confined to small-medium scale farms as unpaid family workers, they have limited mobility and reduced access to education. A woman can only migrate to urban areas as the wife of a male breadwinner, whereas men migrate for education and paid employment. This gendered pattern of rural to urban migration in Turkey is different to that found in other countries which share a similar level of economic development. The comparison of Turkey with Group A and B countries, further, signifies that Turkey did not follow the relatively more *gender equal* path of the middle-income countries (Argentina, Brazil, Chile, Malaysia, and South Africa) which share the same level of economic development to Turkey. Rather, the Turkish trajectory of social change appears to converge towards the more *gender unequal* path of the low-income countries (Bangladesh, Egypt, Morocco, India, and Pakistan) which have similarly gendered patterns of agriculture to Turkey. My analysis, therefore, suggests that premodern domestic patriarchy is instrumental in diversifying trajectories of social change. Under such conditions, it is important to identify the ways in which patriarchal property and labour relations in agriculture shape capitalist development.

7.3 Implications for capital accumulation strategies

Gendered patterns of proletarianisation in Turkey are thus different to those found in Group A countries which share the same level of economic development but have contrasting patterns of agriculture; here I examine the key features of capital accumulation strategies in Turkey relative to other countries. In order to eliminate the differences that might be due to different levels of development, my comparison does not include Group B countries which have a lower level of economic development.

7.3.1 Urban wage levels and labour supply constraint

There are two approaches analysing the relationship between the dominance of small landownership and urban wage levels in Turkey: the first one suggesting that small landownership led to semi-proletarianisation and that access to rural income subsidised the low level of urban wages (Gürel 2011; Köymen 2008); whereas the second proposes that small landownership and rural income put upward pressure on urban wage levels (Oyvat 2016; Keyder 1987). Figure 7.3 demonstrates that manufacturing wages in Turkey were higher than in Brazil, Chile, and Malaysia from the mid-1960s

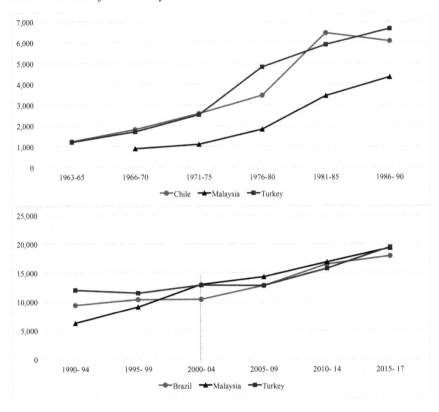

Figure 7.3 Real wages and salaries per employee in total manufacturing, Group A
countries and Turkey (international $)

Notes: (i) For the time period between 1963 and 1990, national currency is converted into the
US$using PPP over GDP (in national currency units per US$) and 1 US dollar (US$)
= 1 international dollar (I$). (ii) For the time period from 1990 onwards, national cur-
rency is converted into international $using PPP conversion factor, private consump-
tion (LCU per international $)

Source: Data is calculated from the databases provided by the UN, Penn World Table and the
World Bank (INDSTAT2 2019; WDI 2020; Heston, Summers and Aten 2012)

until the mid-2000s. Considering that Turkey has had a lower number of
strikes and lockouts in comparison to Group A countries (ILOSTAT 2020a),
class struggle does not seem to be the key factor placing upward pressure
on wages. Furthermore, Cem Oyvat (2016) finds that small landownership
prevents over-urbanisation. The evidence on the rate of net migration to the
largest cities supports Oyvat's original finding; it remains between 5 to 10 ‰
in Ankara, İstanbul, and İzmir) (TURKSTAT 2020).

I suggest that gendered patterns of property and labour relations play
a considerable role in increasing agricultural earnings, preventing over-
urbanisation, and thereby putting upward pressure on wage levels in the

Table 7.5 Labour force participation, Group A countries and Turkey

	Argentina	Brazil	Chile	Malaysia	S. Africa	Turkey
Labour force participation rate, total (% of total working age population)						
1952-55	..	..	36	..	..	51
1960	38	32	32	39	36	47
1970	39	32	28	33	37	43
1980	36	36	27	39	35	43
Labour force participation rate, total (% of total population ages 15+) (modeled ILO estimate)						
1990-94	60	63	55	62	54	55
1995-99	61	64	55	62	53	52
2000-04	62	66	55	61	53	48
2005-09	62	67	57	61	54	46
2010-14	60	65	62	62	53	49
2015-19	60	64	62	64	55	51

Sources: Data between the 1950s and the 1980s are calculated from the database provided by the International Labour Organisation (ILO 1990) and the rest from the World Bank (WDI 2020)

non-agricultural sectors. Established methods of calculating rural income, however, conceal the significance of women's unpaid family labour by measuring productivity rather than household income. Large scale capitalist farms are often more productive than the patriarchal family farms, which thus lead to higher levels of rural income per capita or agricultural value added per capita. In order to assess household earnings in agriculture, I examine the ownership of mechanical technologies, and find that since the mid-1970s, Turkey has had a higher number of tractors (in use) than Argentina, Chile, Malaysia and South Africa. Moreover, since the mid-1990s, Turkish agriculture has the most tractors of any of the Group A countries (WDI 2020). Despite the country's lower level of rural income per capita, small-medium scale farms in Turkey seem to achieve a certain level of accumulation which, in turn, indicates the significance of women's unpaid family labour for household earnings in agriculture.

Relatively high levels of rural household earnings and the absence of over-urbanisation appear to correlate with a certain level of labour supply constraint. Table 7.5 shows that the labour force participation rate has remained more or less at the same level in Turkey, whereas it has increased considerably in Group A countries during the shift from agricultural to non-agricultural employment. Turkey's lower labour force participation rate in comparison to Group A countries implies that the labour supply is constrained. Therefore, the labour shortage problem in Turkey does not appear to have been resolved after the 1950s as others seem to suggest (Düzgün 2019).

Drawing on my analysis, I argue that women's exclusion from landownership in conjunction with the dominance of small landownership appears to have (i) limited women's mobility, access to education, and paid employment,

(ii) constrained labour supply by supporting landowning male peasants to escape proletarianisation, and by developing significant gender gaps within the proletarianisation process and (iii) placed upward pressure on capitalist wages by increasing earnings in agriculture. This analysis therefore suggests that the trajectory witnessed in Turkey cannot be fully explained by the dynamics of capitalist transformation; rather, varieties of patriarchy, particularly premodern domestic patriarchy, need to be considered as the determinants of socio-economic transformation.

7.3.2 Strategies of Turkish manufacturers

Considering the implications of premodern domestic patriarchy for labour supply and manufacturing wages, I continue my assessment by examining the consequences for industrial capacity and quality. Engaging with the guidelines and methodology provided by the United Nations Industrial Development Organisation (UNIDO 2010), I differentiate *industrial capacity* from *industrial quality*. The former refers to the level of industrialisation relative to the size of the economy, whereas the latter measures the ability to produce relatively higher value-added goods (technologically advanced products). Industrial capacity is assessed by examining manufacturing value-added per capita and share of manufacturing value-added in GDP (% of total). I use the following indicators to analyse industrial quality: manufactured exports per capita index, share of medium and medium-high technology sectors in manufacturing value-added (% of total), and share of medium and medium-high technology sectors in total export (% of total).

Evidence illustrated in Figures 7.4 and 7.5 suggests that Turkey's industrial capacity and quality is at the same level as Argentina, Brazil, Chile, and South Africa. This means that Turkish manufacturers appear to have been successful in developing strategies to deal with the factors associated with gendered patterns of proletarianisation, labour supply constraint and higher urban wages.

Table 7.6 shows that the Turkish manufacturers have increased the average working hours per week to compensate for the relatively high level of manufacturing wages. While longer working hours in Malaysia correlate with the country's higher level of industrial capacity and quality (see Figures 7.4 and 7.5), Turkey's longer working hours in manufacturing appear to support the country in catching up with Argentina, Brazil, Chile and South Africa.

According to the evidence illustrated in Figure 7.6, capital investments in manufacturing have also played a significant role in increasing industrial capacity and quality. In comparison to Malaysia, Turkey has generally had a higher level of capital per employee in manufacturing despite its lower level of industrial capacity and quality.

Evidence that I have investigated thus far suggests that in response to the conditions associated with premodern domestic patriarchy, manufacturers

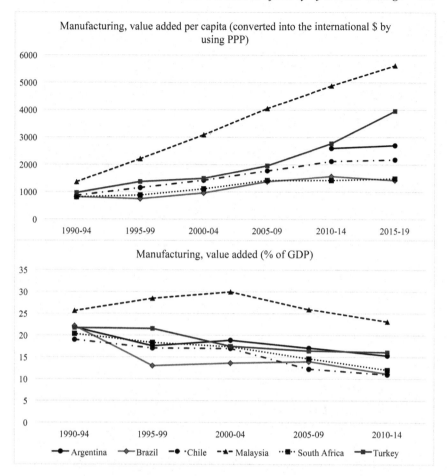

Figure 7.4 Industrial capacity, Group A countries and Turkey (1990–2019)

Notes: (1) Manufacturing comprises the industries between ISIC Rev. 3 divisions 15 and 37.
(2) Manufacturing, value added (in national currency) is converted into international
$using PPP conversion factor, private consumption (national currency unit per inter-
national $)

Source: Data is calculated from the databases provided by the UN and the World Bank
(INDSTAT2 2019; WDI 2020)

appear to have lengthened working hours and increased their capital investments. The former has lowered hourly wages, whereas the latter has
increased unemployment amongst wage workers. These strategies implemented by manufacturers would not be successful without a relatively high
level of state-led coercion in order to quell resistance from the working-class
movement and reduce the number of strikes and lockouts in the country
(ILOSTAT 2020a). Turkey has witnessed a number of army coups (1960
and 1980), successful and relatively less significant military memorandums

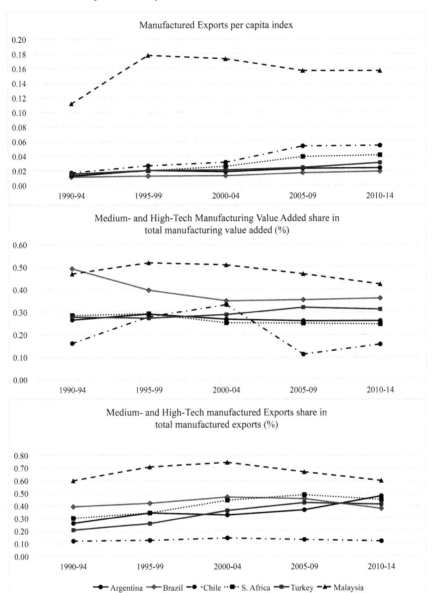

Figure 7.5 Industrial quality, Group A countries and Turkey (1990–2014)

Note: (1) Manufacturing comprises the industries between ISIC Rev. 3 divisions 15 and 37.
(2) Malaysia has higher levels of manufactured exports per capita in comparison to other countries.

Source: Calculated from the database provided by the World Bank (WDI 2020)

Table 7.6 Average working hours in manufacturing, Group A countries and Turkey

	Argentina	Brazil	Chile	Malaysia	S. Africa	Turkey
Mean weekly hours actually worked per employee in manufacturing						
1990-94	..	43	49	..	45	39
1995-99	..	43	48	..	46	43
2000-04	43	44	50	..	46	52
2005-09	43	44	46	49	45	53
2010-14	43	41	42	49	42	51
2015-19	41	40	41	49	42	48

Sources: Calculated from the database provided by the International Labour Organisation (ILOSTAT 2020b)

(1971, 1997 and 2007) and several failed army coup attempts (1962, 1969, 1971 and 2016). In his research, Düzgün (2012a, b) reveals the regressive role that the bourgeois class has played within the historical context of Turkey, but does not pay enough attention to the reasons thereby neglecting the role of varieties of patriarchy in shaping capital accumulation strategies. In light of my assessment, I propose that the significance of premodern domestic patriarchy to the enduring bond between anti-democratic state regimes and the Turkish bourgeois class needs to be considered.

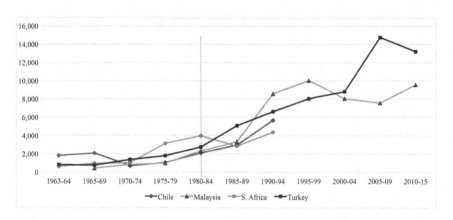

Figure 7.6 Capital per employee manufacturing, Group A countries and Turkey (1963–2015) (international $)

Notes: (i) For the time period between 1963 and 1989, national currency is converted into the US$ using PPP over GDP (in national currency units per US$) and 1 US dollar (US$) = 1 international dollar (I$). (ii) For the time period from 1990 onwards, national currency is converted into international $using PPP conversion factor, private consumption (LCU per international $)

Source: Data is calculated from the databases provided by the UN, Penn World Table and the World Bank (INDSTAT2 2019; WDI 2020; Heston, Summers, and Aten 2012)

To recapitulate, the premodern form of domestic patriarchy in Turkey shapes the proletarianisation process differently to other middle-income countries which share the same level of economic development but have differently gendered patterns of agriculture (Argentina, Brazil, Chile, Malaysia, and South Africa). This shaping of the proletarianisation process, in turn, constrains labour supply and puts upward pressure to capitalist wages. Under such conditions, Turkish manufacturers appear to increase average working hours and increasingly replace labourers with machinery. In doing so, Turkey's industrial capacity and quality catches up with that of other countries. These strategies adopted by the manufacturers, however, require greater state-led coercion to suppress working-class mobilisations. Premodern domestic patriarchy, therefore, constitutes an important factor in varying trajectories of capitalist development and state formation. It is this diversification that needs to be recognised and addressed in order to provide a robust assessment of socio-economic transformation in the global South.

7.4 Implications for culture and religion

By comparing the public perceptions and attitudes towards women's access to education, political representation and paid employment, I assess how far the cultural and religious conditions in Turkey converge towards the more *gender unequal* path found in the low-income countries (Bangladesh, Egypt, Morocco, India and Pakistan) which have similarly gendered patterns of agriculture to Turkey. My assessment, further, enables investigation of the extent to which the predominance of gender-based exclusionary strategies crosscuts different religious and cultural settings, thereby challenging the assumption that the Islamic culture and religion is essentially patriarchal.

Table 7.7 shows that Turkey has a lower level of public support for women's access to paid employment and political representation (Q1, Q2, Q3 and Q4) in comparison to Argentina, Brazil, Chile and South Africa, which share the same level of economic development to Turkey but have differently gendered patterns of agriculture. Instead, people's perceptions and attitudes towards female paid employment in Turkey appear to converge towards Group B countries despite their lower level of economic development.

Evidence illustrated in the table, further, suggests that the dominance of gender-based exclusionary strategies is not inherent to Islamic culture and religion, but instead crosscuts various religious settings. While the public perceptions and attitudes in Malaysia and South Africa are more patriarchal than the rest of Group A countries (see Q1, Q3, Q4, Q5 and Q6), India and Morocco seem to be differentiated from the rest of the Group B counties with their higher approval rates concerning women's access to paid employment and politics (see Q1, Q3 and Q5) and stronger objection to gendered violence (see Q6).

Table 7.7 Patriarchal perceptions and attitudes, Group A and B countries, Turkey (2010–2014)

Do you strongly Agree (A) or Agree (A) or strongly Disagree or Disagree (D) with the following statements?		Q1. If jobs are scarce, men should have more right to a job than women	Q2. Pre-school child suffers with working mother	Q3. Men make better business executives than women do	Q4. University is more important for a boy than for a girl	Q5. Men make better political leaders than women do	Q6. Percentage of women aged 15–49 years who consider a husband to be justified in hitting or beating his wife for at least one of the specified reasons, i.e. if his wife burns the food, argues with him, goes out without telling him, neglects the children or refuses sexual relations (3)
Argentina (2)	A	15	36	23	17	27	12
	D	67	59	73	79	67	
Brazil	A	17	60	29	9	28	9
	D	73	39	69	89	68	
Chile	A	18	36	18	20	27	10
	D	57	59	76	76	69	
Malaysia	A	57	21	58	43	70	42
	D	18	79	42	57	30	
South Africa	A	30	54	49	39	52	61
	D	47	44	48	59	45	
Turkey	A	59	66	64	32	68	13
	D	23	31	32	66	29	
Bangladesh (1)	A	76	88	67	43	62	28
	D	15	12	30	54	34	
Egypt	A	83	63	80	36	86	36
	D	11	38	20	64	14	
India	A	52	76	51	35	52	22
	D	23	17	35	56	37	
Morocco	A	61	63	54	20	57	22
	D	31	26	30	71	25	
Pakistan	A	75	70	73	51	72	42
	D	20	29	24	45	25	

Notes: (1) Data on Bangladesh is calculated from the 2017–2020 wave of World Values Survey, (2) Data on question 2 for Argentina is calculated from the 2017–2020 wave of World Values Survey, (3) Data represents the 2019 figures.

Sources: Q1 to Q5 are calculated from the database provided by the World Values Survey (WVS 2020), but Q6 is calculated from the databases provided by the OECD and the World Bank (WDI 2020; OECD.Stat 2020)

7.5 Conclusion

The patriarchal system of exploitation is as effective as the capitalist system in diversifying trajectories of social change. The premodern form of domestic patriarchy has played an important role in preventing the movement of female labour from agriculture to non-agricultural sectors, supporting landowning male peasants to escape proletarianisation, constraining labour supply, and putting upward pressure on capitalist wages by increasing earnings in agriculture. In response to these impediments, manufacturers seem to have developed alternative strategies to sustain industrial capacity and quality. One such strategy is imposing longer working hours, thereby decreasing hourly wages, and another is increasing capital investments leading to unemployment. Sustaining these strategies requires a certain degree of state-led coercion in order to suppress working-class resistance which thereby increases the bourgeoisie's dependence on the anti-democratic state regimes. Furthermore, irrespective of the dominant religion, patriarchal attitudes in Turkey appear to converge with less developed countries characterised by the dominance of small landownership and women's unpaid family labour in agriculture and, at the same time, similarly gender-based exclusionary norms and attitudes are found in countries with Islamic or Hindu religious backgrounds.

Thus far, I have provided an historical account of the premodern and modern forms of domestic patriarchy (in Chapter 4), examined the post-2000's emergence of neoliberal public patriarchy (in Chapter 5), and analysed the uneven and combined development of premodern and modern domestic and neoliberal public patriarchies (in Chapter 6). I have further investigated the ways in which premodern domestic patriarchy has differentiated Turkey's trajectory of social change from other developing countries (in Chapter 7). The next chapter presents an alternative theoretical framework based on a historical materialist methodology and ontology.

References

Çınar, Mine E. 1994. "Unskilled Urban Migrant Women and Disguised Employment: Home-Working Women in Istanbul, Turkey." *World Development* 22 (3):369–380.

Dayıoğlu, Meltem. 2005. "Patterns of Change in Child Labour and Schooling in Turkey: The Impact of Compulsory Schooling." *Oxford Development Studies* 33 (2):195–210. doi: 10.1080/13600810500137798.

Doss, Cheryl, Chiara Kovarik, Amber Peterman, Agnes Quisumbing, and Mara Van den Bold. 2015. "Gender Inequalities in Ownership and Control of Land in Africa: Myth and Reality." *Agricultural Economics* 46 (3):403–435.

Düzgün, Eren. 2012a. "Capitalist Modernity a la Turca: Turkey's 'Great Transformation' Reconsidered." *Critical Sociology* 39 (6):889–909. doi: 10.1177/0896920512451605

Düzgün, Eren. 2012b. "Class, State and Property: Modernity and Capitalism in Turkey." *European Journal of Sociology* 53 (2):119–148. doi:10.1017/S0003975612000070

Düzgün, Eren. 2019. "The political economy of the transition to capitalism in the Ottoman Empire and Turkey: Towards a new interpretation." In *Case studies in the origins of capitalism*, edited by X. Lafrance and C. Post. Palgrave Macmillan.

Ecevit, Mehmet. 1993. "Rural Women and the Small Peasant Economy." *Turkish Public Administration Annual* 17–19:87–99.

Erman, Tahire. 1998. "The Impact of Migration on Turkish Rural Women: Four Emergent Patterns." *Gender & Society* 12 (2):146–167. doi: 10.1177/0891 24398012002003.

Erman, Tahire. 2001. "Rural Migrants and Patriarchy in Turkish Cities." *International Journal of Urban & Regional Research* 25 (1):118–133.

FAO. 2001. Supplement to the Report on the 1990 world census of agriculture (1986–1995). In *FAO Statistical Development Series 9a*, edited by Food and Agriculture Organization of the United Nations. Rome.

FAO. 2013. World census of agriculture: Analysis and international comparison of the results 1996–2005. In *FAO Statistical Development Series 13*, edited by Food and Agriculture Organisation of the United Nations. Rome.

GDSW. 2000. Kırsal Alan Kadınının İstihdama Katkısı. Ankara: Head Quarter of Women's Problems and Status, Turkish Republic Prime Ministry.

Gürel, Burak. 2011. "Agrarian Change and Labour Supply in Turkey, 1950–1980." *Journal of Agrarian Change* 11 (2):195–219. doi: 10.1111/j.1471-0366.2010.00299.x

Heston, Alan, Robert Summers, and Bettina Aten. 2012. Penn World Table Version 7.1. Pennsylvania: Center for International Comparisons of Production, Income and Prices, the University of Pennsylvania.

Hoşgör-Gündüz, Ayşe. 2014. "Türkiye'de Kırsal Kadının Toplumsal Konumu: Bölgesel Eşitsizlikler, Yasal Müdahaleler ve Kısmi Kazanımlar." In *Türkiye'de Toplumsal Cinsiyet Çalışmaları: Eşitsizlikler Mücadeleler Kazanımlar*, edited by H. Durudoğan, F. Gökşen, B.E. Oder and D. Yükseker. İstanbul: Koç Üniversitesi Yayınları.

Hoşgör-Gündüz, Ayşe, and Jeroen Smits. 2007. "The status of rural women in Turkey: What is the role of regional differences?" In *From patriarchy to empowerment women's participation, movements, and rights in the Middle East, North Africa, and South Asia*, edited by Valentine M. Moghadam. Syracuse, New York: Syracuse University Press.

ILO. 1990. Yearbook of Labour Statistics: Retrospective Edition on Population Censuses 1945-1989. edited by International Labour Organisation. Geneva.

ILOSTAT. 2020a. Employment by sex and age –ILO modelled estimates. In *The ILOSTAT database*, edited by The International Labour Organisation.

ILOSTAT. 2020b. Statistics on working time. Edited by The International Labour Organisation. Geneva

INDSTAT2. 2019. INDSTAT2 Rev. 3 Industrial Statistics Database. Edited by The United Nations Industrial Development Organisation: UK Data Service.

ISCED. 2012. International Standard Classification of Education. Edited by UNESCO. Canada.

Kandiyoti, Deniz. 1990. "Rural transformation in Turkey ad its implications for women's status." In *Women, Family, and Social Change in Turkey*, edited by F. Özbay. Bangkok: UNESCO.

Karkiner, Nadide. 2009. *Feminist Analysis of Rural Woman in a Village of Turkey: Feminist Theory, Method, Research*. LAP Lambert Academic Publishing.

Karshenas, Massoud, and Valentine M. Moghadam. 2001. "Female labour force participation and economic adjustment in the Middle East North Africa region." *The Economics of Women and Work in the Middle East and North Africa (Research in Middle East Economics, Vol. 4)*, Emerald Group Publishing Limited, Bingley, 51–74. doi: 10.1016/S1094-5334(01)04006-7.

Kentel, Ferhat, Perrin Emre-Öğün, and Murat Öztürk. 2017. Kır Mekânının Sosyo-Ekonomik ve Kültürel Dönüşümü: Modernleşen ve Kaybolan Geleneksel Mekânlar ve Anlamlar. Ankara: TÜBİTAK.

Keyder, Çağlar. 1987. *State and Class in Turkey: a Study in Capitalist development*. London: Verso.

Köymen, Oya. 2008. *Kapitalizm ve Köylülük: Ağalar, Üretenler, Patronlar*. İstanbul: Yordam kitap.

Morvaridi, Behrooz. 1992. "Gender Relations in Agriculture: Women in Turkey." *Economic Development and Cultural Change* 40 (3):567–586.

Morvaridi, Behrooz. 1993. "Gender and household resource management in agriculture: Cash crops in Kars." In *Culture and Economy: Changes in Turkish Villages*, edited by P. Stirling. London: Eothen Press.

OECD.Stat. 2020. Gender database. edited by OECD.

Onaran-İncirlioğlu, Emine. 1999. "Images of village women in Turkey: Models and anomalies." In *Deconstructing Images of 'The Turkish Women'*, edited by Z. Arat. New York: Palgrave Macmillan US.

Oyvat, Cem. 2016. "Agrarian Structures, Urbanization, and Inequality." *World Development* 83 (C):207–230. doi: 10.1016/j.worlddev.2016.01.019.

Öztürk, Murat, Beşir Topaloğlu, Andy Hilton, and Joost Jongerden. 2017. "Rural–Urban Mobilities in Turkey: Socio-spatial Perspectives on Migration and Return Movements." *Journal of Balkan and Near Eastern Studies* 20 (5):513–530. doi: 10.1080/19448953.2018.1406696.

Suzuki-Him, Miki, and Ayşe Hoşgör-Gündüz 2019. "Challenging Geographical Disadvantages and Social Exclusion: A Case Study of Gendered Rural Transformation in Mountain Villages in the Western Black Sea Region of Turkey." *Sociologia Ruralis* 59 (3):540–559. doi: 10.1111/soru.12258.

TURKSTAT. 2011a. Statistical Indicators (1923– 2010). Edited by Turkish Statistical Institute. Ankara.

TURKSTAT. 2011b. Summary of Agricultural Statistics. Turkish Statistical Institute.

TURKSTAT. 2020. Regional dataset. edited by Turkish Statistical Institute.

UNIDO. 2010. Industrial Statistics Guidelines and Methodology. Edited by United Nations Industrial Development Organization. Vienna: The United Nations.

WDI. 2020. World Development Indicators. Edited by The World Bank.

WVS. 2020. World Values Survey. Edited by The WVS Association. Vienna, Austria.

PART III

TOWARDS A NEW CONCEPTUAL FRAMEWORK

8 DISCUSSION

THE PATRIARCHAL, CAPITALIST AND RACIST TOTALITY

This book has detailed the ways in which shortcomings in social theory prevent effective feminist strategies and thus maintain the paradox witnessed in contemporary societies whereby patriarchal injustices persist despite active feminist resistance. In this chapter, I propose an alternative theoretical framework that is based on the analyses presented in Part II and which addresses the aforementioned shortcomings. In Sections 8.1 and 8.2, I show that existing arguments on socio-economic transformation and gendered oppression and inequality are not sufficient in analysing the case of Turkey. In Sections 8.3 and 8.4, I then critically assess developments in the approaches over time, including reinterpretations of complexity theory and historical materialism. Finally, in Section 8.5, I discuss the potential contribution of Hegelian Marxist interpretation of historical materialist methodology and ontology to a feminist thought.

8.1 Shortcomings of theories on socio-economic transformation

Classical and Marxist political economists neglect the importance of patriarchal property and labour relations in diversifying trajectories of socio-economic transformation. Countering the view of these economists, my analysis of the case of Turkey demonstrates that the premodern form of domestic patriarchy has a significant role in terms of increasing the initial accumulation necessary for early industrialisation, preventing the movement of female labour from agriculture to non-agricultural sectors as well as supporting landowning male peasants to escape proletarianisation, thereby constraining labour supply and putting upward pressure on capitalist wages.

While Marxist theories on agrarian change dismiss what I call the patriarchal path of agrarian transformation, theories on the respective roles of the non-capitalist classes in shaping development trajectories either draw on an ungendered account of the peasantry or dismiss their significance by assuming peasants' dispossession of land. My analyses, however, show that under the dominance of small landownership, the gendered patterns

DOI: 10.4324/9781003054511-12

of landownership maintain the category of patriarchal peasantry, thereby preventing the hegemony of bourgeois farmers. Subsequently, large-scale capitalist farms and wage labour in agriculture remain restricted. The patriarchal peasantry utilises the gender-based division of labour and appropriates the surplus produced by women leading to a certain level of accumulation. The evidence also suggests that this category of male peasants have had a relatively strong bargaining capacity within the historical context of Turkey and thereby played a significant role in shaping state formation as well as impacting on capital accumulation strategies. My assessment further implies that the dynamics of agrarian transformation cannot be reduced to the question of market dependency. The patriarchal relations of production in agriculture can be integrated with capitalist relations of exchange in the market. This particular path of agrarian transformation, therefore, needs to be considered in order to identify the dynamics of agrarian change in the global Southern countries where gendered dispossession of land is associated with small landownership.

The Weberian analysis emphasises that the illiberal patrimonial states of the global South prevent development of the bourgeois class, whereas the World System and Dependency theories argue that global capitalism leads to weakness of the domestic bourgeoise. However, my investigation suggests that the bourgeois class increases its resilience by adopting a flexible approach and by maintaining its influence over the state. In response to the ramifications imposed by the patriarchal path of agrarian transformation (e.g. constrained labour supply and upward pressure on capitalist wages), the Turkish bourgeoise has increased the length of the working day and replaced labourers with technology to a greater extent than other developing countries. These strategies of capital accumulation, in turn, lead to lower hourly wages and higher unemployment and, as such, require state-led coercion in breaking the resistance of working classes. The enduring bond between the anti-democratic state regimes and the bourgeoise in Turkey therefore needs to be analysed along with the patriarchal property and labour relations.

Finally, both Keynesian and Marxist political economists ignore the ways in which the patriarchal character of the state is significant for socio-economic transformation. My findings indicate that state formation is a process shaped not only by the powers of capitalist labour exploitation, but also by the powers of patriarchal labour exploitation and racist oppression. Holding multiple agendas, the state is in constant negotiation with the capitalist and patriarchal as well as racist collective subjects. State formation cannot therefore be solely explained by the capitalist character of the state; rather, the patriarchal and racist dimensions of the state must also be taken into account. The case of Turkey further demonstrates that both women and men struggle to sustain their influence over the state and, at the same time, the interplay between the capitalist and racist agendas of the state is significant in supporting the patriarchal collective subject.

8.2 Limitations of feminist theories

The findings presented here suggest a different theoretical direction to that followed by the social reproduction approach. First, the case of Turkey implies that the dynamics of gendered oppression and inequality cannot be subordinated to the capitalist system. On the contrary, patriarchal property and labour relations are important in shaping trajectories of capitalist transformation, including capital accumulation strategies and, as such, have implications for state formation and civil society. Second, my analyses challenge the assumption that it is labourers' dispossession of the means of production (including land) and wage dependency that shapes social transformation; rather, the findings suggest that small producers can obtain the means of production and exploit the labour of others (Marx 1976). Immediate producers can defend their ownership of the means of production either by mobilising collectively against the capitalist forces of dispossession or by utilising patriarchal forces of dispossession and exploitation against other producers. The former path makes them into revolutionaries, but the latter into patriarchs and each path has different implications for socio-economic transformation. Third, under the conditions of gendered dispossession of land, men in their roles, as both household heads and small producers exchange the agrarian surplus produced by women's unpaid labour, thereby forcing women to produce for the market. Patriarchal labour relations are thus not limited to the production of use value but also include the production of exchange value. Likewise, household production is not limited to reproductive activities, care work or other forms of non-market goods and services as the social reproduction approach assumes; rather, the findings suggest that the analytical divide between production and reproduction is not applicable to the lives of all women. Fourth, the conditions of the gender-based division of labour in agriculture seem to falsify the biologically determinist accounts adopted by the social reproduction approach. The determinants of the gender-based division of labour in agriculture are not linked to pregnancy, childbirth or lactation. While female peasants are responsible for the heaviest and most labour-intensive and repetitive tasks which require great strength, male peasants handle technical, commercial and bureaucratic tasks.

My analysis shows that theories on varieties of gender regime provide a useful framework for considering historical and geographical variations in gender inequality. Factors signalling the predominance of premodern and modern domestic patriarchies include (i) women's exclusion from paid employment in non-agricultural sectors, (ii) large gendered gaps in education, political representation and public decision-making, (iii) women's limited control over their sexuality, including sexual orientation and reproductive capacity, (iv) the gender-based exclusionary characteristics of cultural and religious settings and (v) a policy framework that confines women's labour to rural and urban household production as well as

(vi) trapping women within violent heterosexual family structures. Conversely, women's double burden of paid and unpaid labour, segregated and subordinated access to civil society, greater control over their sexuality and better protection from gendered violence suggest the dominance of the neoliberal or social-democratic forms of public patriarchy.

My analysis further confirms that the domestic and public forms of patriarchy can co-exist within a single country leading to an uneven and combined development of 'premodern and modern domestic' and 'neoliberal public' patriarchies. The geopolitics of patriarchal transformation in Turkey suggests that the gender-based exclusionary strategies are dominant in agrarian and semi-agrarian cities. The gender-based segregationist strategies are relatively stronger in non-agrarian cities, and while the neoliberal form emerges alongside modern domestic patriarchy, its limited reach leaves the hegemony of domestic forms of patriarchy largely unchallenged. As such, the domestic patriarchal character of the state is pertinent in terms of maintaining the patriarchal gender contract on the grounds of gender-based exclusionary strategies.

The case of Turkey enables assessment of the ways in which varieties of gender regime theories are helpful but, at the same time, it serves to highlight the limitations associated with these theories: First, my analysis suggests that explaining gender transformation in the global South requires an investigation of the premodern and modern varieties of domestic patriarchy. Women's exclusion from landownership in conjunction with the predominance of small landownership lead to premodern domestic patriarchy, whereas conditions of increasing wage dependency and gendered access to a means of subsistence (e.g. a wage, rent, or other forms of income) lead to modern domestic patriarchy.

Second, the gendered division of labour in household production does not lose its significance in the neoliberal and social-democratic forms of public patriarchy; instead, women's double burden of paid and unpaid labour is sustained and the goods and services produced by women in the home are not wholly substituted by market and/or state provision. Therefore, patriarchal labour exploitation within the heterosexual family plays a significant role in all forms of patriarchy.

Third, evidence on the legal dispossession of women from agricultural land contradicts those scholars' differentiation of premodern and modern polity. My assessment reveals the extent to which the Islamic-premodern law and the modern legal framework overlap with respect to legal discrimination against women in land inheritance. Considering that women under Sharia law were entitled to inherit half of what their brothers inherit, it can be argued that the modern civil code of 1926 excluded female peasants from the ownership of indivisible land to a greater extent than the premodern law. Subsequently, female peasants insisted on the Islamic legal and cultural framework to defend their property rights. Therefore, modernity or varieties of modernity based assessments of the shift from domestic to public forms of patriarchy are not helpful in identifying the drivers and dampeners of social change. Instead, I suggest an assessment on the grounds of changes in the forms of patriarchal oppression and labour exploitation. According to my conceptual framework, the predominance of gender-based segregationist strategies along with a shift towards women's double burden of paid and unpaid labour signals the transition to the neoliberal or social-democratic forms of public patriarchy, whereas the predominance of gender-based exclusionary strategies and women's unpaid family labour indicate the hegemony of domestic patriarchy.

Fourth, my analysis of the diversified trajectories of patriarchal transformation distinguishes the gender-based exclusionary and segregationist strategies in order to fully recognise the significance of the patriarchal collective subject. In this concern, the case of Turkey demonstrates that not only male household heads, but also small male producers in rural and urban areas constitute the patriarchal collective subject. The collective acting capacity of men sustains gendered patterns of property and labour relations as well as the patriarchal character of the Turkish state, civil society, and the cultural and religious conditions.

Finally, the inequalities derived from oppression need to be distinguished from the inequalities sustained through the relations of labour exploitation. For example, the religious and ethnicity based oppressions in Turkey do not draw on the relations of labour exploitation; the Muslim majority does not exploit Alevis' labour nor does the Turkish majority exploit the labour of the Kurdish population. Considering the dispossession of non-Muslim minorities within historical context (1920s–1960s) and the religious and ethnicity based discrimination and segregation in the contemporary labour market, I do not deny that Turkish Sunni-Muslim men and women have benefited from the racist regimes of oppression. Furthermore, the history of Turkey is marked by a number of massacres of Alevi and Kurdish people, and speaking Kurdish or listening to Kurdish music in public could lead to lynching in the contemporary conditions of Turkey (Evrensel 2020; BIA News Desk 2021). Being exploited is certainly not as harmful as being killed. What I argue, however, is that the labour of Alevi and Kurdish people is not exploited by the Sunni-Muslim or Turkish majority. Subsequently, those religion and ethnicity based inequalities are maintained in ways different to gender and class based labour exploitations.

The shortcomings of existing social theory, I argue, derive from their methodological limitations. In developing an alternative theoretical framework, it is therefore necessary to assess feminist adaptations of (i) complexity theory and (ii) historical materialism.

8.3 Feminist adaptation of complexity theory

Critically engaging with Weberian and Marxist theories, Walby argues that their concepts of social system reduce complicated social inequalities to capitalism or class inequality and, as such, establish a hierarchy in which class is dominant. She further scrutinises a particular understanding of the social system in which "the whole is made up of parts" as well as Althusserian interpretations of base/superstructure and relative autonomy (Walby 2020: 8). In order to theorise multiple intersecting inequalities, Walby suggests, "it is necessary to theorise more fully the ontological depth of each set of social relations... [and] the relationship between systems of social relations and how they affect each other" (2007: 454). Walby draws on the following key principles of complexity theory:

(i) Each and every institution, including the institutional domains of economy, polity, civil society and violence as well as every regime of (gender, class, ethnicity based) inequality refer to a system. Systems are self-reproducing and thus do not require additional input for their reproduction. (ii) Rejecting the concept of the whole and its parts, Walby argues that "each system takes all other systems as its environment" (2020: 6). For example, the institutional domain of economy should not be reduced to one of the parts of the class regime. The economy is itself a system which takes the class regime as its environment and, at the same time, is taken by the class regime as an environment. (iii) Systems do not necessarily fully saturate a certain space or territory. Multiple systems can be effective in shaping social change. For example, the regimes of class, gender and ethnicity based inequalities are equally significant in shaping the institutional domain of economy. (iv) There are several path-dependent trajectories giving rise to changes within a system and, accordingly, (v) multiple equilibrium points within the context of a system. (vi) The mutual interaction amongst all those systems gives rise to non-linear and bidirectional change. (vii) While the negative feedback loops sustain equilibrium, positive feedback loops move the system away from the equilibrium. (viii) Therefore, a small change may lead to a large effect. (ix) "A project is a set of practices oriented towards change in society", for example, the nationalist, feminist or anti-racist projects (Walby 2020: 13). Multiple competing projects lead the process of societalisation that aligns institutional domains and regimes of inequality.

While invaluable in identifying the systemic characteristics of gender, class and ethnicity injustices and embracing the mutual interaction amongst those systems, Walby's theoretical framework has some problems which derive from the limitations of complexity theory (Luhmann 1995; Capra 1997; Castellani and Hafferty 2009; Maturana and Varela 1980). One such problem is that complexity theory has developed predominantly within the natural sciences, including ecology and mathematics (Capra 1997; Maturana and Varela 1980). By adopting the same concepts, Walby's analysis tends to treat natural and social systems in the same way which leads to confusion regarding those systems' capacity for self-organisation and self-reproduction (Walby 2020). Walby is not the only theorist who has attempted to adopt the same method to analyse both social and natural systems; some Marxists scholars, including Friedrich Engels, also applied the dialectical method to the analysis of nature. However, as György Lukács (1971) highlights, historical and social processes are different from nature and thus cannot be understood by adopting the same method. As I will argue later in this chapter, *self-consciousness* plays a significant role in social systems but is absent in natural systems.

Furthermore, as I argue in the following section, the Althusserian understanding of base/superstructure has greatly influenced the historical materialist concept of over-determination and led to capitalism-based reductionism. In contrast, the concept of mutual interaction between the gender, class and race-ethnicity based regimes of inequality does avoid reductionism and provides for a detailed account of social transformation. And at the same time, as an analytical tool, intersectionality reveals the ways in which the multiple forms of oppressions interact and diversify the experiences of oppressed and exploited sections of society. However, the argument that everything determines everything or the emphasis on the intersecting forms of power, both tends to elide the distinctive features of patriarchy, capitalism and racism to gender, class and race-ethnicity based social inequalities. Accordingly, attention is directed away from the causes and towards the consequences of the patriarchal, capitalist and racist systems or regimes. We need to go further; to develop effective feminist, socialist, and anti-racist strategies, the notion of mutual interaction needs to be considered along with the distinctive mediating categories of each and every system and regime.

8.4 Existing interpretations of historical materialism

While the social reproduction approach provides a limited account of historical materialism, French materialist feminism draws on the historical materialist methodology and ontology to investigate and abolish all forms of oppression and exploitation. In this section, I assess the strengths and limitations of their methodologies.

8.4.1 The social reproduction approach

The social reproduction approach derives a number of key concepts from historical materialism. For example, the notion of historicism is drawn upon to highlight the ways in which the transition from feudalism to capitalism changed the conditions of women's domestic labour within the family. In addition, the emphasis on the capitalist mode of production sheds some light on the determinants of women's oppression. Building on historical materialism, social reproduction scholars also prioritise the work done by women and the relations of labour in their analysis of gender oppression and, at the same time, insist on a theory of (concrete) totality whereby the capitalist system determines but is also determined by the gender and race-ethnicity based oppressions. However, the adaptation of historical materialism used by these scholars has some problems which are discussed next.

First, the social reproduction approach develops a theory of totality (i.e. concrete totality or whole) but in their analysis "[c]apitalist logic is thus determinative... the logic of [capital] accumulation and dispossession invites certain gender relations and not others" thereby subordinating the dynamics of gender-based oppression and exploitation to "a capitalist total-ity" (Ferguson 2016: 51). Despite attempts to avoid a reductionist model of determination, those scholars still argue that a totalising narrative of "the capitalist whole" puts its parts (gender and race-ethnicity oppression) into a place which is necessary for its reproduction (Ferguson 2016: 38). Despite an earlier analysis in which gender, race and sexuality based oppressions and inequalities are reduced to difference and identity (McNally 2015), David McNally has recently portrayed these power relations as partial totalities which have distinguishing features but are not autonomous from "the concrete totality of the whole" (2017: 106). His analysis of totality, how-ever, does not go beyond the limitations of capitalism based determinism; he concludes that gender and race based oppressions are "reproduced in and through the reproduction of the capitalist mode of production", there-fore all other dimensions of these (gender, race and sexuality based) social experiences are overridden by the necessities of capitalist production and reproduction (McNally 2017: 107). Consequently, those theories of totality claim that, depending on its requirements, the capitalist mode of produc-tion determines the rest. Yet, as I will demonstrate, the historical materialist methodology and ontology can be used to avoid reducing various elements of totality to "undifferentiated uniformity" (Lukács 1971: 13). In my theo-retical framework, an adequate theory of totality requires engagement with the Hegelian principle of self-consciousness and the categories of media-tion. My proposed theory can then be deployed to reveal, for example, the benefits white working class men and women derive from racism, and the extent to which men with different class, and race-ethnicity backgrounds are the beneficiaries of gendered oppression and labour exploitation.

Second, once the capitalist character of totality is portrayed as the main determinant of social change, the principle of historicism becomes limited to what capitalism entails with respect to gender and racial oppression. This reduction means that the historically specific dynamics of patriarchy and racism are neglected. In other words, the social reproduction approach fol-lows the principle of historicism only for class societies; gender societies become ahistorical or transhistorical in character. In his critique of histor-ical economism, Antonio Gramsci (1971) emphasises that in searching for historical connections, it is necessary to differentiate what is relatively per-manent and what is passing fluctuation. The principle of historicism thus requires an analysis of the continuities within discontinuities and disconti-nuities within continuities. Consequently, existing research on class societies as well as feminist research on gender societies identifies the continuities and discontinuities within historical context (e.g., Coontz and Henderson 1986; Chevillard and Leconte 1986). An analysis of continuities is accepted within a class context, yet the same effort is labelled as *ahistorical* within the context of gender. In doing so, these scholars not only put forward a limited understanding of historicism, but also dismiss historical accounts of patriarchal domination and labour relations.

Finally, dismissing the historical materialist principle of self-consciousness prevents the social reproduction approach from going beyond the limitations of an Althusserian base/superstructure analysis. Their conceptualisation of the capitalist mode of production, subsequently, draws on a problematic understanding of the 'material'. By detaching the material from the social, those scholars (i) mystify the workings of the material base (i.e. class exploitation, capital accumulation, and the dominant mode of production) that serve to determine the rest and, simultaneously, (ii) fail to recognise that what appears as 'material' is, in fact, a socially constructed phenomenon. While the latter can give rise to a biologically essentialist understanding of sex and the gender-based division of labour, the former obscures the significance of the collective acting capacity of the (gender, class or race-ethnicity based) oppressors and appropriators which leads the mode of production to be portrayed as, what Gramsci (1971) calls, *a Hidden God*.

To summarise, the social reproduction scholars utilise historical materialism to argue for the determining role of the capitalist mode of production thereby making a unifying call for an anti-capitalist movement. Such an account, however, serves to strengthen the portrayal of historical materialist methodology and ontology as deterministic. It is therefore important and urgent to adopt an alternative approach which avoids limiting historical materialism to the capitalist system.

8.4.2 *French materialist feminism*

The French materialist feminist scholars emphasise that the methodology developed by Marx is not limited in its application to the analysis of capitalism and class antagonism; on the contrary, it is necessary in analysing all different forms of exploitation and oppression, including gender, race-ethnicity and slavery. While the pioneering names of French materialist feminism include Christine Delphy, Colette Guillaumin, Monique Wittig, Nicole-Claude Mathieu, Monique Plaza and Paola Tabet, the contribution of other theorists to this scholarship is also significant (see Stevi Jackson, Diana Leonard, Lisa Adkins, Danièle Kergoat and Danielle Juteau-Lee). Here I will elaborate on the strengths and limitations of their materialism with respect to the notions of historicism, totality and the principle of the unity of the material and the social.

In her analysis of the system of marks, Guillaumin provides a detailed account of continuities and discontinuities within the historical context.

She argues that the system of marks drew on historically and geographically diverse symbols, including certain dress codes, bodily adaptations or an actual mark on the body (tattoo, branding, piercing), and functioned in ways which sustained the subordination and exploitation of certain group of people. For example, historically serfs were not allowed to wear certain forms of dress, and slaves were tattooed in some countries. However, during the nineteenth and twentieth centuries, Guillaumin argues, the traditional status of those symbols was largely replaced with *"a sign of a specific nature* for social actors" (1995: 140). While the pre-modern symbols are created by social relations, the natural marks are assumed to precede the social relationship, i.e. they are proclaimed as the origin of race-ethnicity and gender based social relations. With the modern system of marks, "slavery becomes an attribute of skin colour" and "non-payment for domestic work becomes an attribute of the shape of sexual organs" (Guillaumin 1995: 143). According to Guillaumin, the idea of naturalness is, therefore, specific to industrial societies and not the same as the socio-symbolic system of marks imposed on social groups. As well as identifying these changes over time, she emphasises that the socio-symbolic system of marks still exists; gendered patterns of clothing are an example of marking which maintains gendered subordination and exploitation.

Furthermore, Delphy provides one of the very early accounts of changes within the domestic mode of production during industrialisation. In her celebrated article, titled *Main Enemy* (originally published in 1970), she explains the ways in which capitalist production and paid labour became separated from domestic production and unpaid labour. She further suggests that while capitalist transformation undermined family patriarchy, patriarchy did not disappear, rather it changed and resisted (Delphy and Leonard 1992). Despite her attention to changes in patriarchy over time, Delphy's approach has nevertheless been accused of ahistoricism (Barrett and McIntosh 1979). As argued previously, the principle of historicism is not limited to the analysis of capitalism and its historical prerequisites; it requires an investigation of the continuities and discontinuities within different forms of oppression and exploitation throughout history. As such, labelling Delphy's analysis of patriarchy as ahistorical appears erroneous.

Nonetheless, Acar-Savran (2004) suggests that Delphy perceives the domestic mode of production as an enclosed system which thereby constitutes a barrier to historicism. I argue that this problem highlighted by Acar-Savran is linked to Delphy's neglect of totality. As Jackson (1996) explains, Delphy chooses to focus on patriarchy rather than investigating the relationship between patriarchy and capitalism (and racism). In order to analyse the distinguishing features of patriarchy, it is necessary to assess the nature of mutual interaction between systems of exploitation and regimes of oppression. An assessment of changes that capitalist transformation triggers in patriarchy as well as the alterations that patriarchy forces upon capitalism sheds light on the dynamic negotiations between the collective subjects and, in so doing, reveals the level of complexity within the mediating categories of those systems.

Drawing on the historical materialist principle of the unity of the material and the social, French materialist feminists also provide an influential analysis of sex and gender (Wittig 1992; Guillaumin 1995; Delphy 1993; Mathieu 1996). According to these scholars, gender precedes sex meaning that social relations of oppression and exploitation mark men and women by reinforcing the idea of naturalness. As discussed earlier, Guillaumin (1995) highlights that the socio-symbolic system of marks has mostly shifted towards the natural system of marks and, as such, justified race and sex (and class for a while) based oppression and exploitation. While the premodern symbols were accepted as the products of social relations, these race and sex based natural marks are assumed to precede social relations. However, it is gender which reinforces the idea that sex is natural. Delphy et al. (2017) emphasises that nature does not have any values or meaning. Sex in itself lacks any inherent meaning but gender renders sex socially significant (Disch 2015). It is people perceiving nature in particular ways which sustains the categories of men and women and thereby upholds patriarchal relations of power. Monique Wittig (1992) furthers the debate by conceptualising the category of sex purely as a political category:

> The ideology of sexual difference functions as censorship in our culture by masking, on the grounds of nature, the social opposition between men and women... The masters explain and justify the established divisions as a result of natural differences. For there is no sex. There is but sex that is oppressed and sex that oppresses. It is oppression that creates sex not the contrary. The contrary would be to say that sex creates oppression, or to say that the cause (origin) of oppression is to be found in sex itself, in a natural division of the sexes pre-existing (or outside) of society
>
> (Wittig 1992: 2)

By explaining the significance of gender for the 'naturalisation' of sex, these scholars demonstrate the inseparable unity of the material and the social. However, in her analysis of the domestic mode of production, Delphy remains influenced by the Althusserian base/superstructure approach which reinforces a separation of the material and the social. Subsequently, she argues that the material base (domestic mode of production) determines the superstructure (ideology, culture, religion). This approach tends to confound the rules and workings of 'the material base' and, simultaneously, separates the domestic mode of production from patriarchy. The conceptual separation of the mode of production and the system of exploitation constitutes a barrier to understanding the patriarchal system. Conversely, a unified account of the material and the social supports an investigation of systems of exploitation by socialising and politicising labour exploitation.

Adopting this unified concept, in turn, allows an assessment of the distinguishing categories of self-consciousness and mediation within the context of gendered oppression and exploitation.

In light of the strengths and weaknesses of existing adaptations of historical materialism, it seems necessary to go beyond the limitations associated with the Althusserian base/superstructure model which has been influential in the social reproduction approach and, although to a lesser degree, in French materialist feminism.

8.5 Reclaiming the historical materialist methodology and ontology

The Althusserian base/superstructure approach is derived from a particular understanding of materialism, called vulgar or mechanical materialism. While some scholars suggest that the origins of mechanical materialism can be found within the studies of Engels, others stress that it is a product of the Soviet regime. Irrespective of its origins, such interpretation of materialism, including the Althusserian base/superstructure model, has a misleading influence over social theory. For instance, Wood argues that "[i]n one form or another and in varying degrees, Marxists have generally adopted modes of analysis which, explicitly or implicitly, treat the economic 'base' and the legal, political, and ideological 'superstructures'... [as] more or less enclosed and 'regionally' separated spheres" (Wood 1981: 68). No matter how the interactions between those enclosed spheres are analysed, the economic sphere is ultimately positioned as determining the rest. Rejecting the separation of the economic and the political, Wood emphasises that Marx perceives production as a social process by stressing the definition of the material by the social. In his critique of mechanical materialism, Gramsci (1971) further emphasises that the distinction between the material forces and ideology gives rise to economism or ideologism. My assessment also suggests that economism and ideologism are strongly linked meaning that social theory tends to reduce the dynamics of social change either to the necessities or varieties of the dominant mode of production, or to the cultural and religious conditions.

Moreover, Lukács argues that the mechanical understanding of materialism is not only one-sidedly deterministic (i.e. the material determines the rest), but also hinders a detailed analysis of human activity which structures the economy. In this regard, Ágnes Heller suggests that Althusserian structuralism convicts "the philosophy of the subject as guilty of humanism" and, as such, leads to the dismissing of consciousness (1990: 62). She argues that a theory of a collective Subject (with a capital S) needs to be developed. The Hegelian programme of *the dissolution of immediacy*, according to Lukács, is important in theorising the collective subject, therefore the historical materialist methodology and ontology cannot be divorced from the concepts of self-consciousness and mediation (Meszaros 1972; Lukács 1971).

In order to avoid mechanical materialism, a theory of a collective subject along with the notions of mediation and self-consciousness needs to be placed at the centre of the historical materialist methodology and ontology. Such theory prevents the separation of the material from the social thereby avoiding capitalism or culture based reductionisms and, at the same time, provides a detailed account of the totality without losing the distinguishing characteristics of the patriarchal or capitalist systems of exploitation or racist regimes of oppression.

8.5.1 Collective subject and mediation

The Hegelian understanding of consciousness is intrinsic to a theory of the collective subject. Drawing his inspiration from the Haitian revolution, Georg W. F. Hegel (1967 [1807]) developed his influential theory of the master and slave dialectics (Buck-Morss 2009; 2000). The following differentiation between two moments of consciousness is crucial to understand Hegel's theory: consciousness of the object and consciousness of self. What the object is in itself is one moment to consciousness, whereas the-being-of-the-object for consciousness is another moment. Hegel conceptualises the former as *self-in consciousness* and the latter as *self-for consciousness*. In the context of self-for consciousness, "consciousness is not external to the object, but is a part of the object that also changes it" (Burman 2018: 24). In his analysis of the master and slave dialectics, Hegel clarifies these concepts by explaining how the transition from self-in towards self-for consciousness is inevitable: while the master is independent and its essential nature is to be for itself, the slave is dependent, and its existence is for another. Having self-for consciousness, the master becomes capable of asserting his consciousness at the expense of the slave. Under such conditions, the self-consciousness of the slave exists for another self-consciousness leading to the creation of a duplication of self-consciousness. This duplication occurs alongside its unity, the unity of 'existence-for-self' and 'existence-for-another'. This twofold process of duplication and unity leads to a self-for consciousness for the slave, and as such, brings the destruction of this particular social experience and the disappearance of both of the master and the slave.

As well as emphasising the inevitability of the transition from self-in towards self-for consciousness, Hegel stresses the barriers to this transition. He argues that the movement of the appearance mediates the relations of being of the object for consciousness thereby delaying self-for consciousness. According to his principle of the dissolution of immediacy, mediating categories hide the reality of phenomena by presenting them in different forms. Therefore, it is necessary to detach the phenomena from their immediately given form, and investigate the intervening links which connect the phenomena to their core function (Lukács 1971). To emphasise, the conflict between 'existence-for-self' and 'existence-for-another' reinforces a shift from self-in towards self-for consciousness but, at the same time, various categories of mediation prevent self-for consciousness. As the dominant sections of society have developed self-for consciousness, their position refers to, what Heller calls, *the initial collective subject*. However, the transition from self-in towards self-for consciousness is delayed for the subordinated sections of society, therefore their position is identified as *the late coming collective subject* (Heller 1990).

My assessment suggests that the initial collective subjects in contemporary societies are diverse, based on patriarchal, capitalist or racist oppression and exploitation, whereas the position of the oppressed and exploited sections of society refers to the late coming collective subject based on gender, class and race-ethnicity. Having self-for consciousness, these initial collective subjects assert their consciousness at the expense of the gender, class or race-ethnicity based oppressed sections of society. The distinguishing categories of mediation belonging to each and every system and regime, however, impede the transition towards self-for consciousness for the oppressed thereby delaying the late coming collective subjects.[1]

Focusing on class consciousness, Marxist theories provide a detailed account of the mediating categories of capitalism, including the market, wage or the state. For example, Wood (2002, 1999, 1981) demonstrates how the market mediates the relationship between the appropriators and the producers and, in so doing, obscures the fact that private ownership of the means of production sustains capitalist labour exploitation. Although the market appears as a category independent of politics, social relations, and historical and geographical contexts, Wood's analysis reveals its historically specific function in capitalism. The ways in which the state mediates the private ownership of a means of production in capitalism (Poulantzas 1969) and the gendered patterns of property in patriarchy (MacKinnon 1991; Kocabıçak 2020) are also explored in a detailed way. Another example of mediation can also be found within the systems of slavery. While the natural system of marks was used to mediate the race-based exploitation of labour by giving meanings to the appearance of skins during transatlantic slave trade (Guillaumin 1995), the border regulations and policies mediate the relations of labour exploitation under the contemporary forms of slavery. Though a detailed analysis of the mediating categories of capitalism or slavery is not the aim here, my assessment of the case of Turkey does indicate that the cis-gender heterosexual family strongly mediates the relationship between male appropriators and female direct producers thereby delaying self-for consciousness amongst women.

8.5.2 *Totality*

The historical materialist accounts of totality (also named historical bloc, dialectical unity or negative totality) draw on the principle of the unity of the material and the social, and take into account the mutual interaction between the elements of totality and totality itself. Critically engaging with approaches which reduce various elements of totality to homogenous unity, Lukács emphasises that mutual interaction does not mean a one-way causal sequence as implied by mechanical materialists. Rather, it refers to a "reciprocal causal impact of two otherwise unchangeable objects on each other" (1971: 13). This means that the concrete totality is made of totalities subordinated to it and also that the totality in question is over-determined by totalities of higher complexity (Lukács 1948). The historical materialist account of totality, therefore, avoids reductionism whereby the material (economy) is separated from the social (ideology) and, at the same time, allows for the mutual interaction of totalities.

Nevertheless, according to Lukács, mutual interaction between totalities and the concrete totality does not mean that everything determines everything. Totalities of higher complexity have a stronger impact on the concrete totality (Meszaros 1972). The complexity of totality depends on its categories of mediation which prevent the transition from self-in to self-for consciousness among the oppressed and exploited sections of society. Therefore, a higher level of complexity within the categories of mediation means a longer delay of the late coming collective subject. This complexity, in turn, upholds the totality in question without it having to face significant challenge. The more complex its mediating categories are, the stronger the totality is, and therefore the more influence the totality has over other totalities and the concrete totality. Lukács, therefore, develops a theory of totality on the grounds of the Hegelian principles of self-consciousness and mediation rather than intimating the over-determining power of the mode of production, the material base or the self-reproductive capacity of social systems.

Drawing on the Lukácsian understanding of totality, I place the concept of the collective subject – along with its notions of self-consciousness and mediation – at the heart of my theory of totality. According to my framework, the totality having categories of mediation of the highest level of complexity is challenged to a lesser degree than other totalities. As the late coming collective subject of the totality in question is delayed more than others, its initial collective subject has the greatest political power. As a result, this particular form of totality influences other totalities to adopt a flexible approach as well as *over-determines* the concrete totality. An analysis of mutual interaction amongst all totalities therefore entails an assessment of the complexity of the mediating categories belonging to each system and regime.

The key question is whether capitalism, patriarchy, or racism has the highest level of complexity in their categories of mediation, and in what ways such complexity levels vary over time and space. In this regard, the case of Turkey contributes to an assessment of the complex categories of mediation. It appears that nationalism in Turkey has mediated the relations of racist oppression thereby upholding the political power of a Turkish/ Muslim racist collective subject. The complexity level of nationalism, however, seems to be influenced by the imperialist interferences. Initially, the invasion of the WWI allied powers (1919–1923), recently the imperialist expropriation and incursion of the Middle East (since the 1990s) appear to increase the complexity level of nationalism as a category of mediation. Although the mediated powers of race-ethnicity based oppression can have deadly consequences, the categories of racist mediation remain less complex than other perhaps as a result of greater organisational strength in the anti-racist, mainly Kurdish movement.

The case of Turkey, furthermore, indicates that capitalism does not always have the highest level of complexity in its categories of mediation. Under particular conditions, the mediating categories of patriarchy have a higher level of complexity and shape other totalities as well as the concrete totality. The patriarchal collective subject, including male household heads and small producers, appears to have sustained its political power since the early decades of the Republican period. At the same time, the capitalist collective subject has demonstrated a certain degree of flexibility by developing alternative accumulation strategies to circumvent the restrictions imposed by the patriarchal collective subject. Capital accumulation strategies are therefore shaped by the patriarchal control over women's labour within rural and urban household production and the gendered division of labour.

My analyses suggest that the cis-gender heterosexual family has the highest level of complexity in mediating patriarchal labour exploitation in household production. While such mediating function of the family cannot be reduced to an institutional domain or dispersed across four institutional domains, this category of mediation crosscuts all varieties of patriarchy, including the domestic and public varieties, as well as affecting men and women from different class and race-ethnicity backgrounds.

8.6 Conclusion

The historical materialist methodology and ontology is necessary for abolishing the gender, class and race-ethnicity based oppressions and exploitations. However, the influence of mechanical materialism, including the Althusserian base/superstructure approach, must be rejected and instead the Hegelian Marxist tradition considered; in particular, the notion of unity of the material and the social, and the concepts of self-consciousness, mediation and totality. The mutual interaction amongst all totalities must be taken into account, but also the level of complexity in their mediating categories. The more complex mediating categories are, the more influence the totality in question has over other totalities and the concrete totality. The complexity of these mediating categories also varies according to the historical and geographical contexts. The case of Turkey demonstrates that under specific conditions, the mediating categories of patriarchy have a higher level of complexity than those of capitalism and racism, thereby effectively shaping the concrete totality. The cis-gender heterosexual family mediates the relationship between male appropriators and female direct producers thereby obscuring patriarchal labour exploitation. Thus, the family-mediated categories of patriarchy in Turkey have a higher level of complexity than the market-mediated categories of capitalism and thereby prevent the predominance of capitalist relations in agricultural production.

While the mediating categories of the patriarchal or capitalist systems and the racist regimes prevent a shift from self-in towards self-for consciousness, the feminist, socialist, and anti-racist struggles can be effective in promoting this shift. Next, I elaborate on effective feminist strategies that can destabilise the patriarchal system by disclosing its mediating categories.

Note

1 Considering that the late coming collective subject experiences multiple forms of oppressions, Du Boisian concept of double consciousness is important for understanding the complex barriers of the passage from self-in to self-for consciousness. Engaging with Hegel's notion of recognition, W. E. B. Du Bois stresses the alienation and doubleness experienced by Black people and discusses an African American double consciousness (Du Bois 2012 [1903]). While Du Bois himself never really pursued his early theory of double consciousness, the contemporary commentators seem to have different views on his ideas. For details see (Harris 2021; Tangorra 2021; Meer 2018; 2011; Aboulafia 2009; Zamir 1995; Allen Jr 2002; Bruce 1992). Therefore, in my opinion, his important contribution to Hegelian dialectics remains undeveloped.

Reference

Aboulafia, Mitchell. 2009. "W. E. B. Du Bois: Double-consciousness, jamesian sympathy, and the critical turn." In *The Oxford Handbook of American Philosophy*, edited by C. Misak. Oxford, New York: Oxford University Press

Acar-Savran, Gülnur. 2004. *Beden, Emek, Tarih: Diyalektik bir Feminizm için.* İstanbul: Kanat Kitap.

Allen Jr, Ernest. 2002. "Du Boisian Double Consciousness: The Unsustainable Argument." *Massachusetts Review* 43 (2):217–253.

Barrett, Michele, and Mary McIntosh. 1979. "Christine Delphy: Towards a Materialist Feminism?" *Feminist Review* 1 (1):95–106. doi: 10.1057/fr.1979.8.

BIA News Desk. 2021. "Seven people from Kurdish family shot dead at home in racist assault." *Bianet.* Accessed 14.09.2021. https://bianet.org/english/human-rights/247964-seven-people-from-kurdish-family-shot-dead-at-home-in-racist-assault.

Bruce, Dickson D. 1992. "W. E. B. Du Bois and the Idea of Double Consciousness." *American Literature* 64 (2):299–309. doi: 10.2307/2927837.

Buck-Morss, Susan. 2009. *Hegel, Haiti, and Universal History*: University of Pittsburgh Press. Book.

Buck-Morss, Susan. 2000. "Hegel and Haiti." *Critical Inquiry* 26 (4):821–865.

Burman, Anders. 2018. "Back to hegel! georg lukács, dialectics, and hegelian marxism." In *Hegelian Marxism: The Uses of Hegel's Philosophy in Marxist Theory from Georg Lukács to Slavoj Žižek*, edited by A. Bartonek and A. Burman. Södertörn University.

Capra, Fritjof. 1997. *The Web of Life*. London: Flamingo.

Castellani, Brain, and Frederick Hafferty. 2009. *Sociology and Complexity Science: A New Field of Inquiry*, Berlin: Springer.

Chevillard, Nicole, and Sebastien Leconte. 1986. "The dawn of lineage societies: The. origins of women's oppression." In *Women's Work, Men's Property: The Origins of Gender and Class*, edited by S. Coontz and P. Henderson. London, New York: Verso.

Coontz, Stephanie, and Peta Henderson. 1986. *Women's Work, Men's Property: The Origins of Gender and Class*. London: Verso.

Delphy, Christine. 1993. "Rethinking Sex and Gender." *Women's Studies International Forum* 16 (1):1–9. doi: 10.1016/0277-5395(93)90076-L.

Delphy, Christine, Ilana Eloit, Clare Hemmings, and Sylvie Tissot. 2017. "Feminism in Transnational Times, a Conversation with Christine Delphy: An Edited Transcription of Christine Delphy and Sylvie Tissot's Public Talk at the LSE." *Feminist Review*, 117 (1):148–162. doi: 10.1057/s41305-017-0093-4.

Delphy, Christine, and Diana Leonard. 1992. *Familiar exploitation: a new analysis of marriage in contemporary Western societies, Feminist perspectives*. Cambridge, Massachusetts: Polity Press.

Disch, Lisa. 2015. "Christine Delphy's Constructivist Materialism: An Overlooked "French Feminism"." *South Atlantic Quarterly* 114 (4):827–849. doi: 10.1215/0038 2876-3157155.

Du Bois, William E. B. 2012 [1903]. *The Souls of Black Folk*: Dover Publications.

Evrensel. 2020. "7 yılda en az 4 kişi Kürtçe konuştuğu ya da müzik dinlediği için öldürüldü." Accessed 25.01.2021. https://dokuz8haber.net/gundem/insanhaklari/ turkiyede-son-7-yilda-en-az-4-kisi-kurtce-konustugu-ya-da-sarki-soyledigi-icin-olduruldu/.

Ferguson, Susan. 2016. "Intersectionality and Social-Reproduction Feminisms: Toward an Integrative Ontology" *Historical Materialism* 24 (2):38–60.

Gramsci, Antonio. 1971. *Selections From the Prison Notebooks*. London,: Lawrence & Wishart.

Guillaumin, Colette. 1995. *Racism, Sexism, Power and Ideology*. London, New York: Routledge.

Harris, Kimberly Ann. 2021. "Du Bois and Hegelian Idealism." *Idealistic Studies* 51 (2):149–167. doi: 10.5840/idstudies2021624130.

Hegel, Georg W. F. 1967 [1807]. *The Phenomenology of Spirit*: New York, Harper & Row.

Heller, Agnes. 1990. "Death of the subject?" In *Can Modernity Survive?*, edited by A. Heller. Cambridge: Polity press.

Jackson, Stevi. 1996. *Christine Delphy*. London, Delhi: Sage publications.

Kocabıçak, Ece. 2020. "Why Property Matters? New Varieties of Domestic Patriarchy in Turkey." *Social Politics* 28 (4). doi: 10.1093/sp/jxaa023.

Luhmann, Niklas. 1995. *Social Systems*. Stanford: Stanford University Press.

Lukács, Georg. 1948. "A Marxista filozofia feladatia az demokraciaban." Congress of Marxist Philosophers, Budapest/Milan.

Lukács, Georg. 1971. *History and Class Consciousness: Studies in Marxist Dialectics*. London: Merlin Press.

MacKinnon, Catharine A. 1991. *Toward a Feminist Theory of the State*: Harvard University Press.

Marx, Karl. 1976. *Capital: A Critique of Political Economy (vol 3)*. England: Penguin Books.

Mathieu, Nicole Claude. 1996. "Sexual, Sexed and sex-class identities: Three ways of conceptualising the relationship between sex and gender." In *Sex In Question: French Materialist Feminism*, edited by L. Adkins and D. Leonard. London, New York: Taylor & Francis.

Maturana, Humberto, and Francisco Varela. 1980. *Autopoeisis and Cognition*. Dordrecht: Reidel.

McNally, David. 2015. "The Dialectics of Unity and Difference in the Constitution of Wage-Labour: On Internal Relations and Working-Class Formation." *Capital & Class* 39 (1):131–146. doi: 10.1177/0309816814564819.

McNally, David. 2017. "Intersections and dialectics: critical reconstructions in social reproduction theory." In *Social Reproduction Theory: Remapping Class, Recentering Oppression*, edited by T. Bhattacharya. London, New York: Pluto Press. doi: 10.2307/j.ctt1vz494j.9

Meer, Nasar. 2011. "Overcoming the injuries of 'double consciousness'." In *The Politics of Misrecognition*, 45–65. London, New York: Routledge

Meer, Nasar. 2018. "W. E. B. Du Bois, Double Consciousness and the 'Spirit' of Recognition." *The Sociological Review* 67 (1):47–62. doi: 10.1177/0038026118765370.

Meszaros, Istvan. 1972. *Lukacs' concept of dialectic*. London,: Merlin Press.

Poulantzas, Nicos. 1969. "The Problem of the Capitalist State." *New Left Review* 1/58, 67–78.

Tangorra, Manuel. 2021. "Hegelian Heritage and Anti-Racist Horizons: Exegesis and Rewritings of Dialectical Thought." *Idealistic Studies* 51 (2):131–148. doi: 10.5840/idstudies2021624131.

Walby, Sylvia. 2007. "Complexity Theory, Systems Theory and Multiple Intersecting Social Inequalities." *Philosophy of the social sciences* 37 (4):449–470.

Walby, Sylvia. 2020. "Developing the Concept of Society: Institutional Domains, Regimes of Inequalities and Complex Systems in a Global Era." *Current Sociology*. doi: 10.1177/0011392120932940.

Wittig, Monique. 1992. *The Straight Mind, and Other Essays*. London, New York: Harvester.

Wood, Ellen M. 1981. "The Separation of the Economic and the Political in Capitalism." *New Left Review I*, 127: 66–93.

Wood, Ellen M. 1999. *The Origin of Capitalism*. New York: Monthly Review Press.

Wood, Ellen M. 2002. "The Question of Market Dependence." *Journal of Agrarian Change* 2 (1): 50–87.

Zamir, Shamoon. 1995. *Dark Voices, W. E. B. Du Bois and American Thought, 1888–1903*. Chicago: University of Chicago Press.

CONCLUSION
DRIVERS & DAMPENERS
OF SOCIAL CHANGE

We fight against a concrete totality which comprises the patriarchal and capitalist systems as well as racist regimes. The relationship between those systems and regimes cannot be reduced to one of harmony or contradiction, nor can the capitalist system be perceived as the major determinant of the concrete totality. The notions of a mutual interaction and an intersectionality of multiple oppressions are helpful in avoiding such reductionism but, at the same time, tends to obscure the distinctive categories of mediation sustaining those systems and regimes. As such, there is a conceptual shift away from the causes and towards the outcomes, i.e. aspects of patriarchy, capitalism and racism. In order to develop effective feminist, socialist, and anti-racist strategies which aim for complete liberation from all forms of exploitation and oppression, the mediating categories of each and every system and regime need to be investigated. Drawing on the historical materialist methodology and ontology, I argue that a higher complexity level within the categories of mediation sustains the hegemony of the initial collective subject as well as delaying the late coming collective subject. This complexity, in turn, upholds the system or the regime in question without significant challenge.

The case of Turkey suggests that the cis-gender heterosexual family has the highest level of complexity mediating the gender-based division of labour and patriarchal labour exploitation in household production. Focusing on the patriarchal exploitation of labour, feminist strategies therefore need to target the gender-based division of labour in rural and urban household production rather than women's time spent on unpaid domestic work (including care work). The former strategy discloses the given form of family, whereas the latter upholds its mediation. Such adjustment within the feminist perspective further points to the social-democratic form of public patriarchy as an intermediate step towards women's *liberation from* the patriarchal system.

Under the neoliberal form of public patriarchy, the market-led strategies of public provisioning (of domestic goods and services including care) are driven by the rule of compete or go under and, accordingly, promote private decision-making over the entire process. This highly privatised and

DOI: 10.4324/9781003054511-13

anti-democratic character of public provisioning is a barrier to abolishing the gendered division of labour in household production. In the social-democratic form of public patriarchy, however, public decision-making has a greater role in shaping the state-led provisioning. Unlike the privatised and anti-democratic nature of the market-led strategies, the design and implementation of state-led provisioning are accessible to women throughout polity and civil society. Therefore, social-democratic public patriarchy provides an opportunity for going beyond the limitations of women's double burden (of paid and unpaid labour) by targeting the gender-based division of labour in household production.

Nonetheless, the democratisation of public provisioning of domestic goods and services (including care) in itself is not sufficient to challenge the gender-based division of labour and patriarchal labour exploitation in agriculture. Considering those women's limited mobility, access to education and paid employment in non-agricultural sectors, I suggest that the gendered patterns of the movement of labour from agriculture to non-agricultural sectors need to be addressed through an exit package. As I will argue later, the public decision-making mechanisms of social-democratic public patriarchy support feminist strategies in proposing such an exit package thereby challenging those gendered patterns of proletarianization. Therefore, a shift towards the social-democratic form of public patriarchy provides a suitable context for eliminating patriarchal labour exploitation in agriculture.

Focusing on the case of Turkey, my discussion on the political economy of patriarchy ends with a brief assessment of the *drivers* which promote a shift towards social-democratic public patriarchy and the *dampeners* which counter this transition by sustaining the hegemony of premodern and modern domestic patriarchies. The feminist movement is the most important driver which has the potential of challenging this hegemony and reinforcing such shift. Following the 1980 coup d'état which banned socialist organisations, parties, associations, working-class unions and women's socialist organisations, the second wave feminist movement in Turkey was initiated and quickly occupied a significant position within the civil society. Feminist campaigns, demonstrations, exhibitions, and conferences marked the period between the 1980s and the mid-1990s. The following decades (2000s- current) have also witnessed the creation of independent feminist organisations. Addressing various aspects of gendered oppression and inequality, the movement has targeted violence against women and femicides, defended women's abortion rights, reinforced legal changes to increase women's access to property and, at the same time, campaigned against the patriarchal character of the Turkish state and the cultural and religious conditions. The feminist movement has, further, fought for public provisioning of domestic services (particularly childcare provision), equalising the share of housework and care work between men and women, and decent employment for female wageworkers. The movement has established alliances with the Kurdish feminist movement based on the demands of peace and mother tongue education, and the LGBTQ+ movement in fighting against legal discrimination, homophobia, transphobia, and gendered violence. Nevertheless, considering the uneven and combined development of pre-modern, modern, and neoliberal patriarchies, I suggest that the movement needs to reflect on feminist strategies which can strengthen a shift towards the social-democratic form of public patriarchy. Here I provide a detailed discussion of four such strategies which from the evidence appear to be par-ticularly effective in securing change:

1   Diversified experiences of women

The divisions amongst women on the grounds of varieties of patriarchy need to be considered. As argued previously, the division between rural and urban women, state attacks, and equality manipulation prevented the first wave feminist movement from aligning the different demands and strategies of women (Chapter 4). The contemporary conditions of uneven and com-bined development of patriarchal transformation demonstrate that women in agrarian and semi-agrarian cities experience premodern and modern domestic patriarchy, whereas women in non-agrarian cities live under the conditions of modern domestic and neoliberal public patriarchies (Chapter 6). While a relatively small proportion of women experience the double bur-den of paid and unpaid labour (31% of women in working age population in 2021), the majority of women do not have access to paid employment. Instead, their labour is confined to rural and urban household production and, as such, requires special measures (Chapter 5).

In order to engage with the deeply exploitative conditions of premodern domestic patriarchy, I argue that feminist strategies should insist on an *exit package* for women who want to quit agriculture and gain paid employ-ment in non-agricultural sectors. Previously, state-led women-only board-ing schools played a considerable role in increasing rural women's access to secondary education, paid employment, public decision-making as well as control over their sexuality. With a swift U-turn away from neoliberal poli-cies, the re-establishment of these measures should be a priority. Such an exit package would certainly increase women's paid employment but, at the same time, would likely create a battlefield between various actors rather than sim-ply producing a win-win scenario. The loss of women's unpaid labour pre-sents a significant problem for small-medium scale farms. Direct payments could compensate this loss in subsistence farming, but Turkey has a signifi-cant proportion of accumulation-oriented family farms that are integrated into local and international agro-food systems (Chapter 7). The replacement of female unpaid family workers with wageworkers in agriculture would be resisted however by the political power of the patriarchal peasantry.

As well as the experience of women living under the conditions of premod-ern domestic patriarchy, the conditions of women under modern domestic patriarchy require attention. While women with working-class backgrounds have more limited access to education and paid employment than their male counterparts, the domestic patriarchal state insists on keeping those women as unpaid care workers within urban households (Chapter 5). Engaging with the experience of working-class women, accessibility of higher education and care provision appear to be significant feminist strategies.

The divisions amongst women on the grounds of the uneven and combined development of patriarchy therefore need addressing in order to develop effective feminist strategies. The success of the feminist movement in organising women with different backgrounds against domestic violence reveals the capacity of the movement to align women's separate agendas and to thereby promote an exit package of accessible education and care provision.

2   Capitalism or culture based reductionisms

The assumption that capitalist transformation determines the forms and degrees of gender inequality prevents the development of effective feminist strategies in many ways. For instance, one view arising from this assumption predicts that sooner or later capitalist development will diminish the material base of patriarchy in agriculture and pull women into the labour force; a second view suggests that, if not capitalism, it is Islamic culture and religion sustaining the predominance of gender-based exclusionary strategies. While the former points to the condition of underdevelopment or dependent development as the main reason for patriarchal relations of labour, the latter reduces the patriarchal character of the Turkish state to the Islamic conservative character of the ruling Justice and Development Party (2002- current). Both approaches effectively obscure the role of the patriarchal collective subject.

In light of the evidence presented in this book, I argue that varieties of patriarchy diversify the trajectories of capitalist development as well as shape cultural and religious settings and, at the same time, the domestic patriarchal character of the Turkish state is sustained by men in their position as head of households and rural and urban small producers. Critically engaging with the capitalism or culture/religion based reductionist approaches, feminist strategies need to challenge the hegemony of premodern and modern domestic patriarchies.

3   Political power of the patriarchal collective subject

The political power of men in their positions as heads of household and rural and urban small producers remains strong, sustaining the domestic patriarchal character of the state as well as constituting a significant dampener preventing transition towards social-democratic public patriarchy. Considering the extent to which male small producers strengthen the political power of the patriarchal collective subject, it is necessary for feminist strategies to challenge the predominance of gender-based exclusion in small production units across agriculture, services and manufacturing. In addition, the contemporary dynamics between the racist and capitalist agendas of the Turkish state are different to those of the early Republican period. Agriculture is not the main resource of accumulation, nor there is another large-scale expulsion of population, or military conscription faces a considerable resistance. Rather, in contemporary Turkey, the state's multiple agendas have diverse implications for the collective acting capacity of men. For example, in the face of declining fertility rates and rising life expectancy, like many other countries with racist state policies, Turkey has initiated a shift towards the pronatalist strategies (2010s- current) rather than utilising international migration (Chapter 5). These pronatalist policies are strongly linked to compulsory heterosexuality, leading to increased patriarchal control over women's sexuality, including their reproductive capacity. Considering that the majority of women are excluded from the public provisioning of childcare, the pronatalist approach also plays an important role in confining women's labour to household production.

Furthermore, the anti-democratic state regimes in Turkey appear to sustain the political power of the patriarchal collective subject by increasing gender gaps in public decision-making and political representation, and suppressing social movements, especially the feminist and LGBTQ+ movements. Those anti-democratic regimes also sustain capital accumulation strategies which necessitate the weakness of the working-class mobilisations (Chapter 7). While the enduring bond between the Turkish bourgeoisie and the anti-democratic state regimes upholds the above restrictions, strengthening the organisational capacity of the working-class organisations could promote a shift in the current capital accumulation strategies. As well as considering the negative implications of anti-democratic state regimes, as I argue below, feminist strategies need to consider establishing a strong alliance with working-class organisations.

4   Strategic alliances of the feminist movement

The shift towards the social-democratic form of public patriarchy requires the creation of long-term strategic alliances with the working-class, LGBTQ+, and anti-racist social movements. An increased capacity of the working-class movement would play an important role in changing the capital accumulation strategies, challenging anti-democratic state regimes, and initiating a shift towards social-democratic public patriarchy. However, the patriarchal character of working-class organisations needs to be abolished. Engaging with the argument that the gender or race-ethnicity based segregation in the labour market does not only serve to maximise profits but also benefits the privileged segments of working classes, I suggest that the authority of those privileged segments – based on gender and race-ethnicity – over the working-class organisations (e.g. the trade unions, confederations, and social-democratic political parties) needs to be challenged by the increased involvement of female wageworkers. Under such conditions, the feminist movement could challenge the patriarchal character of working-class organisations and thereby promote the demand for state-led provisioning.

The LGBTQ+ movement also has strategic importance in challenging compulsory heterosexuality thus weakening the cis-gender heterosexual family structure. While the elements of biological essentialism in the feminist movement and the dominance of cis-gender gay men in the LGBTQ+ movement tend to undermine an alliance between the feminist and LGBTQ+ movements, the increased involvement of transgender, non-binary, and genderqueer people serves to strengthen it.

In addition, religious and ethnicity based oppression diversifies the Alevi and Kurdish women's experiences of patriarchy. Discrimination against Alevi wageworkers in the labour market and the lack of mother tongue education have maintained the gender-based exclusionary strategies in education, paid employment, and access to legal services, strengthening the premodern and modern forms of domestic patriarchy. Furthermore, the racist agenda of the Turkish state and armed conflict appear to prevent development of non-agricultural sectors in Kurdish populated provinces, thereby upholding premodern patriarchy (Chapter 6). Nevertheless, the Kurdish feminist movement has developed strategies which, to a certain extent, achieve women's liberation from the patriarchal society by revealing the mediating impact of the patriarchal family structure. Alevi and Kurdish wageworkers are also significant in weakening the hegemony of the privileged wageworkers over the working-class movement. Therefore, a stronger alliance between the feminist and the anti-racist social movements is necessary for weakening the political power of the patriarchal collective subject and the domestic patriarchal character of the state and thereby breaking the predominance of premodern and modern domestic patriarchies.

The international feminist movement plays an important role in challenging the hegemony of domestic patriarchy. Thus far, international agreements and initiatives have provided support to the local feminist movement in challenging the domestic patriarchal character of the Turkish state. Nonetheless, those international agreements heavily draw on a top-down approach whereby high-ranking state officers are obligated to follow the international agreements. The lack of engagement between local and international feminist agendas weakens women's overall capacity to achieve long-term permanent gains. Turkey's withdrawal from the Istanbul Convention (in 2021), a human rights treaty against violence against women and domestic violence, indicates that the patriarchal collective subject utilises this lack of engagement to reverse women's achievements. Therefore, it is necessary to establish a transnational feminist movement on the grounds of stronger engagement, one that goes beyond the imperialist and racist agendas of the global North.

To encapsulate, the transition away from the premodern and modern forms of domestic patriarchies towards social-democratic public patriarchy depends on the balance of the above, as well as potential newly emergent drivers and dampeners.

***

Throughout this book, I have elaborated on how far the shortcomings of social theory weaken the capacity of feminist strategies to initiate transformative changes. One important objective of this book is to discuss the necessity of conceptual re-positioning of patriarchal labour exploitation. While men in their position as the gender-based dominant section of society depend on the patriarchal relations of labour exploitation, the cis-gender heterosexual family mediates the relationship between male appropriators and female direct producers in historically and geographically diversified ways. The book has further explored the contribution of the Hegelian Marxist interpretation of historical materialism by theorising the patriarchal, capitalist and racist totality. The case of Turkey offers a case that challenges assumptions and calls for rethinking major feminist categories and theories thereby shedding light on new varieties of patriarchy and the diverse patriarchal actors within the context of the global South.

Index

Note: *Italicized* folios indicate figures, **bold** indicate tables.

9/11 attacks 3, 25

Agarwal, B. 67, 69–70
agrarian change 17–18, 164; capitalist transformation 69; Marxist analyses of 2, 6; Marxist theories on 163
agrarian cities 125, **126**, 128–132
agrarian commercialisation 82
agrarian transformation: in India 67; Marxist perspectives on 15, 18; patriarchal path of 2, 17–20, 21, 27; social property relations 17
agriculture 87, 186; early industrial-isation 87; earnings in 16–17, 27, 151–152, 158; employment in 139, **142**, **148**; female peasant 130; in France 17; gender-based division of labour in 4, 70, 82, 140, 165; Kurdish women in 132; labour migration from 2; mechanisation of 16; movement of labour from 16, 140, 143, 158, 163; non-capitalist character of 20; in North Africa 6; patriarchal control over women in 82, 149; patriarchal exploitation in 62, 69, 140, 183; patri-archal labour relations in 16–17, 21, 69–70, 130–131, 139, 144, 164; prop-erty and labour relations in 16, 144, 149; small units of production in 61; surplus labour in 70; in Turkey 19–20; wage labour in 71, 164, 184; women own-account workers in 116; women's cooperatives in 116; women's unpaid family labour in 16, 18–19, 23, 104, 111–112, 114, 147
Alevi women 8, 124, 130–131, 134–135, 187

Althusserian base/superstructure approach 5, 8, 20, 41, 169, 171, 173–174
anti-Black racism 42, 64, 72
anti-democratic regime 117
anti-Kurdish racisms 64
anti-Alevi racism 42, 64
awqaf lands 80

biological essentialism/determinism 3, 5, 24, 45, 58, 72, 170, 187
bourgeois farmer 17, 19, 164
bourgeois peasant-led transition 19
bride wealth 91–92, 95n3
brothel model 37–38

Capital (Marx) 18
capital accumulation 3, 8, 27, 138, 149–156, 164, 186; anti-democratic regimes 186; domestic labour 43; implications for 149–156; logic of 23; patriarchal labour exploitation 6; patriarchal peasantry for 20; patriarchal relations of labour 47; patriarchy in 155, 165, 178; role of working-class movement 186; in Turkey 149, 164; Turkish manufac-turers 21
capitalism 5, 15, 17–20, 22, 37–39, 41, 43–47; causality 43–47; consequence of 45; determinism 6, 24; develop-ment of 3, 50, 67; distorted, depend-ent 67; distorted and dependent 67; landlord-mediated 17; Marxist accounts of 20; oil-dependent 68; peripheral 3, 67, 69; reductionism 3, 24, 35, 58, 169, 185; reductionist

Printed in the United States
by Baker & Taylor Publisher Services